BUILD A GREAT TEAM
ONE YEAR TO SUCCESS

Property of
Community College of Aurora
Library-Rm. S202

ALA GUIDES FOR THE BUSY LIBRARIAN

BE A GREAT BOSS: ONE YEAR TO SUCCESS
by Catherine Hakala-Ausperk

HIRING, TRAINING, AND SUPERVISING LIBRARY SHELVERS
by Patricia Tunstall

WRITING AND PUBLISHING: THE LIBRARIAN'S HANDBOOK
edited by Carol Smallwood

MENTORING AT THE LIBRARY
by Marta K. Lee

**MANAGING LIBRARY VOLUNTEERS:
A PRACTICAL TOOLKIT, SECOND EDITION**
by Preston Driggers and Eileen Dumas

WHAT THEY DON'T TEACH YOU IN LIBRARY SCHOOL
by Elisabeth Doucett

BUILD A GREAT TEAM
ONE YEAR TO SUCCESS

CATHERINE HAKALA-AUSPERK

AN IMPRINT OF THE AMERICAN LIBRARY ASSOCIATION

CHICAGO 2013

Catherine Hakala-Ausperk is the executive director of the Northeast Ohio Regional Library System. A frequent speaker at national and state conferences, staff days, and workshops, she has a passion for supporting, coaching, and developing successful library staff, including bosses. A 28-year public library veteran, she is also an adjunct faculty member of Kent State University's School of Library and Information Science, where she teaches management. Hakala-Ausperk is the author of *Be a Great Boss: One Year to Success* (2011) and has been a guest editor and author for ALA/APA's newsletter *Library Worklife*. Hakala-Ausperk is an Ohio certified public librarian and an ALA certified public library administrator.

ALA Editions purchases fund advocacy, awareness, and accreditation programs for library professionals worldwide.

© 2013 by the American Library Association. Any claim of copyright is subject to applicable limitations and exceptions, such as rights of fair use and library copying pursuant to Sections 107 and 108 of the U.S. Copyright Act. No copyright is claimed for content in the public domain, such as works of the U.S. government.

Printed in the United States of America
17 16 15 14 13   5 4 3 2 1

Extensive effort has gone into ensuring the reliability of the information in this book; however, the publisher makes no warranty, express or implied, with respect to the material contained herein.

ISBNs: 978-0-8389-1170-9 (paper); 978-0-8389-9575-4 (PDF). For more information on digital formats, visit the ALA Store at alastore.ala.org and select eEditions.

Library of Congress Cataloging-in-Publication Data
Hakala-Ausperk, Catherine.
  Build a great team : one year to success! / Catherine Hakala-Ausperk.
     pages   cm. — (ALA guides for the busy librarian)
  Includes bibliographical references and index.
  ISBN 978-0-8389-1170-9
  1. Library personnel management—Handbooks, manuals, etc. 2. Teams in the workplace—Handbooks, manuals, etc. 3. Supervision of employees—Handbooks, manuals, etc. 4. Library administration—Handbooks, manuals, etc. I. Title.
  Z682.H163 2013
  023'.9—dc23
                                                                     2013005036

Book design in Charis SIL and Interstate by Casey Bayer.
Cover image © Shutterstock, Inc.

♾ This paper meets the requirements of ANSI/NISO Z39.48-1992 (Permanence of Paper).

CONTENTS

PREFACE

It doesn't matter how long you've been the boss or the supervisor or the group leader or whatever you're called. If you're in charge of leading people, you have a team. Congratulations! Challenging and rewarding, frustrating and enlightening, frightening and motivating, every single day that you are lucky enough to do this job and lead other people towards success, you can make a real difference. So, why do you look so nervous?

Well, if you *feel* a little overwhelmed, then you've definitely got a handle on reality. Leading a team is never easy. Discipline will challenge you. Conflicts cannot be avoided or handed off to someone else. After hundreds of performance examples that make you proud, someone will come along and disappoint—maybe even surprise—you and you may not always know what to do next. Here's the good news. You can steadily, solidly, continually, and absolutely build the skills you need to succeed! It's no secret that I'm a fan of lifelong learning. So, as I did in my first book, *Be a Great Boss: One Year to Success,* I have created a workbook here that, as long as you can give it one hour each week of your time, will help you attain that success.

What do you need to contribute? Just commitment.

In my first book, *Be A Great Boss: One Year to Success,* I attempted to accomplish two things. One, clearly the most valuable, was to instill in every boss the commitment to set aside one hour a week for their own, ongoing, never-ending development. The second goal was to help them take a look at the broad, far-reaching role of a boss. In this book, I'm sharpening that look onto your team's success and focusing your weekly development hour on getting better and better at leading your group.

But, that one hour a week commitment, just as in my first book, remains an immutable requirement and, in the end, developing that habit may be the very best gift you give yourself—and others who depend on you.

You may be tempted to just read this book cover to cover in a couple of sittings. If you do that, you'll miss the most important part. On the other hand, if you really do use it to guide you through an entire year of learning, you'll be able to get out of it what was intended:

1. A strong habit, built on repetition and commitment, to always set time aside to learn more and to get better.
2. A chance to really complete each week's exercises, which is the best way to internalize the topic being discussed *and actually apply it to improving your team!*

Make time for yourself. Don't ever stop improving. Long after you've finished working through this book, pick another topic or area where you need to grow and dedicate your one hour a week to that! (Later in this book, you'll get some help figuring out just how to do that.) If you're just getting started in your career, then you have about 1,560 hours of development and improvement ahead of you! Clear your schedule, delegate a job or two, close your door, use a Saturday morning or just work through lunch. It's your career. No one else is going to focus on developing and growing it.

And not only will you personally and professionally benefit from spending a year with this book, but there won't be one member of your team who won't also be glad you did.

After *Be a Great Boss* was released, I heard from many, many readers grateful not only for what they read and learned, but also for the fact that they'd developed a strong habit that they planned to continue to retirement! It worked for them and it can work—and make a difference—for you! So, block off an hour on your schedule (and make it recurring!). Work alone or engage in this process with your whole management team. Prioritize, organize, and dedicate your time carefully, so that, week by week, you can continually get just a little bit better at what you do.

I had a library school professor tell me years ago, in a management class, that any boss who didn't spend at least one hour a week thinking or planning or learning was in more trouble than they knew. Work piles up. Deadlines encroach. No one is suggesting that you're eating bonbons at your desk but, remember this, they do pay you to *think* too. And to grow.

At this point, once you've committed to this team building learning experience, you've taken the first and most important step towards growth. It doesn't matter a bit whether this is your first day on the job or your 1,000th, *today* is the day the real improvement begins.

Walk around first and take a look at each and every member of your team. They're depending on you and you're depending on them. Go on! Build a great team!

ACKNOWLEDGMENTS

It seems like at every major awards event, even though the same people win, they always seem to have a new list of people to thank for their success. Not so with me. The opportunity, encouragement, and ability to complete this, my second book for library leaders, is still the direct result of the love, encouragement, and support of my husband, Dale, and my sister, Susan. Still, I'd be remiss to not acknowledge my teams, current and past, who also deserve my appreciation. It's been an honor to work with each and every one of them and I'm grateful for their patience, forgiveness, and understanding as I've tried to keep on learning. And, speaking of inspiration, I also have to thank beautiful Juliette, the newest member of our team!

INTRODUCTION

"Can I talk to you for a minute?"

Oh, boy. We've all heard that one and grimaced, right? Someone is about to tell you they're quitting. As though your car was creeping ever so slowly up to the tip of the roller coaster and about to slam straight down the other side, reality hits. Your team is about to change!

If this was a happy movie, you'd invite them in, shake their hand, and congratulate them on their newest achievement and wish them well, then go about starting the process of replacing them. But this is the real world, right? Arrrggggh! The paperwork! The arguing! The hours of interviewing wasted on "profession-hoppers" who "love books" and "always wanted to work in a nice, quiet library"! Who will do the work in the meantime? What will they say about you on their exit interview? Will you *finally* get to choose your own person or just take whomever "they" give you? Arrrrggggh! *No!* You cannot talk to me for a minute and shatter my world with this news! I was just getting ready to start making *this* team work!

Wake up. You're having a nightmare. It is not, nor should it ever be this hard to hear the news that someone is leaving your staff. Your team development is ongoing and has been built to withstand and even celebrate these opportunities for growth and change, right?

If not, then *this* is the book for you!

From working effectively with your current team to making room and interjecting someone new into it, week by week, hour by hour, you'll read and practice ideas in this workbook that will have you not only prepared for that next knock on the door—but honestly and earnestly wishing your staff member well . . . and looking forward with excitement to how you can rebuild your team—even better than before!

Being entrusted with the privilege of leading others is, indeed, a happy movie. All you need in order to believe that is confidence in your role and skill.

WELCOME TO YOUR TEAM!

WEEK ONE | ## JAMES MICHENER

Millions upon millions of years ago, when the continents were already formed and the principal features of the earth had been decided, there existed, then as now, one aspect of the world that dwarfed all others. It was a mighty ocean, resting uneasily to the east of the largest continent, a restless ever-changing, gigantic body of water that would later be described as pacific.[1]

There's a little bit of history for you. If you've never read a book by James Michener, first of all, please do. Secondly, this is about how most of them start, with a serious look at history. And, finally, I think I know why. Whether this is your very first day working with your new team or you lost count a long time ago, history is important to understand and it's the very best place to start. I'm not talking about the "We've always done it that way" type of history. At least, not completely. But, still, you can never truly take the helm and lead the ship forward effectively without thoroughly understanding and respecting what has come before.

We all travel with baggage, right? Some of it is lovely and twirls colorfully on well-oiled wheels, while other pieces clunk along, threatening to fall apart with the first stiff wind. The same can be said of people, especially when they've been working together for some time. As the team leader, you need to start with where they've been, what they've learned, and what, in order to build a *great* team, what they may need to unlearn!

While studying the Army practice of holding after-action reviews, authors Parry and Darling emphatically asserted that the past does matter. "The essence of learning is the discovery and use of knowledge," they explained, "and one of the best sources of actionable knowledge is that which emerges from people's own experience."[2]

Especially if you're new to your team leader job, a look back has got to be your first step and it has to be a broad and noncritical look. You weren't there. You can't know why one person was demoted, why certain

< **MONTH 1** | WEEK ONE | WELCOME TO YOUR TEAM! >

ELEMENTS OF SUCCESSFUL TEAMS

- Purpose/Mission
- Team Member Roles
- Real Work
- The *How*
- Deadlines
- Support
- Accountable
- Interdependent[6]

PUTTING THE PAST INTO FOCUS

With a thorough history of your team's structure and past performance in mind, try asking yourself these questions, in order to help define opportunities for improvement.

- Are there conflicts between certain people that are creating divisions within the team?
- Do team members need to get to know one another?
- Do some members focus on their own success, and harm the group as a result?
- Does poor communication slow the group's progress?
- Do people need to learn how to work together, instead of individually?
- Are some members resistant to change, and does this affect the group's ability to move forward?
- Do members of the group need a boost to their morale?[8]

assignments have been held by another for two decades or why no one buys group birthday cakes anymore. If this sounds trivial, I need to work harder to convince you of the value of reflection. Let's start with the organization overall. Believe me, we'll get around to your great team in short order and, with this background firmly in place, you'll be better prepared than you might expect to move it into the future.

Have you seen *Desk Set*, starring Katherine Hepburn and Spencer Tracy? While the number of people shaking their heads "no" to this question used to surprise me, it no longer does. I understand fully that many of today's library staff members actually don't recall what it was like to consider a computer that could answer questions absurd! But, you know what? Within your very team those people are working right alongside others who do remember; and you need to know that!

Libraries are one of those industries that is blessed today with multigenerational staffs, within which you could probably produce both an expert on paper shelf lists and another on iPads. You need to know that, too. Just imagine the different opinions they might hold towards something you might consider quite innocuous, like the dress code, for example. In a 1961 memo to staff called "Personal Appearance," the Boeing Airplane Company explained that female employ-

ees know that "an attractive appearance is important and can be achieved by using intelligence in the selection and care of clothes and the use of proper makeup. The well-dressed girl" [girl??, ed. note] "wears proper undergarments. She knows she does not look well on the outside unless she is dressed correctly underneath."[3]

Puuuullleeease!

What if this rule stayed in effect for many years, even long after the law interceded; it could have become a part of the culture, and one of your team members from that era is now expected to work next to a Generation X-er? See what I mean? You better look back before you set new team standards and then begin struggling to understand why no one is living up to them. "Culture permeates all aspects of any society. It acts as the basic fabric that binds people together. Organizational culture determines how an organization operates and how its members frame events both inside and outside the organization."[4]

And what about the work itself? Do your team members use iPads or No. 2 pencils? Do they arrive socially late or militarily early to work? Who got fired last and why? Or, did they really get fired or did they quit because. . . Why do they all roll their eyes when you use the expression *strategic planning*? What happened during the last plan? Is it true your organization *never* promotes from within? What's been happening around here?

Taking the time to understand the past can give you a solid foundation for moving forward. Test your own assumptions as well. Maybe, just maybe, as a member of the rank and file, even concepts and legends you thought were real might look a little different, once you can check the rumors against the files. "Why do some teams succeed? Why do many teams muddle along?"[5] You have the power, as the team's leader, to not only answer this question but to perhaps change the answer to the former. Use your power for good, instead of evil.

So, how do you approach this archeological dig? Give yourself time. If yesterday was the day you decided to build a great team, either because you just arrived on the scene or you're tired of the ineffectiveness of the past, then today is the day you begin examining where they've been. Tomorrow, you can work on where they're going. Once you've done your homework and envisioned your team's past with open eyes, you can strategically begin to chart out your plan for improvement. One important thing to remember here (and it's often on this one, single point that many team leaders fall flat), you will need to focus on changing *behaviors* and *performance,* but not *people.* Organizational consultant and trainer Marti Peden coined this unique saying to underscore that point and called it her "Attitude and Accountability Version Serenity Statement." "Grant me the serenity to accept the *people* I cannot change, the courage to change the *person* I can, and the wisdom to know it's me."[7]

Work, rules, expectations, goals, communication can all change, and those and more probably should. But people will not. Since teams are made up of people, it's up to the leader—you—to learn and understand that difference. Working effectively, you can define and strengthen culture, outline and articulate achievement, and lead your team to greatness, once you know what you're dealing with and where you're going. Learn about your team's past. Consider it. Ask questions. Encourage reflection. Review, revisit, and analyze the strengths, weaknesses, opportunities, and threats you find before charting a new strategy to move your team forward. Learning all of this and considering it carefully will help bring everything about this wonderful resource you get to work with—your team—into focus for you. It's the best first step you can take.

Michener had it right. The past matters. Your look back will embolden you, encourage you, and help answer the question you've been asking, maybe only of yourself. . .

"Where do we go from here?"

Welcome to your team!

SUGGESTED READING

Ricchiuto, Jack. *The Stories That Connect Us.* Cleveland, OH: DesigningLife Books, 2009.

EXERCISES

-1-

1. **Write "A Brief Team History"** (you don't have to go back as far as Michener would) by interviewing your two longest-term employees. (You use two people so that you can get a broader point of view.) Ask them each to simply tell you the story of the team; don't push for specifics. The issues they mention will tell you something about what they've seen as significant events.

_____

_____

_____

_____

_____

2. **Get lots of opinions** on this one by asking members of other teams, former employees, new staff (to gauge what they hear the most about), and so on. Ask one question: "What's the most significant thing that's ever happened to this team? Why? What was the impact?"

_____

_____

_____

_____

_____

3. **Make a continuum chart** of longevity and note each current team member's years of service. How many have been a part for less than one year? For two to five years? For more than ten years? Comment on how the differences in their levels of experience can help you as you continue building solidarity.

_____

_____

_____

_____

4. **Describe your team's culture.** What's the communication style (open or suspicious), the support system (interdependent or isolationist), the approach to innovation (welcoming or frightened)? By reviewing this, do some goals arise in your mind that need to be addressed right away? What are they?

_____

_____

_____

_____

5. **List at least three** "traditions" recognized by your team. ("Nobody internal ever gets promoted. Our evaluations are meaningless. It's okay to dress down every day.") What do they tell you about the personality of the team? Is there a need for improvement or is the status quo acceptable to you?

_____

_____

_____

_____

_____

WELCOME TO YOUR TEAM!

| ## GRAVEYARD STEW

The attendees had just completed their workshop exercise, during which they had taken and graded their personality tests. In this particular version, the results categorized everyone into one of ten types. To illustrate their differences (and yes, their similarities), the facilitator had half of the group (the J's) gather near one flip chart and the other half (the P's) stand across the room near another. The scenario posed was this: You just got home with a carload of groceries for dinner. How would you have done that?

Following an entertaining and lively discussion, both charts were filled. The differences were amazing.

Described as "people who tend to like a planned and organized approach to life and prefer to have things settled,"[9] the J's had described a process that could have made a government regulator smile. They'd begun at home, with a thorough review of the contents of their cupboards and refrigerator. Following that, they'd constructed a detailed, weekly menu plan and indicated needed items with check marks, some in different colors to indicate quantity needed. After comparing ads and mapping out a multi-store route, they'd efficiently purchased each and every item on their list (and nothing that was not there), then returned home to immediately put the items away, rotating the newer stock to the front.

The P's, "people who tend to like a flexible and spontaneous approach to life and prefer to keep their options open,"[10] up next, dropped their gazes and shuffled their feet before admitting the process (if it can be called that) they would have followed. First, most admitted they would have forgotten

TYPES AT THEIR BEST AND WORST

Don't stop with categorizing the wonderful personality variations within your staff. Rather encourage each and every person to a new level of understanding their strengths and weaknesses; what they can accomplish at their best and challenges or problem areas at which they can improve.

ENNEAGRAM TYPES	BEST	CHALLENGES
Reformer	Wise, Discerning, Noble	Impatience, Resentment
Helper	Unselfish, Altruistic	Possessive, Ignore Own Needs
Achiever	Authentic, Inspirational	Workaholics, Competitive
Individualist	Inspired, Creative	Melancholy, Self-Indulgent
Investigator	Visionary, Big Picture	Eccentricity, Isolationists
Loyalist	Stable, Self-Reliant	Self-Doubt, Suspicion
Enthusiast	Appreciative, Joyous	Impatient, Impulsive
Challenger	Magnanimous, Inspiring	Temper, Vulnerability
Peacemaker	Indomitable, Healing	Inertia, Stubborness[11]

to stop at the store altogether and would likely have to have been reminded at least once or have become very hungry, to have thought of it. Then, with absolutely no thought to menus, costs, or plans, they would have breezed through the first store they passed by, grabbed mostly items on display at the stack ends, and then forgot at least one bag in the car, which they'd put away hours later.

But, the point? Everyone would get to eat. Even though their approaches had been completely different, the job had been done by all. It was a simple exercise and an eye-opening one. If you and your team have never worked through a personality review like this (and you most certainly should), you'd know that the bottom line lesson is always the same. Once we've become comfortable with our own style, it follows naturally that we need to understand and respect the varying styles of those around us, no matter how much we may differ. And, with that accomplished, we can turn our attention to learning how much richer we can be when working together.

It's been said many ways, but bottom line, we are smarter and better together than we are alone, and that's a great place for you and your team to begin your work. A person who arranged spices in alphabetical order, working next to someone whose socks haven't matched in a year will definitely produce a better product than either could have done by themselves. These types of personality tests teach respect for one another's differences. They highlight the need to combine many different types of people on a single team. And, perhaps most important, they leave people emboldened with what their *type* can do at their best—and at what worst parts they need to focus some attention.

So what's the team leader's—your—role in all of this meshing? You are the conductor of a virtuosic symphony orchestra. You bring your team together. You set their goals and clear their paths and help them in this great exercise of appreciation and blending. *You* help make sure everyone comes home with the groceries.

FUN WITH MYERS BRIGGS

The story is made up but the point is clear. "In 1971 English rock icon Joe Cocker told his mother, 'I don't want a job where I work for years and years and get a gold watch at the end' (*Life* magazine, September 24, 1971). Searching for meaning and purpose, Joe Cocker locked himself away in a dank cave in the isles of Sicily to study Myers Briggs codes and psychology. When he emerged, he wrote the following song, expressing his perspective on the unity of all Myers Briggs types." (*Play tune . . . "You Are So Beautiful to Me."*)[12]

Let's get one thing straight, you do not own your team. As wise parents realize about their children, they're just on temporary loan to you and you're to do the best you can with them day by day. I've never liked it when a supervisor introduced me as "my staff member"; have you? It is *my* desk and I can move it to the other side of the room or out into the parking lot if I so desire and the desk has nothing to say about that. It's *my* computer. And it is *my* parking spot (maybe) and my coffee cup. But the *staff* belongs to no one. They are individuals coming together under my leadership for a temporary period and I'm just privileged to be currently directing their work.

Let's talk about why this matters. You are preparing to embark on a yearlong expedition of examination that will result in a renewed and expanded appreciation and understanding of all those individuals who work for you. It seems logical, I hope you agree, to begin with a core value of respect. Apart, your team members possess traits and skills that are unique to their training, background, and attitude. Together, they comprise an impressive and potentially effective group of people whose value to your organization is exponentially greater than its parts. Under your direction, the impact of that value is limitless. As long as you never waver from your dedication to understand, appreciate, and *respect* them as individuals, you're on the right track and ready to get started.

I'm sure you've never had Graveyard Stew before but I bet, if you've been fortunate enough to have eaten at the table of a Depression-era family member, you've had something like it, so this analogy should work. My grandmother, a Finnish immigrant, I swear could turn water into wine after all those years of making due with very little. There weren't different-sized forks on the table and she didn't serve meals in courses. More often, anything and everything handy at dinnertime went into the pot and what came out, somehow, was pure heaven. I think of her Graveyard Stew when I think of managing people. All the ingredients that went into the pot (pieces of beef of questionable origin, homegrown onions, "leftover" potatoes, perhaps a carrot or ewwww, a turnip) were simple on their own and sometimes even bland or worse. But, after coming together and simmering under her skilled eye, they came out as pure ambrosia.

Think of the goals your team has most recently accomplished and consider your one, most outstanding employee. Could she or he have accomplished it alone? Doubtful, you have to admit. There was likely that one other individual (or two, or three) whose complementary talents brought out the best in your expert and, with a few other contributions thrown in, the final result grew larger. Your Graveyard Stew was a success. Or it could have been. Certainly now, with your dedication to improvement, it will be, since you have such a diverse and respected staff to work alongside.

SUGGESTED READING

"Understanding Team Leadership." *Purpose Unleashed*. www.purposeunleashed.com/blog/?p=492.

EXERCISES

2

1. **Think for a moment** of your favorite football team and list at least five different players and the skills they bring. Then, focus on only one and imagine everyone else on the team had only his talents. What would be lost?

    _____
    _____
    _____
    _____
    _____

2. **List all your team** members' names and, next to each, write at least five descriptors of their personality. Review the list you just created. What does the wealth of variation bring to mind about your possibilities for success?

    _____
    _____
    _____
    _____
    _____

3. **You do and will** continue to respect each and every team member, regardless of the similarities or differences between you. Write at least ten ways you can _demonstrate_ that respect.

    _____
    _____
    _____
    _____
    _____

4. **Think for a moment** about the most dysfunctional team of which you've ever been a part. First, list at least ten reasons it was dysfunctional. Next, if individual members' different personalities had been recognized, respected, and utilized, what might have been different about the team's operation and success?

    _____
    _____
    _____
    _____

5. **Get out your calendar** and select a day when you can bring your team together for a Personalities' Summit. (If it has to wait until next year's budget, that's okay. You can still put it on the calendar.) Then, get online or on the phone and find someone who can help you set it up. _Do it_. There can be no stronger foundation for team success than a healthy awareness of what everyone has to contribute.

    _____
    _____
    _____
    _____

WELCOME TO YOUR TEAM!

WEEK THREE | ## THE SETTING

"Job descriptions were invented primarily in situations where communication was at its worst. They divide up all predictable tasks among those available for assignments. This creates an ugly phenomenon called 'my job.' We can accurately credit job descriptions with those famous words, 'It's not my job.' If you have the opportunity to reduce or eliminate these hazards in your organization, get started yesterday. If you don't have the 'power' to impact them, take and make opportunities to suggest ideas aimed at preventing and reducing them. We *can* design work in ways that prevent duplication and gaps and *still* get everyone being collaborative in their creative processes."[13]

You've examined your team's history. You've studied, recognized, and celebrated the diverse talents and characteristics that make up your team's personality and you've noted some areas that could use some work. Now it's time to think about where everything happens. The place. The environment. The culture. The mojo. What's it like to *be* where your team works?

If you're lucky, you'll find that the organization in which you and your team will labor is already open, collaborative, and inspiring. If it isn't, then you'll need to make it so. To start with, how will you know the difference? According to library organizational expert Maureen Sullivan, there are five clear characteristics you'd notice in a healthy, collaborative organization. It would have "an open, fluid, inclusive design, staff would work well with one another—most of the time, work units are teams that focus on activities or processes, contribution and group performance matter more than individual expertise, and teamwork is a way of life."[14]

WHAT DOES IT TAKE?: ESSENTIAL ELEMENTS OF A COLLABORATIVE TEAM

- Decisions are based on accurate, relevant information
- New information is captured and published
- Communication is open
- Staff members have easy access to information
- Three is a strong, competent, committed senior management team
- There is an operational strategic plan
- Human Resource policies are aligned towards collaboration
- Staff members are competent, committed, flexible, and highly motivated
- There is a commitment to continuous learning
- Boundaries (between levels, ranks, and work) are permeable
- There is facilitative leadership
- There is a commitment to individual development[15]

Let's think about how those qualities might look when they're actually applied to the culture of a team. At Zappos, the online retail company, it would seem that everyone truly loves coming to work. Do you think that shows, to the customer? According to Zappos's CEO, there are five basic reasons for his company's positive culture:

1. Everyone, from customers to employees, is treated like family. Every customer (including coworkers) counts and each experience they have must be first-rate.

2. They hire for a cultural fit. Without ignoring skills and abilities, supervisors look specifically beyond those traditional measures and consider personality, friendliness, and passion when selecting new employees.

3. Managers trust their teams. Simple as that sounds, it's too often untrue. Unbound by dictated procedures and over-management, employees are free to simply *wow* customers, again, including coworkers, with every interaction.

4. Everything is shared. Doors aren't closed and there is no whispering. Decisions are open, information is available, and employees are kept in the loop.

5. Staff are encouraged to have fun. The relaxed, supportive atmosphere is a result of the culture and translates into success for the organization.[16]

Does this sound like your library? Do you see your team fitting this description? Take a hard look at the culture in which your employees work before moving forward with your plan to build a great team. If the culture needs to be changed, you can do that. One of the greatest gifts of leadership is that you *can* effect change. One of the greatest threats of leadership is that when change is needed, many look the other way. You may not get to Zappos's level, but without a strong, positive culture in which to perform, you will be building your team's strengths on sand.

Here's a simple place to start. You need to understand what organizational culture is. Culture is the culmination of what you say and do and of what staff members think you say and do. Although some academics would cringe at this simplification (you'd have no trouble finding shelves of organizational development books that can make this a lot more complicated), that's it in a nutshell. Now, here's the hard part. You cannot change the latter (what people think) but you *can* change the former—what you say and do—and, over time, your team's culture will shift with you.

Noted expert Edgar Schein tells us there are three components to culture: artifacts (things you can see), values (based on strategies and goals), and assumptions (perceptions, thoughts, and feelings that are taken for granted).[17] Understanding how you, as the team leader, can influence these elements and begin to drive your team's culture should start now and continue every single day. You've probably heard lots about these three concepts before. Artifacts can be everything from dress code to signage to meeting minutes (or the lack thereof). Values can be represented by your organization's mission or the fact that you haven't had a formal strategic plan in ten years, and assumptions can include the dreaded *organizational memory* or a synonym for that—gossip. There is no switch to flip or *Easy* button here. There will probably be dozens if not hundreds of small changes and actions you'll need to take over the coming year and beyond in order to create and sustain a culture that's "good (i.e., would one like to work there) or bad (would one not?)."[18] There will be signs to take down, bad habits to discourage, outright fallacies to correct and more. But there is one very simple and inescapable way that you can begin your efforts to create a sustainable, positive culture that allows you to move forward.

"Stories. Excuse me? You change the culture with stories. If you want to change the culture, you have to change the stories. (Don't) change the performance review system, the rewards packages, and the training programs. Don't change anything. Not yet anyway. For now, just change the stories. Do dramatic story-worthy things that represent the culture (you) want to create. Then, let other people tell stories about it. Find other people who do story-worthy things that represent the culture (you) want to create. Then, tell stories about them."[19]

Successful teams don't have walls, like immutable job descriptions and long-standing rumors that guide them. They don't have threats hanging over their heads, like unsubstantiated gossip about what will eventually happen because *it always has*. And they don't have a commitment

---

CHANGE TO A WELCOMING CULTURE

There can be no debate that, where in the past libraries have focused on their stuff, often to the point of making users ask permission to see it, they're now focusing on the people and finding new ways every day to invite them in. This paradigm shift illustrates a major cultural change! How have they done it? Here are some things they have done that have told the story that libraries are changing!

- Downsize service desks, removing old barriers to staff members
- Use roving reference service, where staff members go to the customers, rather than wait for customer to come to them.
- Have a greeter/concierge at key service points (and make sure they smile when they say hello to everyone)
- Focus on comfort for people of *all* ages, not just the polite, quiet ones
- Have multiple staff (not just the director) get out into the community and get to know the people they're serving[20]

---

to past practices that clearly haven't worked, just because no one has been brave enough to take them on. Successful teams have leaders who are committed to remembering the power of corporate culture and to reshaping it, day by day, through their words, their actions, their support, their encouragement, and their intent to build a greater team. The results will tell their story.

SUGGESTED READING

Schein, Edgar. *Organizational Culture and Leadership*. San Francisco: Jossey-Bass, 2010.

EXERCISES

-3-

1. **List at least ten** artifacts (visible, tangible things or events) that reflect your team's current culture. Some examples might be having a Reference "pod," where librarians sit together, rather than individual desks spaced throughout the building. Another example might be holding annual, mandatory Staff Development Days or Summer Picnics. Leave room to note after each one whether you want to continue and strengthen it or make it go away.

_____
_____
_____
_____
_____
_____
_____

2. **List at least ten** cultural values (shared standards or goals) that impact your team today. Some examples might be that only staff members with library degrees can supervise anyone or that customer confidentiality must be protected at all costs, regardless of expense. Again, after each one, comment on the positive or not-so-positive influence each has and which you would like to see changed.

_____
_____
_____
_____
_____
_____
_____

3. **Assumptions can be thought** of as values without proof. While values are institutionalized because they actually happen over and over, assumptions can be based on little more than what the longtime staff say they are. Think, "if you complain, they'll put you in charge of the solution" or "if you're doing well at your current position, they'd never promote you." List ten cultural assumptions that are affecting your team and, again, think about and comment on how you feel about them and which ones you'd like to erase from your team's collective memory.

_____
_____
_____
_____
_____
_____

4. **Look back at the** three lists of changes you want to see, list them here, and, next to each, identify at least one concrete action you can take to begin telling a new story.

_____
_____
_____
_____
_____
_____
_____
_____

WELCOME TO YOUR TEAM!

WEEK FOUR | **THE ARCHITECT**

The very best description of leadership comes complete with dishes and silverware.

"When Frances Hesselbein became CEO of the Girl Scouts of the USA, a *New York Times* columnist asked what it felt like to be on top of such a large organization. With patience, like a teacher pausing to impart an important lesson, Hesselbein proceeded to rearrange the lunch table, creating a set of concentric circles radiating outward—plates, cups, saucers—connected by knives, forks, and spoons. Hesselbein pointed to a glass in the middle of the table. 'I'm here,' she said. Hesselbein may have had the title of chief executive officer, but her message was clear: *I'm not on top of anything.*"[21]

Because of the work you've done so far in this book, you have come to understand the team's history, its people and its culture. In the process, you likely encountered some changes, some stability, and some surprises and, guess what? They're going to keep on coming as you and your team move forward. There's only one piece missing before you forge ahead, adding to the team, strengthening its core, and blending new and longtime employees together—and that's a leader.

You.

There's a definition for that, you know. "Some people use the words interchangeably, but for most of us the traditional boss is someone who turns employees off, while a leader turns them on."[22] If you remember the earlier silverware and dishes example, this comment won't shake you. Be part of your team, show the way by taking on tasks you're asking them to do, before delegating them permanently to the right people. Don't get

LEADERSHIP LESSONS FROM GEESE

This oft-repeated list should give "human" teams a lot to think about. The correlations from geese to your own staff are clear—and so is the call for your group to work together, at all costs.

FACT As each goose flaps its wings, it creates an "uplift" for the birds that follow. By flying in a "V" formation, the whole flock adds 71 percent greater flying range than if each bird flew alone.

LESSON People who share a common direction and sense of community can get where they are going quicker and easier because they are traveling on the thrust of one another.

FACT When a goose falls out of formation, it suddenly feels the drag and resistance of flying alone. It quickly moves back into formation to take advantage of the lifting power of the bird immediately in front of it.

LESSON If we have as much sense as a goose, we stay in formation with those headed where we want to go.

FACT When the lead goose tires, it rotates back into the formation and another goose flies to the point position.

LESSON It pays to take turns doing the hard tasks and sharing leadership. As with geese, people are interdependent on each other's skills, capabilities, and unique arrangements of gifts, talents, or resources.

FACT The geese flying in formation honk to encourage those up front to keep up their speed.

LESSON We need to make sure honking is encouraging. In groups where there is encouragement, the production is much greater. The power of encouragement (to stand by one's heart or core values and encourage the heart and core of others) is the quality of honking we seek.

FACT When a goose gets sick, wounded, or shot down, two geese drop out of formation and follow it down to help and protect it. They stay with it until it dies or is able to fly again. Then, they launch out with another formation or catch up with the flock.[26]

LESSON If we have as much sense as geese, we will stand by each other in difficult times as well as when we are strong.

---

bogged down (or allow your team to be) by small details. It's going to be your job all along the way to keep everyone focused on the larger mission. And hold the bar high! Leaders who expect—and deliver—a lot themselves can expect the same from those they lead. Motivate and demonstrate but, by all means, *lead!*

Don't be afraid to demonstrate strength and decisiveness. Better you should fear the opposite, leaders whose legacy is one of inaction, apathy, or worse, cowardice. While hundreds of books have been written about how to lead well, making the concept seem inextricably complicated and unreachable, many simple people have accomplished it with little more than basic skills and a passion for their work.

Consider William Bratton, the New York City police commissioner who, in "less than two years, and without an increase in his budget, turned New York into the safest large city in the nation."[23]

How he did it now outlines a process that leader-training seminars are copying all over the nation and hopeful team leaders are turning into their own blueprint for success. Basically, he followed four simple steps. First, he helped his team realize there were real issues that needed to be resolved. To accomplish this, he used new communication models (including more effective meetings) and real statistics and data to back him up. In many teams, even this simple beginning could be quite a foray from information trickled out to a special few and decision making that's been kept in the dark. Next, he sought to understand the background and environment (sound like history and culture?) in which his team labored, and he used it to his advantage by getting key people on his side. When team members met with success, he celebrated them. When they began to contribute to limitations, he held them accountable. Finally, realizing there were not resources to put out every fire, he focused people and the budget where they could do the most good and, after they had, he moved on to the next challenge.

Armed with an understanding of how he did it, any aspiring *great* team leader can imitate Bratton's success. Think of the parallels in your organization to his four-step approach and match that with the groundwork you've already laid for your own success.

1. STEP ONE is to study the past and identify the real issues that need to be resolved. As you did in week one of this workbook, that calls for a look back at history, not to dwell on past mistakes but to clarify and separate the healthy from the unhealthy impacts on your team.

2. STEP TWO saw him tackle the current environment, making sure it was fit and matched to the kind of progress he expected to see. Contrary to popular opinion (usually voiced by those who want to keep the status quo), old habits do die, even if they die hard. Throughout this development year and beyond into the future of your career, if you keep sharp your awareness that culture matters and can be adapted, you'll be able to maintain your team's environment as a fertile place in which to grow.

3. STEP THREE is all about awareness. Many leaders stray off course at this point because they labor under the illogical concept that before they can move on or even make a decision, everyone needs to be happy. In tough spots, that's not what leadership is all about. If you know your team members' strengths and possible contributions and support, then you'll be able to see derailments coming and make the right and courageous decisions that keep the team on track. "Leadership is not about being 'soft' or 'nice' or purely 'inclusive' or 'consensus-building.' The whole point is to make sure the *right* decisions happen—no matter how difficult or painful—for the long-term greatness of the institution and the achievement of mission, independent of consensus or popularity."[24]

4. STEP FOUR, finally, will keep all of your team's energy and now-sharpened focus and motivation on the right things that can actually be impacted by them. A friend used to often remind me, "You've got to pick the hill you want to die on."[25] Same message, said differently. Later in this workbook, we'll talk about planning and giving your team targets to aim for. This step is why that planning is so important. But success begins here, with you as the team's leader acknowledging all that has to be done and parceling it out in achievable steps, so that each success can help pull your team up to the next one.

As the architect of your team's future, you're almost ready to begin building, blending, and growing your staff members' skills and ambitions, all while meeting your organization's goals.

ELEVEN SOLID WAYS TO IMPROVE YOUR TIME MANAGEMENT SKILLS

1. **MAKE LISTS**: Write as much down as you can. If you don't carry a planner or notebook already, start.

2. **MAKE USE OF DOWN TIME**: Use walking, driving, showering, or otherwise "dead" times to plan. Prioritization is the key.

3. **REWARD YOURSELF**: Whenever you accomplish something, especially the important things, make sure to take the time to reward yourself.

4. **CONCENTRATE ON ONE THING** : The human mind works more efficiently when it is focused. Take care not to bleed tasks into each other. At times, multitasking may seem like a more efficient route, but it is probably not.

5. **AVOID PROCRASTINATION AT ALL COSTS**: It is the ultimate productivity killer.

6. **SET PERSONAL DEADLINES**: Set earlier, personal deadlines than the actual deadline. Not only will this save you time and make you more productive in the long run, but you will also have a buffer time with little to no penalties compared to those received for missing a real deadline.

7. **DELEGATE**: It is not uncommon for people to take on more than they can handle. To avoid this unnecessary stress, do not feel bad about delegating tasks.

8. **SET UP A LONG-TERM PLANNER**: In the everyday drab of life, we can often lose sight of our goals. Setting up a long-term planner will help you envision your long-term goals and rationalize your current objectives. (You can revise the long-term planner monthly to keep goals up-to-date.)

9. **EMPLOY A PROGRAM LIKE "RESCUE TME"**: This is a lightweight app that records and graphs how you spend your time on your computer. Those "two-minute" breaks to check out Digg, or play a flash game on some website, or e-mail Aunt Betty, can add up to quite a bit of wasted productivity and wasted time.

10. **WORK IN A TEAM**: Although giving up responsibilities is a scary thought for some, it is an invaluable method to increase the average team productivity of all involved. Make sure the team goals are clear and make sure everyone knows who is responsible for given tasks. Make sure, also, that all lines of communication are always open.

11. **BE CAREFUL TO AVOID BURNOUT**: Burnout occurs when your body and mind can no longer keep up with the tasks you demand of them. Always be sure to leave time for relaxation and reflection. *(Editor's Note: There's that one hour a week!)*[27]

A final, practical tip before moving forward to build your team. You're going to get busy. There's going to be more tasks to accomplish than time. Small problems are going to magnify themselves as the pressure of day-to-day survival mounts. The easiest, the very easiest thing to do in reaction to all of that is to forget everything you've read here so far and just start treading water. Don't do it.

Keep these pages handy. Paper clip them if you have too. And when you hear yourself saying, "Sure, I'd love to improve my skills, but I'm just too busy to get better," reread the advice and help in this chapter. And, while on the topic of business, remember one other inescapable and rescuing fact about time . . . *you* are in charge of *it.* If you've never taken a time management course or read a book on the subject, now would be a great time to start. Your time will be limited, your demands will grow, and your priorities, if you're not careful, could slip. There's no shame in relearning how to file, sort, schedule, and juggle your time. One of my favorite managers identified a staff member with incredible organizational skills. She sent the young woman to time management training and then scheduled her to spend a week at the office of each branch manager in her region. The result? Effectiveness increased, frustration decreased, and there was more time for leadership—real leadership, not pencil sharpening, than ever before.

"It's too easy to get intimidated by a daunting workload and sometimes too much work is discouraging to the point of people avoiding it completely! Putting it off generally just allows more to pile up, which in turn make you want to work on it even less. When you aren't able to get enough done every day, a number of things could be affecting your productivity. Some things, such as procrastination, distractions or inefficient work methods can be helped with the proper time management techniques."[28]

If you want to have a great team, it will need to have a focused and available leader. The work ahead of you is rewarding at the least and life-changing at best. Clear your desk. Get organized. Get ready. Your team, with all its past, present, and future, is waiting.

Lead.

SUGGESTED READING

Collins, Jim. *Good to Great and the Social Sectors: Why Business Thinking Is Not the Answer.* Boulder, CO: Jim Collins, 2005.

Kim, W. Chan, and Renee Mauborgne. "Tipping Point Leadership." *Harvard Business Review* (April 2003).

EXERCISES

-4-

1. **Leadership is very much** about decision making. List the *usual* steps you take when making a significant decision. Look at your list. Is it logical? Open? Do you communicate the process and the decision well? Is it data-driven or based on hearsay? If necessary, add some steps in to make it all of these things and then try it out on a pending decision.

   _____

   _____

   _____

   _____

2. **Describe the three strongest** elements of your team's culture and the three most threatening to future progress. Next to each one, add some notes about how to keep and/or improve the situation.

   _____

   _____

   _____

   _____

3. **Your team members will** have to be held accountable for their demonstrated commitment and actions. One way to do that is by rotating leadership at team meetings. For however many team members you have, sketch out a calendar of the same number of upcoming team meetings and assign each team member one meeting to lead. Then coach the group on your expectations. As part of each meeting, ask them to include an update on one of their own pending projects or services and invite their fellow team members to help them make improvements.

   _____

   _____

   _____

   _____

4. **If you're going to** begin by focusing on the most important issues pending before your team, first you need to know what they are. List at least ten decisions or actions facing your team, and then put them in priority order. Build your next team meeting around issue number one.

   _____

   _____

   _____

   _____

   _____

5. **How do you stay** organized? With so much work ahead of you and so many competing priorities, if you're not already good at this you need to make some changes. Describe steps you could take to start making improvements and applying your time where it's really needed.

   _____

   _____

   _____

   _____

   _____

RECURITING

| ## GAPS

"Can I talk to you for a minute?"

Oh boy. As I mentioned early on in this book, that particular phrase can send your stomach plummeting—or not. Now that you've had a chance to get your feet under you by getting to know your team better, understanding the hurdles they've faced in the past, and preparing to meet tomorrow head-on, you just might feel a bit different when you hear this knock at your door. As you should. The opportunity to reexamine your staffing levels, assignments, and personnel strengths can provide a very positive benefit to balance the loss of a valued employee. If your staff member is leaving by choice, you can be happy for them as well and, better yet, if they're leaving to accept a promotion, then you can be happy for both of you! That's the kind of opening every team leader should welcome and savor because what it means is that you've successfully helped someone to grow, stretch, succeed, and move on in their career's next challenging step.

Congratulations to you both!

Now, let's talk for a minute.

After the cake and gifts have been cleared away (or, if this isn't an amicable departure, then the sooner you get started, the better), it's time for you to take a hard look at the gap that's going to be left on your team and to begin considering what you're to do about it. The days of the automatic posting are gone and not likely to return. Nowadays, great bosses pause to consider the opportunity before them, and they look hard at *all* the options it represents.

Get out a piece of paper and number it one through three.

THE VALUE OF UPDATING JOB DESCRIPTIONS

Besides the obvious, there are many reasons that taking the time to review and update job descriptions with every opening can improve the entire hiring process, from start to finish.

- If it's a rule that you have to do it, then it gets done.
- It ensures that the job you're advertising really does exist.
- It makes for a stronger recruitment tool, when potential applicants don't read out-of-date descriptions or terminology.
- The option to change—any part—from the title to the salary presents itself.
- It results in a better match and hire, which is the whole point of the hiring process.[5]

One. Consider what work will *not* get done once your employee leaves. It's no secret that, over the years, some staff members will create enough work to fill their paid hours, whether that work is really key to the organization's mission or not. While you might have had to tolerate that situation initially, don't perpetuate it. Make sure that when the task list you create is complete, it truly reflects a viable position. If the person leaving was responsible for retyping the invoices into an in-house database, be sure to measure the value of that task. While that practice was ongoing, was another option invented? Or is the entire list still needed? Don't fill hours, fill work.

Two. Imagine what work you *wish* the person in this position would do that hasn't been done before. You may or may not have been already engaged in performance evaluations and goal setting with your soon-to-be-departed employee that, one day, you hoped would result in new achievements and contributions. Now is your chance to build those in as expectations and not

just blind hope. Perhaps customer needs have evolved to where new programs or services would be appreciated? Now is the perfect time to build them into performance expectations and standards.

And, finally, three. Think of the personality of the team in which this person will work and what would help to make it stronger. Perhaps earlier replacements have left the group a little heavy on the introvert scale and some new, more communicative staff would provide a fresh balance? Or, maybe due to retirements or other openings, you find yourself a little short of risk takers and a bit heavy on the status quo? One human resources (HR) consultant reminds us that "in a highly effective team, skills are complementary. Everyone brings something to the table that makes the whole bigger than the sum of the parts."[1] This is your chance to (carefully) add to that sum.

When you've finished this exercise, you will have begun to craft a new perspective on what might just be an outdated job description. You will also have created a personalized (to your library) gap analysis that will direct the rest of your decisions in filling (or not filling) this position. Where, traditionally, "organizational gap analysis is a process by which a business or organization identifies ways to improve performance,"[2] usually by reviewing skills, service needs and the like, this particular style of that process looks at *your* staff and its particular, new opening.

It's important to break here before you really get rolling on the process ahead of you to remember that *not* filling this new opening must remain an option. As you'll see as you move through your three steps, you might find that there's not a lot of work that's going to be left undone, that there really isn't anything special you'd like added (although that's a stretch), and that the balance of your team environment might actually improve as a result of this change. If so, find another way to use the money, either within your department or another or by holding it, in order to strengthen your library's financial future. If you've finished your analysis and you're just not sure, wait. Let the dust settle and see how your organization shakes out with one person gone, then repeat these steps a little way down the road. Often, unforeseen implications in staffing will arise and announce themselves given time, making your hiring decision easier and clearer.

But let's assume the answer is: hire! There's still a lot of work to do before you run the ad. As the boss, it's critical to remember what John Donne said, "No [wo]man is an island."[3] Now would be a great time to consider how that updated job description and your new hire can enhance the overall work team. "If you're thinking of adding more people to your team, first assess the kind of team you have. It would be nice if you could hire the right people for your team by answering a few check-off questions on a form, but it's not quite that easy. As a hiring manager, part of analyzing the open position is to understand not only the role the candidate will play, but how the organization and the team affect that role."[4]

So then, with the needs and fit of your team clearly in mind, let's get back to the job description. Without reinventing the wheel, look over what's already in use. Of course, essential functions of the position are critical and need to be totally current. But, so too should you be able to find mention of emotional intelligence, communication, motivation, initiative, creativity, and flexibility. Carefully review what's already there, add what you need (new job demands may well have come along since this was last done), then add what you want (if you can) and be prepared to find what you hadn't even imagined yet. You're adding a team member! With all of these opportunities now open, that sinking "can I speak to you for a minute" feeling is probably long gone!

One last thing: don't spend too much time polishing the diamond. Openings on any staff can be a source of dismay at best and fear at worst for all those left behind. Still, one way you can get a team benefit even out of that unsavory situation is to give some *interim* opportunities while

"MONEYBALL" HIRING TIPS

Hiring managers who assured me they "could just tell" which applicant to pick made me nervous then and still do. Don't get caught up in your own ego. Delineate needed skills and attributes, use tests and questions that accurately measure them, and then consider the results. *Then*, add your gut feeling. Here are some "knowledge discovery" or data evaluation tips.

1. Keep descriptions bare-bones. Do you need an accountant or a bookkeeper who is good with numbers?
2. Soft skills totally matter. Seek proof of them, not just claims.
3. Demonstrations can be cheap. If you're looking for a teen librarian, have them come in and spend an hour after school with the kids.
4. Don't underspend. Explains hiring consultant Daniel Dworkin, "You want your workers to start fired up, and not be planning an exit as soon as the economy turns around!"
5. Seek a blend of skills, some from each team member, not one person who has them all.
6. Look for a corporate culture fit, not misfits.
7. Design a hiring plan, stick to it, and make a decision. Don't overspend on the process before getting to the solution.[6]

you're moving the process forward as fast as you can. In professional sports, no player wants to be injured and no injured player wants to be out for too long. Why? Because they know there's always an understudy in the wings who can fill in and maybe even show them up, while meaning to just keep the bench warm. For you, the boss, this can be a great thing. If you've been developing your staff professionally all along, you'll have learned in previous evaluation meetings who's ready to step up and is just waiting for a chance like this. Don't let tasks go undone when you can keep the team's work moving forward *and* stretch and grow the next generation of success stories at the same time. Consider making some temporary assignments, with adequate training and support provided. To beat the sports metaphor up just a little more, you might just be surprised to see who steps up to the plate.

And when's a better time to learn that than now . . . when you're about to start your replacement search?

EXERCISES

-5-

1. **Make a list of** the key duties of the person who is leaving your staff. (If no one is leaving right as you reach this exercise, then complete it thinking in general terms of the person who might logically leave next.) Then number them in priority order. List everything! Finally, cross out the things that (1) someone else already does; (2) no one really needs to do anymore; or (3) still need to be done but could be streamlined. Finally, do your best to put time estimates next to each. This will give a good estimate of whether or not there's time left to add the new jobs you'd like to see tackled.

   _____
   _____
   _____
   _____
   _____
   _____

2. **What are some of** the new tasks that changes in your library or the economy might have brought forward? List them. If there's someone already on your staff who you think would enjoy and do them well, jot that down. You can always "take" other jobs from them and give them to your new person. With this kind of forward planning, you'll know the talents and interests for which you should be looking.

   _____
   _____
   _____
   _____
   _____
   _____

3. **List, in general terms,** the personalities/quirks and strengths already present within your work team. What elements would complement them? Which types might be fuel to the fire? With these two lists in hand, craft a description of the person you haven't even met yet, who would be a perfect fit!

   _____
   _____
   _____
   _____
   _____

4. **Think back to the** last time you filled a position. Even with the best intentions, you probably made some mistakes. Jot down some things you didn't do quite right and make notes about how you can do a better job throughout the process this time around.

   _____
   _____
   _____
   _____
   _____
   _____

RECRUITING

| ## THROWING THE NET

"We'll try ANYTHING that can improve customer service!"

"Grumpy people need not apply."

"If you like computers better than people, keep looking!"

Without mentioning any names, these are some of my favorite job ads I've seen. Why? Like libraries, they're not just full of words, they're full of feelings.

Since it's now time for you to begin thinking about how to advertise your open position so as to attract the type of person your library needs, it's time to consider the creative and valuable recruitment tools at your disposal. It's time to throw the net.

Everything, absolutely everything you do and use to lure the perfect person into your open position should keep you focused on your goal of developing a great team. Primary on your list should be creating a group of people not by their sameness but by their differences. Someone once asked in an advocacy class, "When is the right time to begin preparing to pass a property tax levy?" The answer was "The morning after you passed the last one." I'd suggest the same ongoing approach should be in place for support and development of diversity on your staff.

In order to be prepared to recognize and support and champion diversity, first you have to recognize it. Several suggestions for how to do this well were offered in *The Diversity Tool Kit.*[7] Do you belong to clubs or professional organizations where membership is diverse? Do you subscribe to publications whose emphasis is diversity? Do you attend (or sponsor) community functions that honor the diversity in your existing staff? If you can't answer *yes* to any of these, then, long after you've filled this position, keep working at it, so you're better prepared for the next one. But, for now, this *Diversity Tool Kit* and other publications like it can help

5 TIPS FOR WRITING GREAT JOB ADS

1. **Write a Great Job Title:** You can test the value of this next time you post a job ad by posting it twice, once with a boring title (Front End Developer) and once with something more creative (Do You Dream of CSS Classes and jQuery Functions?) and see what type of applicant each delivers.

2. **Portray Your Culture in the Company Description:** You're looking for a perfect fit for your team, so describe what life in that team is like! Do you bring your dogs to work, are there flexible hours, are neckties and stockings required? For many, the culture of an organization can be as important as the pay.

3. **Be Realistic about the Requirements:** The applicant should be able to scan a (not too long) bulleted list of required qualifications and tell right away if the skills listed are ones they have—and are ones they want to spend all day doing.

4. **Be Realistic about Experience Needed:** Often-used models for this were arbitrarily created so long ago no one still on staff can remember why. Back when computers in libraries were new, for example, you'd never think of hiring a PC person without at least five years' experience. Now, young adults right of college are likely just as qualified. Be reasonable and accurate in your estimates.

5. **Keep It Flexible:** Don't be afraid to use the word *preferred*, both so you can keep your options open and so you can be delighted by some extra quality you hadn't even thought about before! Remember, you're building a team, not widgets.[15]

ing schools and churches. They can often help fill you in on demographic changes going on in the community that you are attempting to serve. If you already have some diversity represented on your staff, tap those employees for referrals or for suggestions for *nontraditional* advertising venues you might use.

When they visited the director's office to announce their final selection for the new librarian, she stopped them at the door and said, "Let me guess, she's white, kind of quiet, in her early thirties, with long, blonde hair?" Both selection team members, each white, kind of quiet, in their early thirties, with long blonde hair, gaped in amazement! "How did you know?" they asked.

True story. Listen, all hiring supervisors mean well. All have one goal in common (or should have) and that is to hire the right person. As with life in general, we fear what we don't know and gravitate towards what is like us. But beware of this temptation. With an opening in front of you you've decided you will fill, you have a golden opportunity to seize. Cast that net wide and look for people who can enrich, broaden, stretch, and differentiate your team. By doing so, your community members will begin to see the library for what it is—or should be: an image of themselves.

One definition of diversity explains, "Diversity means variety. It influences all aspects of our environment and encompasses all of those qualities that make us the same, similar, different, and unique."[8] So how do you attract that variety? Let's talk a bit about the job ad you're about to write.

What's the first rule of advertising your opening? It's *Don't* use the ad the library has always used. At least, don't use it automatically. If it truly describes the person for whom you are seeking and it has all the other hallmarks of an attractive, relevant, exciting description of the opportunity you're offering, then, by all means, go ahead and get some more mileage out of it. Consider, though, if it meets all of those qualifications. Does it *sell* the job—and the library—to the applicant?[9] In an article for managers in the hospitality indus-

suggest some immediate steps that might help in your broadened search. For example, check with contacts you have in local organizations, includ-

try, some very specific examples were presented to demonstrate this point. Consider how to sell the job. "Sales manager needed for 60-bedroom, three-star hotel in New York. Job will also cover restaurant" doesn't sound half as good as "The Grand Hotel in picturesque York needs a dynamic new sales manager. With 60 bedrooms, we're one of the biggest hotels in the city and our restaurant has won the Yorkshire East Out award for the past three years. Have you got what it takes to make us even more successful?"[10]

Remember, "the job advertisement is the potential applicant's window into your [library]. If you want to attract the right people, you need to make sure they know you're there, know what you're about and why you need them."[11] "If you write a lousy job description, chances are you'll get a lousy response rate."[12] Don't let that happen to you. Most likely, you're hoping for a breath of fresh air, a new set of eyes, eager and unfettered by old habits and grudges. So, write *to* that person. Don't be afraid to include creative, honest words that one might not normally see in an ad. Let the potential applicants out there know that *this* job is special and is just what they're looking for! "For an ad to get you the very best candidates, it needs to break the mold of every employment ad you have ever seen!"[13]

Once you've written the part of your ad that describes the library and the job, you've got one more decision to make. Other than an application or resume, for what *else* should you ask? First of all, it has to be something! These days, in the competitive world that is library work, dozens if not hundreds of applications could bury you if you don't start that self-selection process early, with the application! You'll notice I said "self-selection" because you've got to start thinking of this process as just that. From now until you introduce your new hire to the staff, remember—let them select or de-select themselves!

This is important! Too often, I've heard bosses, while flipping through a pile of applications that are blocking out the sun, comment: "This one used to be a teacher. They don't do well in

WHAT DIVERSITY REALLY MEANS

Once upon a time, diversity was used as a euphemism for race. Today, that richness has grown, as the cultures of our communities have broadened. Consider all of these characteristics when seeking diversity in your team and feel free to add more. After all, it's your community!

- First Language
- Education
- Work Style
- Communication Style
- Family Status
- Organization Role and Level
- Geographic Location and/or Origin
- Work Experience
- Income
- Religion
- Military Experience
- Age
- Race
- Ethnic Heritage
- Gender
- Mental/Physical Abilities and Qualities
- Sexual Orientation[16]

libraries." Or, "This one lives too far away; we'd almost certainly have attendance problems." Don't fall into that trap. First, you're not Carnac the Magnificent (look it up!), so you don't *know* any of that for a fact. And, second, those comments reflect you, rejecting someone based on an unsupported impression. Maybe the person who lives far away is so committed to their work that they'd end up being the best employee you've ever had. You don't know that they won't! So, rather than rely on intuition or (worse) assumption, ask them for things that will *show* you, at each step in the process, if they should stay in or out of the running.

Bosses often agonize over what to ask for that can best reveal those special features they need to see. Should you require a cover letter? (Can you be certain the applicant wrote it herself? No.) References? (Are they honest or just someone wanting to move their problem somewhere else?) Answers to written prescreening questions? Now we're getting somewhere!

As long as you ask questions that truly reveal a person's knowledge, skills, abilities, and background, you're going to be learning things that will really, truly matter. While some people might characterize these pieces of the package as barriers, I say bring them on! How else can you have confidence that the "weeding" you're doing through the applications is getting you closer to the right fit? "Creating reasonable barriers to entry has two important benefits: it weeds out the unmotivated and ill-fitting, and it increases the perceived cache of the role."[14]

Envision the perfect team fit that this opening is giving you the chance to fill, write your ad, and place it where the people you're seeking will find it. There's still more work to do before the responses start coming in, but at least when they do, both you and they will be in the right ballpark.

SUGGESTED READING

Gardenswartz, Lee, and Anita Rowe. *The Diversity Tool Kit*. Irwin Professional Publications, 1994.

EXERCISES

-6-

1. **First, make a list** of the cultural differences already in existence within your team. Then describe at least one special contribution the team enjoys, based on each one.

   _____
   _____
   _____
   _____
   _____

2. **Pick a position to** use as an example for this exercise (if you have a real position open right now, use that!) and write the most creative description of it that you can. Remember, you're "selling" the position to someone.

   _____
   _____
   _____
   _____
   _____
   _____
   _____
   _____

3. **Now, write a compelling** description of your library and team, one that would make an applicant have to be crazy not to want to work with you!

   _____
   _____
   _____
   _____
   _____
   _____
   _____

4. **List all the titles** of positions you supervise, which might become empty. Next to each, write an alternative, more creative way of naming the job. These could become the next headlines for your job ads!

   _____
   _____
   _____
   _____
   _____

5. **Using that same list** of positions on your team, note at least three "extra" components you might request, should you advertise that position to candidates. Supplemental applications materials wouldn't necessarily be the same for different jobs. Be creative. What could they do/provide/bring/present that would really help you learn more about them. What could you learn from each tool?

   _____
   _____
   _____
   _____

RECRUITING

WEEK THREE | **THE HIRING TEAM**

Any day now, those large, yellow envelopes stuffed with application materials are going to start flowing into your library's HR office. You can picture them. You can't wait to get your hands on them. You're anxious to tear them open and start checking out the . . . wait a minute. Eager as you may be to see the fruits of your advertising labors, you've still got a lot of work to do before you can slice open that first package. Namely, you have to get your hiring team in place!

Involving other staff members on a hiring team can be almost like teaching a course in teamwork. While it's their opportunity to become even more invested in the group, it's also your chance to set the stage for success, for everyone involved. Think of the elements of blending that you can highlight throughout this process. You can emphasize existing team members' strengths and weaknesses and recognize openly that it's okay to have both. Together, you can identify the core skills and contributions that will strengthen your team so that, once you've found them, an initial level of respect and appreciation will already exist. And, perhaps most important, you can be growing leadership qualities and skills for all involved, by coaching them to develop openness, communication, and decision-making skills.

HR professional Joan Lloyd suggests some clear guidelines to keep in mind when assembling your hiring team. "First," she begins, "decide who the interviewing team will be. It might be peer managers, along with the person who is to be the person's manager. It could be a combination of peers, employees and 'internal' customers, who will be interacting with the new person. (If) the group will make the ultimate decision by con-

WHO GETS TO MAKE THE FINAL DECISION?

If you're wondering why no hands go up when some bosses ask for hiring team volunteers, it may be because they've been there before and they think their input was ignored. Often, that's not the case, but it might look that way. Take the time, up front, to clarify why you need their input, how it will be used, and, ultimately, who will make the decision. One definition of decision-making offers five choices.

- **LEVEL ONE:** The leader makes the decision alone.
- **LEVEL TWO:** The leaders make the decision, with input.
- **LEVEL THREE:** You are seeking consensus, but the leader gets the final say.
- **LEVEL FOUR:** The leader will delegate the decision to another person or team.
- **LEVEL FIVE:** True consensus must be reached (i.e., everyone must, if not agree, at least be able to live with the final decision).[21]

WHAT ACTUALLY HAPPENS BEYOND THE INTERVIEW ROOM DOOR

Here are some tips on how to assemble, include, and utilize the strengths of your team and not just end up with a room full of confused people—your applicant included.

- Use a room that's large enough to allow everyone to be comfortable and see one another clearly.
- Make sure team members are appropriately dressed, uninterrupted, and not rushed. To do otherwise would send a clear message that "you don't really have a chance here, we're just going through the motions."
- Place the applicant where he can easily make eye contact with all members of the team. Provide him (and team members, if they desire) with a beverage. Your goal is to make everyone as comfortable as possible.
- Before each applicant arrives, allow time to recap their qualifications, strengths, and weaknesses. Don't let team members be sifting through paperwork for reminders of who this is during the interview.
- Applicants should have been provided a list of interviewers' names before the event, but take the time to introduce everyone again, face to face.
- Lighten up. Interviews are incredibly stressful, no matter how experienced the applicant. Encourage your team to be relaxed and welcoming. Your goal, again, is to make your potential new hire comfortable so you can learn as much as is possible about them and them about you.[22]

sensus . . . if there is *anyone* who could veto the choice, they should be included from the beginning."[17]

A word here about veto power; specifically, yours. Right after the coffee and donuts are shared at your first hiring team meeting, you need to clarify who gets to vote, which votes matter, and who will make the final decision. Then you have to stick by that. Period. If the situation calls for you to analyze input and then make the call, say that. Out loud. If the decision will lie with group consensus, explain exactly what that means. Often, people confuse consensus with majority or, worse, unanimity. Be clear from the beginning about how the process will end or you'll face the possibility that you'll do much more harm to the team than good by including

them. And certainly, if you proclaim there is individual autonomy for hiring supervisors within your organization and you're not that person in this case, then step aside. Regardless of the fact that you outrank the hiring supervisor, if it's their job to make the final decision, let them make the final decision. To do otherwise will leave them feeling betrayed, mistrusted, perhaps used, and certainly deflated. Not exactly the kind of team spirit you're looking for, for sure.

But wait, what if their decision is wrong, you might be thinking. Then so be it. Throughout your career as a boss, your charge will remain largely the same. Coach, train, develop, trust, motivate, and encourage your staff members to grow. Mistakes will be an unavoidable and, often, beneficial aspect of that growth. But only if you allow your staff to make them—and fix them—and move on. "You don't lead by hitting people over the head—that's assault, not leadership,"[18] Dwight D. Eisenhower once said.

So then, with your team in place and your process for decision making clearly articulated, you can move on to make certain each hiring team member understands what the procedure is and in what way they will be contributing. Lloyd suggests that several steps make up this part of your process, including reviewing the qualifications for which you're looking (perhaps even including putting "musts" and "preferred" on a flip chart for discussion) and deciding on what the questions will be and how they'll be asked.[19] There's room,

and reason, for a few more steps in this process. First, remembering that this is a coaching and development exercise for your team members as well as a hiring process for your organization, consider adding some formal training into the schedule on topics such as behavioral interviewing or active listening. Because the interview process is fraught with nerves and tension, it pays to have super-vigilant interviewers, who can see beyond the trembling hands to the real answers, skills, and background the applicants have to share.

If this sounds like a lot of work, then you're paying attention. It is and should be a considerable process to seek, identify, evaluate, and select a new member of your team. "When you consider the high cost and emotional destruction that comes from hiring the wrong person for the job, the time spent on the front end is well worth it."[20]

Remember your ultimate goal is to *Build a Great Team!* While working day-to-day with the people you already have will offer many chances to accomplish this, those golden opportunities to bring in a brand-new person, perspective, and contributor cannot be overestimated. Grow your team with your team involved and you'll be building foundational synergy that will move you all forward—together.

EXERCISES

7

1. **Carefully evaluate the current** members of your team and list the names of those whom you might want to add to a hiring team. Next, think outside of your department or branch or, perhaps, even library and add other names of people whose expertise, experience, and insight could bring a fresh eye.

   _____
   _____
   _____

2. **Looking back to the** list of names from question #1, make notes after each person about what they would contribute to the team. (This part of the process helps keep you from selecting people just because "they've never been on a team before." While an honest sentiment, it's rarely a good reason for inclusion. This process will also help prepare you for that first hiring team meeting, when you share with everyone exactly why they're there.)

   _____
   _____
   _____

3. **With what type of** hiring decision would you be comfortable? Do you make the final call on your own, after considering input? Do subordinate hiring supervisors make their own call, after considering your input? (And, if they don't, this might be a good time to consider why you don't allow that and change your practice.) Describe the decision-making process you want to use and make notes to explain it here, so you can better explain it to the team later.

   _____
   _____
   _____

4. **Imagine you have given** decision-making authority to another hiring supervisor and you fear they're about to make the *wrong* decision. What would you do? How would you counsel them? How would you approach helping them with that wrong decision, once you've let them make it, to minimize impact?

   _____
   _____
   _____

5. **From where do you** get interview questions? While you're not at the stage in this workbook yet to write them, think about sources you have used and might use in the future and list them.

   _____
   _____
   _____

6. **Finally, research and locate** a well-reviewed article on behavioral interviewing, currently a popular approach, and read it carefully. Even if you've used this method before, this review might help remind you of why it should or shouldn't work in your environment.

   _____
   _____
   _____

RECRUITING

| **THE RIGHT FOOT**

Since almost a full four months had gone by since she'd submitted her application for a certain opening, a librarian once told me she was shocked when she answered the phone one day to hear the HR person inviting her in for an interview. She'd never received confirmation that her application had actually arrived, she'd been transferred from department to department when she'd called to inquire, and finally, when she stopped by one day to ask in person about the status of the search, she'd been met with rudeness at best and disdain at worst. Because of all that treatment, she said she wanted to respond by saying that she wouldn't work for an organization that would treat potential employees that way if it was the last job open on earth. Instead, she politely told them she'd retired.

Again, true story. But since you're in charge of your own hiring story, you can write a better one.

If you read a lot about management, you might be getting sick of hearing that communication is the key to everything. You'd better get over that, because it is. An individual's decision to apply for a place on your team is step one of a process in which you have the opportunity to put your best foot forward. Through your ad, the job can shine and your organization can shine and attract only the best. Through the communication that takes place from the time that first application arrives, you can go a step further and showcase how people who join your team are treated.

"We all have our moments, but think about how you feel when you meet or speak with someone. Their tone, demeanor, presence, energy—all inspire a feeling. That feeling is as powerful as the words and actions themselves.

COMMUNICATE POTENTIAL NEGATIVES
CLEARLY TO YOUR APPLICANTS

One HR specialist stated that "most companies which are looking to hire new workers take the approach of trying to sell the job and the organization to candidates by telling them all the positives." He goes on to suggest, however, "that by allowing candidates to preview the job and by showing them the negatives, a sizeable proportion will screen themselves out before they are hired, rather than after."[26] Some examples of cons to consider include:

1. Let applicants actually observe employees working at the same job for which they're applying. (If you're hiring someone to work with teens, for example, don't just take their word that they love that age group. Invite them to spend an hour or so in your teen room after school before the interview begins and observe their behavior.)
2. Describe the potential downsides of the job. A cable installer, for example, once told all applicants about not only the work they did, but all about the heat and insects they had to suffer through.
3. If the work is highly repetitive, let the applicant try doing it for a couple of hours straight, just to see if they're suited to the job.
4. If the environment is high-pressure or features constant interruptions, ask them to explain how they'd stay sane in such a setting or, better yet, how they've handled it before (experience speaks louder than intentions).
5. Make sure your "type A" applicants know how quiet your smallest branch is, before they're in it and are frustrated at the lack of action. Again, having them spend some time actually seeing the setting can go a lot further than just hearing about it.

"If the applicant is intrinsically better suited to one rather than the other, then clearly it is preferable that she/he knows what to expect in advance, so as to make an informed decision and, hopefully, stay in the post longer."[27]

I believe we should all pay attention to this concept—and determine what feeling we are trying to invoke to complement our message."[23]

This great advice should guide your every action as you and your organization begin the important process of interacting with a potential new team member. Specifically, what should you consider? The following steps, which have actually been used by organizations for some time, might get your list and your imagination going.

1. Respond immediately to the receipt of an application with a message that doesn't just acknowledge that you got it but conveys excitement and appreciation for the applicant's interest in your organization.
2. Continue open, formal or informal communication (depending on your culture) that keeps the applicant apprised of the process and progress. This doesn't have to take a lot of staff time, since one letter, carefully crafted, can be sent (or, these days, even more effortlessly e-mailed) to your entire pool of applicants.

3. Avoid tricks and traps. Review the applicant materials quickly and notify the sender if pieces or parts are missing. While many hiring managers will use those lapses as a reason to exclude the application (*If they can't follow application directions, what would the rest of their work be like?*), it's often better to save that reaction for tie-breakers or too-close-to-call elimination techniques. After all, your primary goal should always be to attract the richest group of candidates possible, before the elimination process begins.

4. Describe the interview experience completely, ahead of time. When notifying your lucky few that they've been chosen for actual interviews, help them be well prepared and, therefore, able to show you their best side, by telling them where the interview will be, who will be involved (including titles), what the interview will entail, how long it will last, and anything else unique about the event that might otherwise catch them off guard. Remember, you're communicating with someone who might well end up being the very best employee you've ever had! If you treat them that way from the start, you're closer already to making it a reality.

5. No sandwiches. One high-level interview was interrupted constantly by hiring team members refreshing their soft drinks, searching for just the right sandwich condiment, and otherwise busying themselves with dinner! Show respect for the applicant's time, efforts, and interest in the position by eliminating any possible distractions during the interview, so everyone can pay undivided attention to the answers being offered. *What you DO communicates as much or more about your organization as what you SAY in a well-worded letter.*

6. Communicate in writing following the interview if there is going to be an

COMMUNICATE CLEARLY TO YOUR HIRING TEAM

Everyone is busy. While being invited to take part in the hiring process is a compliment and, often, an exciting prospect, it's also more work added to often already overworked employees. Be clear about what you'll be asking them to do, when they'll be doing it, and when they'll be done. Here's an example of how communication can seem clear, when it's really not. Don't let this type of communication guide your hiring team!

Aoccdrnig to rscheearch at Cmabrigde Uinervtisy, it deosn't mttaer in what order the ltteers in a word are, the olny iprmoetnt thing is that the frist and lsat ltteer be at the rghit pclae. The rset can be a total mses and you can still raed it wouthit a porbelm. This is bcuseae the human mind deos not raed ervey lteter by istlef, but the word as a wlohe.

So…

1. Clearly define the task or project.
2. State the deadlines, standards, and format.
3. Give time frame.
4. Check progress periodically.
5. Give feedback.[28]

unusual delay in the decision-making process. If your time line remains normal, there may not be a reason for this step (although it is still a nice thing to do), but when, as sometimes happens, a decision maker is out of the office or another candidate's interview is delayed, your communication can be a welcome and stress-reducing gesture to someone who is counting the days until the phone rings.

7. Keep your options open. Don't ever tell a candidate they did not get the job until the one who did get it signs on the dotted line. You don't want to burn bridges you might end up revisiting or leave an

impression of confusion or wavering on the part of your leadership team.

8. Finally, saving the biggest and most important tip for last, banish all gossip, comments, winks, eye rolling, and large, heaving breaths between every member of your hiring team and absolutely anyone else. Anywhere. "How many applicants did you get?" should be answered with "It's not appropriate for me to discuss that." "Did she apply again?" should be answered with "It's not appropriate for me to discuss that." "Do you think he has a chance?" should be answered with "It's not appropriate. . ." You get the drill. *It's not appropriate for anyone involved in hiring to discuss any part of the process outside the hiring team.* Why? Beyond legal considerations and many employment laws, it's not nice. Also, "Breach of confidentiality cannot only be a legal problem. Perhaps more importantly, it can create a breach of trust that is difficult, if not impossible, to repair."[24]

One inarguable goal that will contribute to the greatness of your team is that ever-tilting windmill, the perfect fit. Many an eager, unemployed applicant has brushed away the advice to be sure and interview them, while they're interviewing you, and both sides have suffered as a result. Your communication process at every single step of the hiring process should be part of your perfect-fit-quest. So, tell them everything. Spend time just talking in the interview, before the more serious questioning begins. Tell them what's good about the place and the job and what's challenging. Give examples, if you can. And think outside of the box to find ways to explain the special features that make your organization one anyone and everyone would like to join. Some features to consider describing might include: being listed on a "best place to work" list; having a culture of innovation, risk-taking, and the celebration of diversity; demonstrating employment stability and security; having high values and a strong culture, offering great training and development opportunities; or sponsoring lifestyle benefits, such as flex time, wellness programs (that work), or even lots of parties![25]

And while you're busy communicating positively to your applicants, remember to be doing the same to your team members. Don't *say* you want their input, then cut them out of the information chain. Don't surprise them, as though you don't respect their time and other duties, by hurriedly scheduling quick interviews, and don't leave them wondering how the last step went and, most important, what will come next.

Everyone, from the applicants to your existing team to that wonderful new person you're going to be adding, will be looking at your feet throughout this process. Communicate openly, be excited, be honest, and put your best one forward.

EXERCISES

-8-

1. **Sketch out the process** you and/or your organization currently uses when you begin receiving applications for an advertised opening. Write it as though you're reporting in a time line and include all the actions that take place.

_____
_____
_____
_____
_____
_____

2. **Review your time line** from the above answer but, this time, edit it. Make sure it follows a professional pattern and has all the steps necessary to showcase your organization in the best possible light to the applicant. Then, make a "to do" list of changes you need to make to get this new system in place.

_____
_____
_____
_____
_____
_____

3. **How can you improve** this system? Remember, you're being given the opportunity to accomplish two things when working with a hiring team. One, you're going to hire the very best employee you've ever had; and two, you're going to be coaching, developing, and growing new skills in your existing team members, making them more valuable employees as well. Write the process you need to follow to make this happen.

_____
_____
_____
_____
_____
_____

4. **Finally, draft a plan** that will showcase your library in its best (and worst) possible light. Once you've created this description, you can adapt it for various positions and use it over and over in future hires. List the best reasons to work there and describe, honestly, some of the challenges. When your applicants read this, they're going to be able to decide if they want to turn back or not, before everyone's time is wasted. (You can also use parts of this description to craft some very useful interview questions.)

_____
_____
_____
_____
_____
_____

NARROWING

WEEK ONE | **FIRST IMPRESSIONS**

The hiring team had been selected but they weren't present in the office on that fateful day when the HR director decided it was time to begin the application review process. Hurriedly, overconfidently, and unfortunately, carelessly, he quickly scanned through the document pile, tossing pages quickly into one pile or another with comments like, "She used to be a teacher, they don't fit well in libraries"; "This one lives too far away, they'd never want to drive this far"; "I think my friend knows this one and doesn't really like her much"; and "I'll bet she's almost ready to retire."

His intention was to present the hiring team with the *top* five or so candidates, even though they would have made it into that pile based solely on his biased, unbalanced, and opinionated review. Not a great start to effective team building.

After all the careful thought and analysis that's (hopefully) gone into this opportunity to bring in a new team member, the process shouldn't speed up at this point but should begin to slow down, as it carefully and strategically hones in on the perfect new fit. Too often, in a rush to fill a challenging opening, steps are jumped over, as in the above example. How can you keep this from happening? Think "team" and, at every juncture, keep everyone involved. There's a lot more at stake here, as you build a great team, than just filling another seat at the desk. Let's consider for just a moment the role of support staff at this juncture.

Many organizations aren't blessed with large enough staffing budgets to employ trained human resources personnel, so administrators fill that role. Others have entire departments dedicated to HR and personnel operations.

THE "COST" OF A BAD HIRE

No one wants to pick the wrong applicant but it happens. Fortunately, more often than not, it can be avoided by investing time, talent, thought, and skill into the hiring process. If you're thinking, at this point, that you don't want to spend so much time on just one hire, consider the implications of making the wrong choice.

1. You would *waste the resources* of the organization. The time spent on recruiting, interviewing, and processing a new employee is considerable.
2. You would *reduce staff morale* when the new employee fails to perform up to expectations.
3. You would *waste the time and energy of the supervisor*, who must devote unnecessary attention to evaluate, correct, or limit unproductive behavior.
4. You would *waste the time* taken to train the employee.
5. You might end up with *increased absenteeism and accidents*, which increase organizational costs.
6. You would *expend the time of administrators*, who must deal with deteriorating performance.
7. You would *decrease the quality of service* delivered to the public.

Both options can work, as long as their contribution to team development remains in *support* of the team leader's autonomy and not in *lieu* of it. Why does this matter? From the beginning to the end of this book, you'll learn about the myriad of ways that teams are built, developed, challenged, and balanced by you, their leader. Throughout this process the leader, too, is growing and improving. What if a golfer, when he's just about to swing his driver at the first tee, is replaced by the local pro who claims, "I know this hole better than you do, I've been playing it for years. Let me hit this first shot for you." Sure, the pro would argue, the ball might fly a little straighter—or it might not. But how much did the golfer learn and how valuable overall is that person going to be to his team?

If an organization cannot give hiring autonomy to its team leaders, then it should do everyone a favor and replace or eliminate them. Hopefully, that's not the answer. The answer is patience— and process. Right or wrong, good hire or bad (and you'll read about what to do with those later), leaders need to be able to build, rebuild, and continually *lead*. Good golfers do need their pros and their coaches, just as team leaders need support from other professional staff. But before you go any further, make sure everyone knows exactly who is driving the bus. Hopefully, all will be present to lend their valuable support but will be in their proper place when that fateful day finally does arrive . . . and it's time to begin the application review process!

Once assembled, the hiring team, its professional support personnel, and the team leader need to work together, with a road map, in order to effectively move forward. Those aren't just pieces of paper with lots of writing on them in that in-box. They are lives. They are people. They are experiences and potential. That one that you just glanced at, in case you don't know this (and, at this point, you don't), just happens to belong to the very best employee this organization might ever have. The other one, that someone else at the table likes, would result in the worst team fit you can imagine. Are you ready to get started? Almost. First, you need to create that map.

"The interviewing process, even when carefully structured, is a distinctly human process. There is nothing intrinsically wrong with this. The problem arises when the decision-making process is tainted with considerations that are not relevant to determining the ability of the candidates to perform the job."[1] While "no set rules exist for evaluating job applicants—other than common sense, your business needs some kind of applicant-evaluation system or protocol in place before resumes or applications"[2] can be assessed. If you've got that wonderful job ad you ran handy, you can get to work creating your system.

Several very simple and, likely, obvious rules should guide you in the creation of your evaluation tool. First, rate what you asked for. This point should underscore, again, the importance of writing a complete and accurate job ad that truly reflects the skills, knowledge, and abilities you're seeking in your new hire. One option is to create a spreadsheet or "grading" chart that, along the left side, lists every applicant by name (or number, if you want to protect anonymity and assure fairness in rating internal applicants). Along the top, create a column for each of the criteria you specified in the ad. If you asked for a college degree, assign that element a column. As you review applicants, put a check mark in that space for everyone with the required or requested education. Did you ask for specific experience? There's another column. How about certain, specific skills? Review your entire advertisement and, if you referred to it in the ad, the position's job description, and allow room to *count* the number of qualifications met.

A word of warning here: don't let yourself get too caught up in the formality of this process. While it's important to assure that your top candidates are bringing what you seek to the interview table, leave a column or two open as well to allow yourself to be surprised by a quality you hadn't even thought of, which would help round out the skills of your team. Even though you're attempting, at this point in the process, to fairly compare apples to apples, adding a new variety once in a while might be just what your team really needs! Remember what Henry Ford once said: "If I'd asked people what they wanted, they would have said faster horses."[3] Prepare to be delighted and surprised by your pool.

Once everyone on the team has had a chance to evaluate the applications themselves, get together

INITIAL MEASURING STICKS

Your job advertisement and your first review format should contain the nuts and bolts of the position requirements. There will be time later for unique accomplishments and incredible experience to be shared. Start by making sure that the basic building blocks for success are in place.

Measure to be sure the following key elements are present:

THE PREREQUISITES FOR THE POSITION

These should track with the qualifications listed in the job description (or ad).

SPECIAL REQUIREMENTS

In an accounting firm, for example, perhaps only applicants with a CPA credential would be considered.

DELINEATED QUALIFICATIONS OR ATTRIBUTES

Identify those attributes that you feel will produce superior performance in functions critical to your library's competitive strength and look for these attributes in prospective employees.

Whatever you do, don't rush this step![4]

and review the resulting scores, reflections, comments, and reactions. This might be your first chance to really feel the team synergy that a new member could add. This step is precisely why a good leader doesn't want the packets reviewed clinically and dispassionately by another department member, who might just be looking to see if all the required elements are present and in order. This step is also the reason you're working with members of your team, and not just by yourself. Sure, you know what you *think* is needed, but how can you expect the rest of your team to openly and appreciatively accept any new member without having this chance to begin building excitement, anticipation, and appreciation for their skills early on?

Often, this grading process results in a pretty clear division between the top candidates and the rest of the pool. Just as often, though, this grading process is where team members can get stuck and can be reluctant to eliminate a perfectly good (but not perfect) candidate, so that your process can move forward. The best way to avoid this glitch is to present the review process not as an elimination (with an "A" pile and an "F" pile) but as a narrowing (between, for example, the "Cs," "A minuses," and the clear "As"). With assurance that the group can always go back, if not completely satisfied with the interview results, and reconsider some of the borderline contenders, many will be more comfortable extracting the true stars from the group and starting from there.

Your team is forming first impressions at this point. This is your first look, your first chance to reflect and really listen to one another, and your first opportunity to be as fair as you can be. This process is also logical and replicable; both are considered hallmarks of a professional hiring system. Clearly, lacking the manpower, time, and energy to personally interview everyone, some discriminating measures must come first. The best ones to use are the ones you've already identified, which happily leaves room for even more surprises down the road, since you're almost ready for the first interview.

SUGGESTED READING

Rubin, Richard E. *Human Resource Management in Libraries: Theories and Practice.* New York: Neal-Schuman, 1991.

Rubin, Richard E. *Hiring Library Employees.* New York: Neal-Schuman, 1993.

EXERCISES

-9-

1. **Last month, you selected** staff to join you in your search process, primarily making up your hiring team from within the immediate department or branch. It's time to think of who else from your organization it might be wise to include for support. Or, if you have no choice in the matter, then how might you productively use those who will also be taking part in the process, without minimizing either your or your team members' valuable input? List their names and describe their optimal roles.

   _____
   _____
   _____
   _____

2. **Who makes the final** hiring decision in your organization? If it's not you, then make some notes about how you can work with that person to assure that your valuable insight as the team leader is heard and considered. Even if it isn't customary for you to write a formal recommendation for hire, outline one anyway, so that you can be sure your voice and input will be presented.

   _____
   _____
   _____
   _____

3. **Thinking of the entire** hiring team, both coworkers and support personnel who will be involved, what might get in the way of their objectivity? List as many variables as possible and, next to each, begin to note how you can ameliorate the impact of these challenges.

   _____
   _____
   _____
   _____

4. **Once the initial review** is completed, what if the team comes together only to find major disagreements on the assessments? List at least three tactics you could use to bring the group to consensus. (Remember, consensus isn't the same as majority rules. It means reaching a decision everyone involved, whether they totally agree with it or not, can live with.)

   _____
   _____
   _____
   _____

5. **While you have members** of your team gathered together for this review process, describe at least one exercise or activity you can build in, not only to sharpen their impressions of the applicants but also of the team overall, and how the team can be strengthened with this new addition.

   _____
   _____
   _____
   _____

NARROWING

| ## A BOOK BY ITS COVER

Although paying for a plane ticket, rental car, and hotel hadn't been on their radar before, the hiring team was overwhelmed by the outstanding quality of application materials one person had submitted from across the country. Almost every single aspect of her application was perfect. Actually, there really wasn't a need to meet her in person, since they'd be happy to just offer the job to her over the phone, but one experienced member of the team insisted on not skipping that step, so they flew her in.

At the appointed time, they eagerly opened the door to the outer reception area to welcome her in. But no one was there. Ten minutes later, still no one. Finally, a half hour after her interview was scheduled to begin, someone called from the front door to say she'd just ambled in and had headed for the cafeteria to finish her written assignment. Huh? Finalists had been instructed to bring a draft of the agenda they might use at their first staff meeting as branch manager and, apparently, two weeks hadn't been enough time for her to complete it? A full forty-five minutes after the planned start of the interview, she knocked on the door. No one could believe it was the same person standing before them. She was casually disheveled and non-apologetic as she ripped her handwritten agenda from the spiral pad and handed it over. Without even introducing herself, she demanded, "So, where do I sit?"

I know I keep saying this but, true story.

Whoever originally said you can't judge a book by its cover must have done a lot of interviewing. Truly, in this example, those transportation costs represented money very well spent! There can be many explanations for the

WHAT TO LOVE ABOUT TELEPHONE INTERVIEWS

- They can help you develop a strong pool of applicants at which you want to take a closer look.
- The cost is far less (especially in staff hours) than managing multiple in-person interviews.
- They can help you eliminate applicants based on high-priority considerations, such as availability and schedule flexibility.
- By using standardized questions, they can be delegated to a lower-level (less expensive) support staff member.
- They can be done much more quickly than in-person interviews.
- They can give you extra insight into the applicant's attitude, based on his or her responses, enthusiasm, and preparedness.[9]

contrasts this applicant presented. You and your hiring team need to be aware of these tendencies, so that you will always vigilantly watch for and test against them. In short, you need to find a way to look behind the paperwork.

Let's start with that impressive cover letter. I once had a journalism major *friend* (get it?) who helped her fellow students write cover letters in exchange for beer. It was the 1970s and she felt the experience was about as close to a creative writing exercise as they might get. Here's why that's important. In a hiring workshop once, a small work group was given a pack of five applications and asked to select the top candidate from among them as an exercise. "I'd take this one, for sure," one person announced. "This is the most creative cover letter I've ever seen." The only question, she was asked by the instructor, is who wrote it?

Cover letters do have value but, like all other elements of the application package, they must be kept in perspective. Specifically, cover letters should be of value only because of *what* they say, not *how* they say it. How about those outstanding written responses our candidate submitted for the preinterview questions? Again, ask yourself who wrote them and, even if the answer is the applicant herself, did she have help, advice, or even an *insider* to consult, who knew what the *right* answers might be?

Don't be discouraged. It's not all smoke and mirrors. But you better be on the lookout for both. You can do that by utilizing any of a number of effective and, sometimes, fun prescreening tools that can show you a little more about the book— behind the cover. Even the experts agree that "although the job interview is the most common way by which employers determine the suitability of a candidate, the validity of the interview has been questioned. For this reason, other techniques have been applied . . . [such as] tests or tryouts."[5]

Once you've narrowed your pool down to the top candidates, you might want to consider bringing them in for a preinterview screening before subjecting them and your team to the full-blown interview. One library has had success involving them in actual role-playing exercises, to judge their ability to think on their feet, especially if they're applying for a challenging position. "We decided we needed more than a list of interview questions, especially because people can practice for an interview. Our intent was to test a person's customer service skills by simulating an environment where he or she is expected to remain calm in a stressful interaction with a patron."[6]

After applying the same technique when filling a managerial position, they were even more convinced of the value of looking under the cover. "What we found most surprising in using the role-play . . . was that, although the final three candidates had all given strong interviews, one person excelled in the role-play. The role-play uncovered his natural leadership ability, his ability to remain calm in stressful situations, and his talent for communicating and being persuasive."[7]

Another library, which was known for its focus on strong, positive attitudes towards customer

WHAT TO LOOK FOR IN PREINTERVIEW TESTS

Written, preinterview tests can help you further narrow your field of applicants down to a manageable number, based not on guesswork but on actual responses. Remember, at every step of the hiring process, you should not be eliminating applicants but allowing them to eliminate themselves, based on criteria you've established.

Q: Do you have experience with _____?

LOOK FOR: Short or yes/no answers might indicate the applicant is in a hurry or not really interested in the position. Look for a solid answer that shows real experience.

Q: Have you ever _____?

LOOK FOR: Again, look for details and real examples that match the experiences that would reflect the open position.

Q: When is the last time you _____?

LOOK FOR: Look for the answer—a date—plus additional information on the experience and how it might relate to your open position.

Q: Write a short paragraph on why you want to work for us.

LOOK FOR: Look for something specific to your organization, not a generic response about loving libraries or enjoying customer service. Consider the communication style and ability. Does passion show through?

Q: Reply back to abc@123.com by (a certain date) and include your name, the position for which you're applying, a phone number, address and e-mail address, plus a list of three references.

LOOK FOR: Look for the ability to follow simple directions! Some hiring supervisors will use the inability to follow directions or meet deadlines as an automatic elimination tool. Wiser heads will use it to break a tie but, if the candidate is qualified, will still consider them. In any case, it's good to know before their first day if you can expect professional, detail-oriented work from them.[10]

service, innovation, and people skills, borrowed from an elementary school project when they invited applicants for several very different positions to come together for a very unique prescreening event. With no hidden agenda, they billed the evening as an "Attitude Prescreening" and introduced the observers as the hiring supervisors for all the open positions. Then, in small groups, they gave two to three assignments to see how people responded to challenges and to others around them. For one exercise, they were provided several empty paper towel rolls, some masking tape, and a stack of old newspapers. The team, they explained, that could build the tallest "bridge" in ten minutes would win. The prize, of course, was chocolate.

One applicant, whose resume and application had initially impressed the hiring team, immediately rolled her eyes, heaved a great sigh, and announced to her teammate that this was the stupidest thing she'd ever seen. Yes, you read it correctly. The leader *had* introduced the evening as an "Attitude Prescreening" event. She was immediately disqualified. Another woman, whose resume wasn't particularly impressive, smiled as soon as the word "*Go*" was spoken, immediately tore off her shoes and, laughing, got down on the floor and announced to her teammates she had an idea to try. Her enthusiasm was contagious and, of course, they won; she was interviewed, hired, and promoted.

There's no limit to the creativity your team can apply to these unique evaluation tools! Another library went even farther—and introduced toys. "Timothy A. Toomer, director of the Alexander A. Buttersworth Memorial Library, describes a very unorthodox testing technique that he utilizes as part of his interviewing process. During the middle of a job interview he gets up and says, 'Please excuse me. I have a very important phone call to make.' Then he hands the job candidate a new Lego box and says 'Here's something to keep you busy while I'm gone.' Then, he leaves the room for twenty minutes. What's the method in this madness? Very simple. According to Toomer, 'If you're a conventional person, someone who obediently does whatever you are told to do by an authority figure, you will meticulously follow the designs prescribed in the Lego blueprints. But, if you are a creative person, you will rip the box open and either ignore the blueprints or more probably lose them.' So, when Toomer returns to the interviewing room, he checks to see what the candidate has done with the box of Legos. If the candidate has either not opened the box at all or has opened the box and simply followed the canned instructions, he or she will not get the job."[8] Toomer is looking for creative thinkers and, for him, this process works.

Whether or not your hiring team should employ one of these screening techniques depends on your answer to one simple question. What do you want to know? You've read the cover letters, reviewed the standardized application form and, perhaps, even evaluated written answers to prescreening tests. You have an A+ pile that may or may not be what you consider the right number to interview. Still, do you know all you want to know about each person? If the answer is yes, then you're making progress. But even if the answer is yes, think about what *else* you could learn from either a simple, straightforward prescreening tool or something more elaborate and creative. Remember, the person you select could be either the best or worst employee you've ever had. Maybe you and your team need to take the time to dig a little deeper and strengthen your understanding of the potential team members you are considering.

And there's one more benefit worth mentioning. The prescreening event would also provide you with the opportunity to show your organization's culture, spirit, and even personality to the applicants, so they can eventually make the right decision as well. If your library is fun-loving, creative, and spontaneous, you just might have one person in your pile who decides to look for a more conservative match or vice versa. They are interviewing you, too, and just as the applicant needs to put all of her or his cards on the table, you also need to be certain to demonstrate what your group is all about. Eventually, both the library and a candidate will have an important decision to make, and the more each knows about the other, the better the outcome is likely to be.

SUGGESTED READING

Manley, Will. *The Manley Art of Librarianship*. Jefferson, NC: McFarland, 1993.

EXERCISES

-10-

1. **Take a good look** at your organization's current employment application. List some qualities, characteristics, or attributes that it does *not* tell you.

    _____
    _____
    _____
    _____
    _____

2. **Think back to a** hiring experience you've had or have heard about in which there was a big difference between what was on paper and what showed in person. What were the differences? How might they have been identified before the person was brought in to interview or—worse—hired?

    _____
    _____
    _____
    _____
    _____

3. **Pick one prominent position** within your team and imagine, if you had an opening and were going to do a telephone prescreening, what questions would you ask? List at least five and be sure to write the answers you'd be seeking.

    _____
    _____
    _____
    _____
    _____

4. **Using the same position,** write at least five questions you'd use if you were bringing the entire pool in to take a scheduled, preinterview written test? Again, include answers. And add comments about what *else* you might be able to learn by actually seeing the candidates, which you'd miss if you mailed the test out.

    _____
    _____
    _____
    _____
    _____

5. **Finally, again using the** same position, describe a prescreening "event" you could hold. What would you do during it and what would you hope to learn?

    _____
    _____
    _____
    _____

NARROWING

WEEK THREE | **FLAGS**

A library security expert and former FBI agent once pointed out that every time you see reporters on TV interviewing the neighbors of a recently arrested criminal, they always crack the front door just a bit, peer suspiciously out, and say something like "I always thought there was something weird about him!" His point? Trust your instincts!

Admittedly, most hiring supervisors get a gut feeling after their very first review of the applicant pool about who is likely to get the job and who isn't. You can't fight city hall or human nature. It happens and, especially with very experienced team leaders, there's no avoiding it. Still, those same experienced leaders know that all the other careful steps in the hiring process are critical and they don't step over them in a rush to take action on their intuition. With their initial reactions tucked firmly in their minds, they continue diligently through the process that you've been reading about, fairly evaluating the application materials at each step along the way and listening to input from their hiring team.

Where those instincts that we all need to be alert to show up is in the *flags* that we sometimes see waving at us during these structured, analytical steps. Whether those flags might either support or challenge our original, gut reactions, our original opinions, they need to be recognized and the information they represent brought into consideration. Sometimes, unfortunately, less experienced bosses or those in a hurry or, worse, those whose egos get in the way will brush those flags out of their path like a downhill slalom skier going for a new record. Those who are truly intent on building

SLOW DOWN FOR RED FLAGS

While they shouldn't cause an applicant to be eliminated outright, these warning signs should definitely result in careful review and, perhaps, a few direct interview questions for clarification.

1. **IGNORING A REQUEST FOR SALARY HISTORY:** There's an argument to support both sides in this age-old debate, which pits employers who want applicants to have a clear understanding of potential pay against applicants who don't want to paint themselves into a corner. The bottom line is, if you have asked for a salary history, then you need it to further your process and if it is not supplied, this red flag could result in contention at best and wasted time at least.

2. **SUBMISSIONS THAT TAKE ADVANTAGE OF A CURRENT EMPLOYER:** A resume or application that is e-mailed from a current employer's address (during work hours, especially) or mailed in their envelopes, printed on their stationery, or stamped on their machine is a red flag that could be telling you the person is probably searching on their current employer's time. If they'll take advantage of their current employer, you know they'll take advantage of you.

3. **LACK OF CUSTOMIZATION TO YOUR POSTING:** Sometimes, applicants who are unqualified for positions tend to spam employers with resumes. They know that taking the time and energy to custom-write a cover letter, when they have little chance of obtaining an interview, is a waste of their time. Well-qualified applicants write a custom cover letter that draws a direct connection between the skills and experience you seek and the applicant's qualifications.

4. **OVERQUALIFICATION:** You walk a fine line in selecting an overqualified candidate for your job, since this selection might result in a quick turnaround and more time and expense in rehiring for the position. It's possible that their lifestyle, expenses, and family budget were developed with the expectation of a higher salary. So they may continue their job search after accepting your offered position. Alternately, your organization could benefit from their long-term experience and knowledge. Thus, red flags don't mean "stop," they just mean "caution."

5. **UNUSUAL HISTORY:** Job hopping does not carry the stigma that it did in the days of the corporation man. However, a series of short-term positions is still a red flag to examine. When you consider such an applicant, request an explanation for each job change. Probe and listen carefully to the answers. And, as always, trust your instincts.[13]

a great team will slow down and let the flags do their job—to make us think, maybe beyond what we can even see or prove.

It's a delicate dance. Team leaders have to listen to opinions and reactions (theirs), without ignoring contrary thoughts (their teams'), while also watching for subtle signals (flags) and keeping all these elements in objective balance.

Green flags or good surprises are, understandably, the easiest to spot. Every once in a while, a manager hears or reads or sees something about the applicant that makes him sit up and think, "Wow, now *that* would be a great thing to add to our team." One of the best surprises you'll find is energy or an undeniable fervor, passion, or zeal for the work involved. Lots of applicants want *a* job. A demonstration of this type of unfiltered, authentic enthusiasm usually indicates that this applicant wants *this* job! That's what you're looking for and, if you find it, you should tuck it away in your notes to use in later comparison to a more lackluster, yet perhaps better experienced, candidate.

ONE EXPERT'S ADVICE ON GOOD BEHAVIOR

As both a recognized library and human resources expert, Dr. Rubin shared some of the following tips during training for new library school grads looking for work. Other tips here were collected the old fashioned way—through experience. They are just as helpful as tips for employers looking at candidates.

- **NO PARTY PAGES:** Yes, employers do (and should) surf the Web to get a clear picture of their applicants. "Party" pages on social networks can serve as a personal reference, not to mention a reflection of common sense.

- **GOOD GRAMMAR AND PUNCTUATION:** Communication, at any position, is critical in today's job market. Watch for people whose work would need to be continually edited and corrected.

- **DON'T BE IRRITATING DURING AN INTERVIEW:** Personalities differ, but if an applicant leaves you feeling frustrated, just in that first hour of conversation, what do you think the future might be like?

- **HAVE PROFESSIONAL AFFILIATIONS:** Dr. Richard Rubin goes as far as to say that he won't consider professional applicants without professional affiliations. They reflect dedication to the work and the industry and a commitment to ongoing development.

- **KNOW—AND AGREE WITH—THE CULTURE AND VALUES:** Intellectual freedom questions often fall under this category, as would inquiries about diversity. Make sure you paint a clear picture of your culture and then probe to see if the applicant shares your organization's values.

- **PREPARATION, PREPARATION, PREPARATION:** A favorite question of many interviewers is "Tell me what you did to prepare for this interview." The response, which will vary from "I checked out your web page" to "I've visited several times, I attended a board meeting, I've spoken to several staff *and* I've reviewed your web page," will tell you how invested they are in getting your job.

- **BE ON TIME:** Needs no further explanation.

- **ANSWER THE QUESTIONS:** Ditto. Except, watch for tangents that will take an applicant off in a direction other than the answer that you seek. This could be unintentional, and you can steer them back with a follow-up, or it might be a dodge because they don't have an answer. You need to determine which.

- **HAVE AND DEMONSTRATE GOOD MANNERS:** Robert Fulghum, author of *All I Really Need to Know I Learned in Kindergarten*, once said, "It doesn't matter what you say you believe—it only matters what you do." Rubin said, "Likeability is everything!" Do you and your team members need to be best friends in order to be productive? No. But how far would your team building get if the person you ultimately hired wasn't even likable?[14]

It's the red flags, though, that should give you the greatest pause. These are the instances that could later cause you to figuratively crack the screen door open a bit and say, "I had a feeling there was something not right about this applicant." Keep in mind: these flags are cause for caution and consideration, not elimination in and of themselves. Poor answers, innocent omissions, and other minor flaws in the applicant's presentation of her credentials could reflect stress from "the current job market, bad advice from career or placement experts, or desperation. They may not represent the applicant's entire career. That said, certain flags, you cannot ignore."[11] One of those is outright lying.

Hard as it may be for new bosses to believe, people lie. That's why references should always be checked—with no exceptions! One employee, who had been on the job for years, was found to not really have the bachelor's degree she'd claimed to have and which was a basic requirement for the job. No one had checked. Another employee, who claimed a strong friendship with a favorite colleague of the director's, had never even met him before. No one checked. And finally, the new cataloger, who had claimed more than ten years' experience in technical services, couldn't even begin to classify the very first title handed to her. She'd processed invoices only. No one had checked. Hard or not, all information provided by applicants needs to be verified, examined, considered, and clarified before your final, very important and expensive decision is made.

Sometimes flags, red or green, don't jump out directly at you during an interview, but you have to watch for them while the process is under way. The applicant shouldn't be the only one answering questions! While your hiring team is taking their turn at querying your next potential superstar, ask yourself these questions:

1. Is the applicant nervous? Too much nerves might indicate inexperience or poor communication skills. Or it could tell you how badly the applicant wants this job! No nerves showing could mean she is a skilled, articulate communicator, or she couldn't care less if she gets the job or not. You'll need additional questions and observations (and insight from your team) to determine which answer is correct.

2. Is everything about them? "I'd like a shorter drive to work," "I want to make more money," or "I have friends who work here" are poor responses to the question, "Why do you want this job?" Watch for answers that demonstrate the value the individual will bring to you, not the other way around.

3. Are they leaving something behind with you to remember them by? Professional applicants should prepare a portfolio representative of their work and should leave it with the hiring team for later review. From that, you should be able to get a strong sense of their creativity and skill level. No matter how many notes you take, after a while, all candidates begin to blend together in your memory. Having a personal portfolio handy to remind you of their skills will help them—and you.[12]

The goal in hiring, as in life, is balance. It's a strong and professional team that can sit back after all the appointments are over and carefully and fairly evaluate the entire mass of collected information. By reviewing everything from cover letter to the work experience, from the prescreenings to the personal interviews, and from instincts to references, one applicant will always rise just a bit above the rest. Next week, we'll consider further those final two steps in this challenging and exciting process: the actual interview and the final review and decision-making process. The great team you are building is about to get a little bigger.

EXERCISES

-11-

1. **Think back to a** time when someone was hired, either by you or another manager, and they turned out not to be a good match for the position and the organization. List what red flags *might* have presented themselves with this person and where and when they could have been recognized. Also, list what could have been done to look into them further.

   _____

   _____

   _____

   _____

   _____

2. **Keep thinking back but,** this time, recollect a great hire that was made, who ended up being an excellent fit and an outstanding employee. What green flags were probably seen and how did they end up becoming part of this employee's success?

   _____

   _____

   _____

   _____

   _____

3. **In an interview, imagine** the applicant answering a question about their rapid job changes by stating, "I often get bored at work after I've completely mastered the task at hand." List at least three things you could do or say to investigate this curious comment further.

   _____

   _____

   _____

   _____

   _____

4. **Next question, same interview.** In response to your query about their background, she or he replies, "It would seem I've been successful at all the people-centered jobs I've ever had." This statement begs for more detail! What could you say or do (three things) to find support for this claim?

   _____

   _____

   _____

   _____

5. **After deciding to quickly** check just one reference for an applicant everyone on your hiring team already knows and loves, you get a very critical and negative response. What three things would you do after that, to either verify or dispute this input?

   _____

   _____

   _____

   _____

NARROWING

| **SETTING THE STAGE**

It's almost interview time. For days now (or longer), you've been wrapped up in reviewing paperwork, "scoring" qualifications, and rating applicants. You and your hiring team have been meeting behind closed doors to compare notes, share insights, discuss reactions and opinions, and now it's almost interview time. Is everyone ready? At this point, you might want to push the paperwork away for a short time and refocus on the team you already have working for you. They need you right now to provide assurances, direction, information, and leadership as you all grow together.

Reflecting on your goal to build a great *team*, this is the perfect time to make some other preparations, still well before that new person arrives for their first day, to make sure that you're laying the best groundwork possible for everyone's success. And those preparations will require everyone's involvement. "Renewal is accomplished only through the inclusion of all . . . personnel in transformation efforts. Total participation and collaboration is critical to healthy and lasting change."[15] It's time to get your team involved in setting the stage.

Let's examine a hypothetical instance that could leave a new employee doomed from the very start and where, in all likelihood, she or he might quit after just a few weeks on the job (and after all the work you put into a hire? Imagine!). Department members who had been excluded from the hiring team had gone ahead and made up their minds about the new hire before she even set foot in the library. Based solely on a lack of input and information, also known as gossip, they were unwelcoming, belittling, unhelpful, critical, and distant to the new person from day one. Greedily,

LET THE TEAM DEFINE WHAT "WELCOME" MEANS

If you had spent time sourcing and choosing an expensive new piece of machinery, you wouldn't just leave it in its box when it was delivered, and hope it would just start being productive! And who better to help initiate that productivity—and building early bonds at the same time—than your existing team! Spend time together and allow them to help plan your new employee's first days. By discussing these questions together, their role in the future success of the "new" team will be reinforced as well. They can start by answering questions like these:

- What will the new team member need to know about our environment, in order to feel comfortable?
- What can we do to make he or she feel confident?
- What impression of our team do we want the new person to have on her first day?
- What can we do to create that impression?
- How can we be certain to not appear intimidating to the new person?
- What can we do to let her know we welcome her to our team?
- How can we show that we value what she'll add to our team?
- How can we make certain that we'll all be there to help, in any way, so our new team member doesn't feel left to sink or swim?[20]

ORIENTATION TASKS FOR TEAM MEMBERS

While there are certainly some orientation procedures that are best performed by administrators or the direct supervisor, many other steps could be more meaningful to both new and existing staff, if performed by team members themselves. Here are some options. Perhaps you could ask current team members to volunteer for one or more, in order to involve everyone in that critical first week.

HAVE A TEAM MEMBER:

- Prepare a "New Employee" departmental/team announcement.
- Prepare a personal, "New Employee" welcome letter.
- Ensure the work area to be assigned is cleaned and stocked with needed supplies.
- Share organizational information about the team such as titles, structure, and the primary responsibilities of team members and goals.
- Greet the new team member and take him on a tour, complete with personal introductions to others.
- Arrange for lunch (surprisingly, a number of new hires are left to fend for themselves for lunch on their first day).
- Explain how the new person's role will interact and intersect with other team members.
- Provide reassurance! Spend some time at the end of the first few days with the new person. Assure him you're glad he's there and answer any questions.[21]

they hung onto their previous assignments and reacted with disdain when asked to share duties or, worse, to instruct the new team member on procedures to achieve them. Why?

They were scared.

Without adequate preparation, explanation, and assurance as to how the team would morph into a new entity, they were afraid for their own stability and success. And their fear would cost them all dearly.

Back to the real world, how can that unfortunate turn of events be avoided? The answer to that is one of the keys to great teams. Effective leaders recognize the basic needs shared by all their team members. As expert David McClelland proposed, those needs include "four major sources of motivation for employees. Beyond the need for power, there are needs for achievement, affiliation and autonomy."[16] Further, he explained that employees want to control and influence their jobs, receive supportive feedback, feel acceptance, enjoy independence and, as all experts agree, realize success. It's the team leader's job to assure staff that, even after a new, unknown member is introduced in their midst, these basic needs will continue to be met.

On an ongoing basis, whether you're facing an opening on your team or not, you should have been providing continual feedback on the skills, accomplishments, and goals of each member of your team. Now is a great time to meet with each person and reexamine your shared mission, recognize their contribution towards it, and assure them that their opportunities for continued success will be enhanced—and not threatened—by the new person you'll be bringing on board. Further, by emphasizing the critical role they will all play in the new person's success, you could outline as a group the induction procedures and processes planned for your new hire. By the time that person arrives on her first morning, everyone on your team should have an assignment and a role to play in the orientation, which can cement not only the new person's sense of belonging but also the individual value each person feels towards their own place in the group.

Ask for ideas. Design your new employee's first week as a group. Let *them* tell *you* what's important to team success, and together you can find ways to impart that knowledge to the new person. The bureaucratic, paperwork stuff can fill in the cracks, but should definitely take a back seat to this golden opportunity to provide a team welcome and a real chance to begin to forge those new alliances. All too often, team members don't even shake hands until hours upon hours of HR videos, forms, and insurance forms are out of the way. Let the state-mandated videos on the dangers of blood-borne pathogens wait—and put the new team bonds first. Investing in the success of a new team member—and the future success of the team overall—needs to be a shared objective.

"There is a responsibility on both sides to create a shared purpose. Leaders can't do it alone. Employees must also make an effort to tie their personal skills and desires to the company's objective."[17] Remember the Frances Hesselbein example from the first month of this book? After arranging concentric circles radiating outward with dishes and silverware, she said of her position as CEO of the Girl Scouts of the USA, "I'm here,"[18] and she pointed to the middle, not to the top. The thing about circles is that they shouldn't be broken, in order to assure a continued, steady, and strong connection.

By taking the time, at this point of the hiring process, to address your team's fears, confirm their value, and involve them in the exciting changes, you will be employing a shared strategy, intent, and responsibility to move your team forward to success.

"We cannot predict the future, but we can create it."[19]

SUGGESTED READING

Collins, Jim, and Morten T. Hansen. *Great by Choice: Uncertainty, Chaos, and Luck—Why Some Thrive Despite Them All.* New York: HarperCollins, 2011.

EXERCISES

-12-

1. **Think back to the** worst first day on the job you've ever had. How could it have been improved? List three beyond-the-call-of-duty things that other team members might do to say welcome.

_____
_____
_____
_____
_____

2. **List all the parts** you can remember of your first day, the last time you started a job. Note which if them might have meant more if a team member, rather than a supervisor or support staff person, had handled them.

_____
_____
_____
_____
_____

3. **Get out a list** of existing team members and, next to each name, note one or two parts of their job they are most protective of. Before introducing a new team member, how might you reassure them about keeping those assignments?

_____
_____
_____
_____
_____
_____

4. **In question #3, if** you are going to have to reassign one of those favorites, make at least five notes about how you can do it, without putting the new team member immediately behind the eight ball.

_____
_____
_____
_____
_____

5. **Draw up a sample** team meeting agenda that could be used to bring everyone together, before a new person has even been selected, to voice concerns, ask questions, and generally look positively into the future.

_____
_____
_____
_____
_____

INTERVIEWING

ANSWERS

As clichéd as it might sound, you would really never know if you've arrived at your destination if you didn't know where you were going to begin with. Most traditional interview questions are proficient at leading you down that proverbial, albeit purposeless path. While listening to applicants offer the same, predictable answer one after another, you can find yourself wondering why you asked the question in the first place. What did you hope to learn? The reason this often happens is because most interviewers don't begin their question writing by considering what they are hoping to hear! More often than not, they just pull an old interview out of the drawer, blow the dust off, and dive right in.

"Tell me about your background."

Admit it, you've asked that, right? More often than not, that's the first question out of the gate. We ask it even after just reviewing the person's cover letter, application, and resume! It would be fair (but surprising) if the candidate were to answer, "Well, since you've just read most of my life story in the paperwork I submitted, can you be a bit more specific about what else you'd like to know?" Even though I've run into interviewers who feel otherwise, I think that is a completely wasted question. To those who would suggest it's a good *ice breaker* because it lobs the applicant an easy one to warm up with, I say try harder.

I'm not against ice breakers, don't get me wrong. But if you want to put your applicant at ease with a question whose answer will be of more value, try just letting them talk about themselves, but in a way that will demonstrate something you need to know. For example, you could instead try opening

QUESTION WHAT'S IMPORTANT[6]

Assuming the following list of competencies and characteristics (taken from Rubin's book, *Hiring Library Employees*) were identified as being critical to the new hire's success, here are some questions you might craft to really learn something about the applicant's ability to succeed.

COMMUNICATION SKILLS

- THINK: How can we know this person will communicate well?
- ASK: In three sentences or less, explain to a third-grader what an integrated library system is. (*NOT: What kind of a communicator are you? That's just asking them. Let them show you!*)

AMBITION

- THINK: How can we be sure this person is really driven?
- ASK: If you won the lottery tomorrow, how might that affect your career? (*NOT: Where do you want to be in five years?*)

PROFESSIONAL APPEARANCE

- THINK: In our community, it's critical that managers look professional. How can we be sure the applicant will be okay with that?
- ASK: How would you explain to an unsuccessful candidate for a manager's job that their unprofessional dress affected their final applicant score, and why you feel that's justified? (*NOT: How do you think managers should dress?*)

ABILITY TO COOPERATE

- THINK: Even when it's not easy to do so, how can we be sure the person we select will be able to succeed with our team and not just give up?
- ASK: No one on your new team will answer your calls or e-mails and the project you've been assigned is due in one week. What would you do? (*NOT: Give us an example of a successful team you've been a part of.*)

POSITIVE ATTITUDE

- THINK: Initially, the new staff member will run into some negativity. How can we know they'll be able (and willing) to overcome it and not just look the other way?
- ASK: You notice a member of your team is displaying negativity, excessive criticism, and high drama, which is affecting internal and external customer service. You call her into your office. What do you say? (*NOT: Why do you think a positive attitude is important?*)

MATURITY

- THINK: Is the applicant really ready to lead and not worry about "being one of the gang"? Do they know the difference?
- ASK: For the fifth time in one week, you were the only person not invited to join the gang when they went out to lunch. For the purpose of this answer, you've got to do something. What would you do? (*NOT: How close a relationship should a manager have with team members?*)

RELIABILITY

- THINK: Can this person be trusted?
- ASK: Tell us about a time when something good happened that couldn't have been completed without you. (*NOT: How reliable are you when faced with a deadline?*)

CONSIDER QUESTIONS THAT DEMONSTRATE ... [7]

IS THE CANDIDATE HIGHLY ADAPTIVE?

A GREAT QUESTIONER HER/HIMSELF?

VORACIOUSLY CURIOUS?

ABLE TO DISCERN PATTERNS IN CHAOS?

ENTHUSIASTIC ABOUT PEOPLE?

ABLE TO ADMIT MISTAKES?

A LOVER OF LEARNING?

with "What's the coolest thing you've gotten to do lately?" It's relaxed, it's fun, and it lets them jump into the interview with both feet by sharing a recent success story and making themselves look good. And you've learned what they think of as an accomplishment, what really gets them energized, and whether the work they most enjoy is a realistic match for your current opening.

Next, "How would you resolve a difference of opinion with a coworker?" Huh? Consider what you could possibly learn by the traditional response to this, which is usually "I'd talk things over, we'd find a way to work it out, blah, blah, blah." These inane questions, which I believe waste the time and energy of everyone at the table, remind me of a favorite oldie but goodie from the 1980s, which was "How do feel about diversity?" I was always dying to, just once, come across a courageous, smart-aleck applicant who might reply "I'm for it." Now, from that answer, I *would* have learned something—that this person could recognize what an empty nod towards inclusiveness such a question represented. I'll bet everyone would hope the questions got better from then on.

There's an easy way to avoid these pitfalls in interviewing and that is to begin by knowing where you need to go. You'll know quite a bit about your interviewees by the time they've been selected. But what *else* do you need to learn? Remember all the work you did back when you were confirming that you did, indeed, need this position filled? Remember all the gaps you identified in your current team? Use those needs! Make sure you're selecting the person who can fit into your team best and bring the skills and abilities that will make it a stronger unit! Resumes and applications give you the nuts and bolts of a person's skills, knowledge, and abilities. What's missing? Make a list of those questions unanswered, either by inconsistencies or omissions in their application, and then formulate questions that will address those points.

The last thing either of you (or your hiring team members) need to be doing right now is wasting everyone's time.

So, in addition to the applicable skills and experience you've identified, what else should you be looking for? As most managers and administrators are well aware, traditional library funding is shrinking. Everywhere, we need to be doing more with less and stretching our staff to support innovation. In short, libraries need to "get creative. We're on the verge of a second Renaissance that will make the first Renaissance appear half-hearted."[1] If we embrace this reality, then "library staff would be hired based on the creative talents, as well as their other competencies."[2]

Richard Rubin further supports the notion that the entire hiring team needs to be on the lookout for those *other* traits that tell you more about the person than the name, rank, and serial number questions we're all used to hearing, while still keeping the key elements of the position in mind. "All staff involved in the hiring of a particular position should have a good idea of what they are looking for in a candidate. To accomplish this, each selector should carefully review the job description, with special attention to the job tasks to be performed and the required knowledge, skill and abilities for the position. In addition, the selectors should reach a consensus on the character of the job. Finally, the selectors should also consider any other job related traits that they consider important for a candidate to possess. These traits may be less tangible and more difficult to measure, but they should not be ignored."[3]

All of these steps are well and good for your organization *today* and the role your open position plays *today* within it. But remember, a larger question needs to be addressed in the interview that can position you and the candidate for success or failure *tomorrow*. How good will they be in dealing with what might happen next? Ask yourselves, "Is the candidate sitting in front of you right for this job?" How do you know, when market conditions are so volatile it's hard to predict all the qualifications and attributes you're going to need six months or one year down the road? "Old command and control work environments didn't demand the kind of flexibility, adaptability and broad business knowledge that new, dynamic work environments do. Desirable candidates, even ones who have the right qualifications—must be flexible, rapid and eager learners"[4] as well!

There's one very good reason that "Tell me about yourself" has been around as long as it has. It's safe and what you've been reading about is . . . not so much. It's always been *easier* to ask (and answer) the simple, straightforward question than to paint someone into an awkward situation and then ask them to get out of it. But, it's worth it, if you really want to know what you need to know about your candidate. "Don't be afraid to address the elephant in the room and have the difficult conversations ('tell the kind truth')—you can't solve the real problems without doing this."[5]

This is *your* team that's developing. Rare is the opportunity to enhance it, to grow it, and to prepare it for a strong and successful future. Just ask a team leader you know who is struggling with bad hires, dysfunctional groups, and dismal performance how much they'd appreciate the chance to do it over again and select the right addition to their group. With that in mind, consider what you *really* need to know about that perfect person and then get writing. What's next? How to write the perfect question!

SUGGESTED READING

Rubin, Richard E. *Hiring Library Employees: A How-to-Do-It Manual.* New York: Neal-Schuman, 1993.

EXERCISES

-13-

1. **Write the three dullest** and most pointless interview questions you've ever heard or asked and then rewrite them in a way that will tell you more.

   _____
   _____
   _____
   _____
   _____

2. **Pick one position on** your team and then consider, after reviewing traditional application materials if that job was open, what three qualities or characteristics might you not be able to learn from that paperwork? Write questions to investigate each. If you have a real job opening right now, great! Use that position.

   _____
   _____
   _____
   _____
   _____
   _____

3. **Write at least three** different questions that might help you find out whether or not your candidate is creative.

   _____
   _____
   _____
   _____
   _____
   _____

4. **Now, because of the** changes we all face today, write at least three different questions that might help you find out if your candidate is innovative.

   _____
   _____
   _____
   _____
   _____

5. **Finally, let's consider an** elephant. Suppose your candidate has answered a question during the interview with an answer that you absolutely, positively know to be false. How would you approach that? What could or should you ask next? What _else_ might you then need to know?

   _____
   _____
   _____
   _____
   _____

INTERVIEWING

| ## QUESTIONS

"If you were a tree, what kind of tree would you be?"

In over 25 years, this is by far the most debated interview question I've ever heard. And the talk wasn't very kind. People complained, "What was she thinking to ask this?" "What kind of stupid question is that?" and "What a terrible interviewer!"

I disagree. Actually, I think this is an excellent interview question because it accomplishes something that very few *standard* questions can claim—it tells you something you don't already know. This book could literally double in size if it were to list for you the thousands of potential interview questions you could ask. But there are hundreds of books available out there that can provide that information, if you'd like to read them. Before you do, though, I would suggest you keep one very important criterion in mind when making your selections—with every single question you ask, you need to be able to learn something new, something important, and something that really makes a difference from every answer!

With the famous tree question, you could do just that. You might learn, for example, if the applicant had a sense of humor. Or it might demonstrate just how creative they are and how open they are to innovation. Certainly, you'd see how quickly they can think on their feet, when faced with something unexpected. On the other hand, you might learn from a curt, negative answer that they're not comfortable with the nonconventional. Would that be important to you?

This might sound good, but, still, you might be wondering how to even create such revealing questions? The answer isn't as difficult as you might

THERE ARE MANY TYPES OF QUESTIONS!

Choose the right ones for the right reasons!

DIRECT

- What is your salary requirement?

REFLECTION

- Why do you think you didn't get this job the first time you tried?

INTERPRETATION

- Help me understand what you mean by a commitment to diversity?

ELABORATION

- Tell me a little more about that.

CLARIFICATION

- So, am I hearing you correctly? You said . . .

REPETITION

- Let's revisit your comments about supervision. What, again, are your main goals?

LOOPING

- Let me give you a bit more time to think that over; we'll come back to it later.[11]

come to think about. He suggests using *wide*-open or leading questions which, while "based on a predictable topic, often [have] several correct answers and can lead the person to a place of discovery."[8] Consider these options:

Is it raining? (closed)

What's the weather outside? (sort of open)

What is going on outside? (wide open and leading!)

So, let's get writing. Here are a few tips and some sample language to keep in mind when crafting your questions. You've picked the topics in order to learn what you need to know. Try using some of these ideas to pose your questions in ways that can get you the results you seek.

1. HOW? While "What is your approach to management?" might elicit a somewhat dry and rehearsed response, consider asking "How did you come to develop your approach to management?" Including *how* in any questions can open it up far enough that your candidate has a chance to really share a part of herself.
2. CONVINCE ME! Use your hiring team as guinea pigs and watch the different answers you can get by asking one "What's your customer service approach?" and the other "Convince me you are dedicated to outstanding customer service."
3. THEIR OWN WORDS. We put a lot of words into the mouths of our candidates, even when we don't mean to, when we're really there to hear what (and how) they have to say! Instead of "Why should we hire you for this job?" try "When the other candidates call me and ask why we picked you, what should I tell them?"
4. EXAMPLES. Back in the 1980s, one of the interviewing rules of thumb was that no

think. You've already completed the first step by defining what it is you need to know. Around those concepts, you can now craft your questions. Before you begin, keep in mind that while *what* you ask will be critical, *how* you ask it will be just as important. In a workshop called "How to Problem Solve, Manage and Lead with Powerful Questions," Ned Parks introduced an expansion to the standard open/closed questions we've all

follow-up or clarification questions were allowed. Thankfully, those days are gone. Any time and every time an answer leaves you asking for more, one great follow-up technique is to ask for examples. For example, try following "I'm a great team player" with "Can you give us a couple examples that demonstrate that?" Don't just ask for one example. Take them beyond that simplicity to really delve into the truth. I recently asked an applicant to tell me ten (yes, ten!) ways our organization could demonstrate outstanding customer service. Believe me, once they get past five or six, they're really thinking and you're really learning a lot about them!

5. BE CREATIVE! Not only will your team's interviewing creativity likely result in a better picture of your candidate, but it will also demonstrate to *them* what kind of an organization (free-thinking, innovative) you have. A manager friend recently shared with me that, instead of "How can you remain patient when a telephone question might seem frivolous?" she posed "You're working at the busy desk when someone calls and asks how to make a peanut butter sandwich. Please let us hear your answer."

6. WHAT IF? After a perfect answer to a tough, situational question, throw them for a loop (just as life often does) and see if you can figure out what their Plan B would be. "How would you handle a staff member who is consistently late?" will probably elicit a programmed response. "I'd talk to them; remind them of our rules, etc., etc." Follow that with "What if that didn't work and they continued being late?"

7. SILENCE. Know when to stop talking. No matter how good your question, sometimes it's best to ask it and then sit back and be quiet and let the silence be filled with their comments, not yours.

8. DRILL DOWN. As mentioned, don't be afraid to follow up! Don't accept half answers and don't leave yourself wondering what was really meant by an answer. A favorite technique of mine is the *Five Whys*. Originally developed by Sakichi Toyoda (and later used by Toyota Motors), it was thought that "by repeating why five times, the nature of the problem as well as its solution becomes clear."[9] Consider this generic application:

My car will not start.

1. Why? The battery is dead.
2. Why? The alternator is not functioning.
3. Why? The alternator belt has broken.
4. Why? The alternator belt was well beyond its useful service life and has never been replaced.
5. Why? I have not been maintaining my car. [10]

How might this work in an interview?
I would make an excellent branch manager.

1. Why? Because I'm good with people.
2. Why? I've worked with the public most of my life.
3. Why? Office jobs have never appealed to me.
4. Why? I don't do well in repetitive situations.
5. Why? I thrive on diversity, multitasking, and surprises!

9. USE REAL LIFE. Scenario questions accomplish a multitude of good. First, they provide an opportunity to let the applicant know what your job is really like. Second, they allow you and your team to see how all the qualities, skills, experience, and PR you've been hearing about might really be applied—day-to-day. Be creative, but don't scare them away. I remember one manager who, in

an attempt to determine a candidate's support of intellectual freedom, slammed a book down with the page open to a vulgar (albeit artistic) picture of a young girl and screamed "How *could* you let my child check this out??" A little over the top? Perhaps. But, better the candidate know what might really happen—and you all know how they might react.

10. TRICK QUESTIONS. A final tip as you begin writing your next interview: skip the tricks. You don't need them, if you approach this exercise honestly and carefully. People are rattled enough on interview day. They are nervous, overstimulated, (hopefully) excessively prepared, and likely prone to not catch the nuances you might build into your questions to trip them up. If you do, what have you accomplished? You'll learn less about them and they'll learn the worst about you. So stick to the plan. Identify what you need to know, creatively craft wide-open, creative questions, and enjoy getting to know one another. It just might be the beginning of a wonderful relationship!

By the way, it's Birch. That would be my answer to the "tree" interview question. Why? Because white birch trees remind me of my Finnish grandmother and of her strength and resilience, two qualities I've always tried to emulate. No matter what harsh or demanding elements the environment might hand them, they persevere. If that says something about me, as well, then I'm lucky.

SUGGESTED READING

This book has been around for a while, but it still contains the most intriguing questions you'll find for very specific information needs.

Kador, John. *The Manager's Book of Questions: 751 Great Interview Questions for Hiring the Best Person; Questions Guaranteed to Identify: Leadership, Initiative, People Skills, Stress Management, Organization, Technical Competence & Creativity*. New York: McGraw-Hill, 1997.

EXERCISES

14

1. **Write two questions, one** *"How"* and one *"Convince me"* to inquire about a candidate's past management experience.

    _____

    _____

    _____

    _____

    _____

2. **Write two questions, one** *"In your own words"* and one *"Give me an example"* to inquire about a candidate's experience managing a budget.

    _____

    _____

    _____

    _____

    _____

    _____

3. **Write a scenario question** you might ask someone applying to work with teenagers.

    _____

    _____

    _____

    _____

    _____

    _____

4. **Write a scenario question** you might ask someone who would be supervising former peers.

    _____

    _____

    _____

    _____

    _____

5. **Answer this question as** if it was being of asked of *you* right now, "In what way do you feel more confident about the success of the next interview you'll manage?" Answer it with a single sentence, then drill down through the 5 Whys.

    _____

    _____

    _____

    _____

    _____

INTERVIEWING

| ## THE BIG DAY

On the day of her job interview, the applicant wasn't quite sure where to go and there didn't seem to be anyone around to ask. Finally, the third person she asked figured out whom to call and she was sent "upstairs." After wandering around up there for a while, the manager found her and asked her to wait a while, since the interview team wasn't all there yet (it was already fifteen minutes after the interview was to start). Once in an empty room that they managed to find, other staff straggled in, one still finishing a sandwich and the other two on cordless phones. At least, she thought they were on the interview team, but they could have been customers, given the casual way they were dressed. With only a handful of interruptions from phone calls, they managed to get all their interview questions answered and they walked her to the door—of the room, not the library. Confused, she left with no understanding of what came next or when she might hear any results.

At the next library to which she applied, the e-mail came only hours after she'd sent in her application materials. It seems they were looking forward to meeting her and she was supplied with specific instructions on where to park, where to check in, and the names and titles of those who would be interviewing her. A smiling face was waiting to greet her as soon as she entered the building, and she was escorted to a quiet, neat meeting room where the professionally dressed, friendly team was already waiting. While each took turns asking questions, the others stayed focused only on her and her responses. She sipped from the water she'd been provided with and,

AN EFFECTIVE INTERVIEW IS AS SIMPLE AS "ABC"

A is for Attitude

■ Project an image of energy and enthusiasm. For you and your team, that means dressing, arriving, and behaving as if this interview is truly important to your organization. It means being attentive, welcoming, and interested.

B is for Behavior

■ A positive attitude will drive positive behavior. Your team should arrive before the applicant and be thoroughly prepared for the meeting. They should know their role, what questions they're asking, who is meeting the applicant at the door, who is getting them a glass of water, and who is showing them out or around afterwards. *No* interruptions should be allowed during the interview. In short, they should be on their best behavior and treat the applicant as they would like to be treated.

C is for Compatibility

■ You and your team should consider each and every interview as an opportunity to look for overlaps in two circles: the first being the skills and persona of the applicant and the second being the personality and needs of the team. The interview should always be a positive search. Look for compatibility in these circles, not for reasons to support your predisposed, negative, or judgmental thoughts.[15]

put the applicant at ease, so that you can learn as much about them as possible and they about you. Unavoidable nervousness can be reduced by a comfortable setting, friendly surroundings, and a general, welcoming environment.

Remember, the applicants are interviewing your library, too! Given these two scenarios, where would *you* rather work?

"Most people consider job interviewing a very stressful experience. Unfortunately, the stress itself becomes our greatest enemy, preventing us from creating a positive connection."[12] As the team leader, reducing this stress—on both sides of the table—is up to you. The best way to do this is with thoughtful preparation and execution of the interview itself, again, on *both* sides of the table.

Even with all that preparation behind them, interviewers often next make the innocent yet critical mistake of rushing the process along. Consider the team that schedules more than three or four interviews in one day, in an effort to make it easier on the schedule to have so many people missing from their posts. How long should an interview take? As long as is needed to truly, thoroughly, and fairly assess if the candidate is right for your team! At all times, "the candidate should be given plenty of time to think about responses and to reflect on her or his answers. From time to time, especially talkative candidates might have to be redirected by the interviewer in charge but, generally, the more a candidate talks, the more information that is obtained."[13]

So, everyone is present and looking professional and pleased to be there. Your very carefully thought-out questions reflect what you and your team have pre-decided that you really need to know. The candidate is seated across from you and is relaxed and ready to begin. So far, so good. Naturally, either one person or the entire team will be taking notes during the interview itself. Expecting to be able to recall the often subtle reactions to each query is a fatal mistake. But, before just passing out the paper and pencils and issuing the instruction to write, make sure you prep your team on what they should be recording.

relaxed, she smiled back at each person in turn as she gave her thoughtful and comfortable answers.

What's the difference? Again, start with the end in mind. Your goal in *any* interview is to

ENHANCING THE INTERVIEW

Once you've reached the end of your questions, your opportunity to learn about the candidate—and they about you—shouldn't end. There are many more ways to explore a person's appropriateness for the job available to you and, while you have them in your building, you should take advantage of as many of these ways as possible. Later, when you're potentially facing a tough decision between a few contenders, you'll be glad you did. Consider:

- **SHOWING THE CANDIDATE AROUND:** It is the practice in some organizations to give the individual a tour of the library. This also may involve meeting and talking with staff members. This gives the candidate a better idea of the actual working conditions and staff atmosphere of your organization. Although there are some advantages to this process, you must be scrupulous about ensuring that any questions asked by staff conform to the law. What can *you* learn from this exercise? How about how the candidate interacts with other staff members or what their casual impressions are of your library? These few extra minutes of your time can prove invaluable in giving you an extra, unscripted chance to get to know the person you may very well be adding to your team.

- **GIVING THE CANDIDATE A WRITTEN TEST:** Paper tests can vary widely and can include standardized personality, integrity/attitude, or specific knowledge tests. Often, the knowledge tests can be the most telling. If they're going to be providing readers' advisory services, for example, ask them to list ten popular authors in several different genres. If they'll be answering students' questions, ask them to give short definitions of several pop culture concepts. If they're going to be providing business reference, ask them to match investment and banking questions with the source they'd most likely check first. It's easy to say you can do a job or that you've done it before. But nothing can match showing a bit of the skills and knowledge you profess to have.

- **OBSERVING THE CANDIDATE IN A JOB TRYOUT:** If your candidate actually saw what story times are like in your inner-city library, would they still be enthusiastic about the job? Although there's no way to know for sure, one good test method is to take them into one and see how they react. One manager had a librarian attend a computer class for seniors, given by a potential teammate, and was surprised and delighted to see her jump right in and creatively help to answer questions from other students. The two seemed as though they'd been comfortably working together for years! A moment like that might provide *just* the tipping point that can help you later separate those top two, closely scored written interview results.

- **ASKING THE CANDIDATE FOR A PRESENTATION:** If communication skills, the ability to answer questions, and the ability to organize materials are essential functions of the job, then the presentation should be evaluated for these factors. Once, when interviewing for a branch manager position, I asked candidates to provide a sample agenda for their very first staff meeting and to present what the first five minutes might be like. Not knowing ahead of time what to expect, or even if this exercise would prove helpful, I was delightfully impressed by one presentation and ended up hiring that person. While all the other applicants had focused on who they were, what they were like, and what they wanted to do with staff, our ultimate selection explained there would be lots of time to get to know her—but she wanted to begin by getting to know them! She asked them to go around the table, share something about themselves, and say one thing they were looking forward to seeing happen in the near future. We could have asked interview questions all day long and not learned as much as we did with that simple demonstration.[16]

Discuss what to look for, what to listen for, and what to note, so that your post-interview discussion can paint a complete and thorough picture of each applicant. Other than how they answer the questions, counsel your interview team to evaluate:

1. BODY LANGUAGE – Experts tell us that more than 90 percent of the message candidates convey to potential employers is through nonverbal communication. Do they make eye contact with all the team members? Do they shake hands? Do their gestures, posture, and tone of voice convey a positive, upbeat, and enthusiastic attitude towards your organization? By and large, interviews are not just about how well the candidate answers questions, but about what kind of person they are and whether they'll *click* with the team.

2. ATTENTION TO TIME – Candidates simply cannot miss the bus, be stuck in traffic, misjudge commute time, or forget to set their alarm clocks. If the candidates aren't at the interview early, then they're late. Period. This is the simplest way to judge how really sincere they are about wanting to join your team.

3. PREPARATION – Once, with two very different positions open, I received an e-mail that stated a resume was attached for my review. I didn't even know for what position the person was applying. When I opened the document, the objective line described a desire to hold a position that wasn't even close to either of our open jobs. Obviously, absolutely no preparation went into this application beyond hitting the SEND button on the keyboard. When recording answers to

specific questions, I'll often write little about the answer itself and more about what obviously went into preparing the answer. If it's obvious that nothing did, then that fact is the most important to note.

4. SELF-ASSESSMENT – Experts suggest that, before new employees can positively contribute to your organization, they have to have a clear understanding of their own goals and priorities. Candidates who can't adequately explain what they hope to accomplish in your position or where they see their own careers going in the future should raise red flags, possibly indicating they haven't thought this match through very carefully.

5. OVERALL IMPRESSIONS – An interview should not just tell your team whether or not someone is suitable for the position, but should also pass on a feeling of comfort. This is by far one of the most important factors that needs to come through because, someday soon, you might all find yourselves working together. To this end, encourage your hiring team to make broad, thoughtful notes not just on specific answers, facts, and dates, but on feelings and overall impressions as well.[14]

Interview day is a special time for everyone involved. It is the culminating opportunity to grow and enhance your team, making your organization and the service you offer more valuable to your stakeholders. Prepare for it. Handle it well. Get everything you can out of it. After all the candidates go home, you and your hiring team will be left with a difficult decision to make, and you're going to want to have collected the best and most information possible to make it well.

EXERCISES

15

1. **Think back and recall** the worst interview experience you've ever had or been part of. List at least five explanations for why it went wrong and, next to each reason, note how each mistake could have been avoided. Next, think back to the best interview experience and list five reasons why it was great. These are the five steps you'll want to remember and emulate!

_____

_____

_____

_____

_____

2. **Hopefully, you agree that** making the interviewee comfortable will help elicit from her or him the most useful information. List five things you _should_ do to create a comfortable atmosphere and five things you _should not_ do.

_____

_____

_____

_____

_____

3. **If you are hiring** a person who will manage people in your organization, what type of presentation might you ask them to do during the interview? Write the instructions you'd give them in order to prepare.

_____

_____

_____

_____

_____

_____

4. **You want someone who** is interested in landing _your_ currently open job, not just _any_ job. What five indicators might help assure you of this?

_____

_____

_____

_____

_____

5. **It's critical for you,** as the hiring team (and team) leader, to maintain a positive, enthusiastic attitude through what may well turn out to be interview after interview after interview. How can you do this?

_____

_____

_____

_____

_____

INTERVIEWING

| **DECISION TIME**

I will look at any additional evidence to confirm the opinion to which I have already come.[17]

—Lord Molson, British politician (1903–1991)

We've all seen it before. In a hiring scenario that is unfortunately all too commonplace, every single step of the process—all the hard work of so many people—is for naught at decision time, when the boss picks the person he planned to hire all along.

Shame on him.

After all the interviews are completed, it is *not* the time to ignore evidence, brush aside impressions, forget about experience, ignore the team dynamic, and just pick your best friend for the job. It's time to listen and to reflect and to focus and to make the best call you can. That's why you're the team leader. To do any less would be to let down your colleagues, your organization, and ultimately your customers. You'll have a lot of collected data to consider. Thanks to the contributions of time and talent of your hiring team members, you'll have a lot of input to listen to. And because of your overall understanding of the function and role of your team, you'll have practical objectives and goals to weigh. Author Harold Messmer Jr. suggests putting all of these criteria under your microscope according to a few guiding principles.[18]

1. *Anchor yourself to the hiring criteria.* They should serve as your guiding force throughout the valuation process.
2. *Take your time.* The more pressure that you're under, the greater the likelihood of rushing the decision and ending up with an employee who not only isn't your best choice, but who you're

IGNORE YOUR BIASES

As human beings, we cannot help but bring biases into evaluation and decision making. Especially when called upon to judge others, beliefs we have developed in our lives creep in and need to be recognized and considered appropriately—or dismissed, if inappropriate. Consider the belief vs. reality possibilities when candidates do the following:

SPEAKS TOO LOUDLY

- COULD MEAN: They're overly bold and pushy.
- Or: They're hard of hearing.

STANDS TOO CLOSE

- COULD MEAN: They'll cause personal space problems.
- Or: They're hard of hearing.

STANDS TOO FAR AWAY

- COULD MEAN: The like to work alone.
- Or: They don't want to appear pushy or overbearing.

ASKS MORE QUESTIONS ABOUT TIME FOR FAMILY THAN WORK

- COULD MEAN: They're not going to care about doing a good job.
- Or: They want to be sure the job is a good match for their lives.

WON'T INITIATE QUESTIONS

- COULD MEAN: They don't really care about your organization.
- Or: They've already done a thorough investigation of your library.

SMILES AND LAUGHS NERVOUSLY

- COULD MEAN: They're silly and won't take the work seriously.
- Or: They're nervous, like 99 percent of people during interviews.

WON'T MAKE EYE CONTACT

- COULD MEAN: They're insincere.
- Or: They're not used to speaking in front of such a formidable group.[24]

probably going to end up firing—with all the disruption that entails.

3. *Cross-verify.* Try not to rely solely on any one source of information, whether interview impressions, resume data, reference checks, testing, and so on. Spread a wide net and pay careful attention to discrepancies. Always, always, always check references, even when it seems obvious you shouldn't have to.

4. *Don't force the issue.* The recruiting process sometimes uncovers a "dream" employee—except for one problem: the candidate's skills and attributes don't

HOW TO MAKE REALLY BAD HIRING DECISIONS!

A tongue-in-cheek look. If you can find yourself in these examples, just try harder.

1. **MAKE EMOTIONAL DECISIONS AND JUSTIFY THEM WITH FACTS:** Most interviewers make quick judgments about a candidate based on the four "A's"—how attractive, articulate, assertive, and affable the candidate is. Candidates who don't meet the appropriate first impression standard are assumed incompetent. If you do this, why waste your valuable time with further questions? Instead, just conduct a five-minute interview and forget collecting any facts. It won't make any difference in your final decision, anyway.

2. **DO NOT SEEK OUT OBJECTIVE DATA IF IT CONTRADICTS YOUR BELIEFS AND IGNORE IT IF YOU FIND SOME:** Its' very tough to eliminate a candidate you like, and even tougher to seek out positive information for candidates you don't initially think would fit. So, rather than get to the truth, go the easy route and trust your gut feelings and first impressions.

3. **MAKE SURE NO ONE KNOWS THE REAL JOB:** The purpose of the interview is to determine competency *and* motivation. When you look at the underperformers in your company, you'll discover most of them are quite competent, they just don't find the work satisfying. So, to make sure you hire more of these people, go out of your way to *not* tell the candidate anything about the job until the day she starts. What a surprise that will be.

4. **MAKE SURE YOUR ADS ARE HARD TO FIND:** When top people begin the job-hunting process, they seek out tools such as Google and social networking sites. If your job can't be easily found there, you'll never see the best people. To continue not seeing any good people, make sure you continue to post your ads on the major job boards, where the best people look last.

5. **MAKE SURE THAT INTERVIEWERS ARE UNTRAINED AND CAN ASK ANY QUESTIONS THEY WANT:** Hiring mistakes are no big deal (right?), so why not let anyone interview the candidate, ask any questions they want, and then ask them whether you should hire the person? To make matters worse, only let untrained interviewers meet your candidates. This will certainly impress those top candidates you see regarding your company's level of professionalism.

6. **ADD UP THE YES AND NO VOTES:** Here's a sure-fire way to get the hiring decision wrong . . . let each untrained, biased, emotional, and superficial interviewer have a full yes or no vote on who should get hired. To make sure the process works as described, do not challenge anyone's assessment, just in case the person might get offended. This is more important than reaching a healthy consensus or making the tough decision on your own, after hearing all the team's input.[25]

match the hiring criteria for the job. Remember Rule # 1 (above)—anchor yourself to the hiring criteria! Don't try to put a "good" employee in the "wrong" job.

A library school student once shared with me the single most useful thing she learned from an entire semester class on management. When you have to make a decision, her instructor had said, it doesn't matter if you make a good decision or a bad decision. *Just make a damn decision!*

And now it's your turn to do just that. With all the data you now have to wade through, start wading and pick your most likely candidate. Then review your decision by starting back at the beginning, just to test the validity of your choice. Where is the beginning? It's your organization's overall strategy, vision, and goals. With the hiring materials for your candidate of choice in front of you, remember that "a staffing strategy does not exist in isolation. It's one part of what is required to achieve your organizational goals and strategies and to fulfill your organization's mission."[19] Does your candidate support this? Then, with those basics out of the way, you can move on to some of the softer skills assessments.

One description of "soft skills" could be, simply put, personality; and that's not a dirty word in hiring. Consider this example of need in a small company of "three partners, hiring their first support person. They knew what skills they needed, but overlooked the fact that the most important trait in a support person is their willingness to help. They needed someone who could get along in this small office of four. Answering to three bosses requires patience and resilience. They needed (someone) to be centered enough to demand the bosses prioritize tasks, and flexible enough to switch tasks continually."[20] Even with outstanding typing, filing, and computer skills, a person without these specific personality traits would have been unhappy with—and likely unsuccessful at—the job.

If you've seen this lopsided match of all skills and no heart, you know this can be a true disaster. In one library, a support person with outstanding technical and professional traits and background failed miserably because she felt demeaned in a largely postgraduate environment. While her *skills* were aptly suited to her support role, her *personality* was not and, hence, her lack of satisfaction with the work and the resulting negative impact that had on workflow, morale, and productivity. How can you interview for personality? It's not easy but, also, not impossible to assess. "Irritability and complacence, dominance and curiosity show in facial gestures, in tone of voice, in speed of speech and movements. [If you're not comfortable with your strengths in these areas], work with a coach to learn more about reading

nonverbal communication."[21] Once you know what you're looking for, note it, and then be sure to give these qualities fair consideration in decision making.

You now have amassed a considerable amount of information, from the application, the interviews, maybe some tests, and you and your team's impressions. What's left before you confirm your decision? Making sure it's all true. "If possible, the same number of reference checks per (final) candidate should be made . . . Given the rather large percentage of applicants who falsify information on their applications, this amount of verification may prove valuable. Employers should also consider letters to educational institutions, verifying the conferring of degrees (or ask for copies.) Stories of individuals who have claimed to have graduated from prestigious institutions are common in the business literature."[22]

"In a conference room on the first floor of the Houston Hobby Hilton, Jose Colmenares surveys a group of 13 women and 3 men and wonders which—if any—have the 'right stuff' to become flight attendants with Southwest Airlines. Colmenares is not looking for a fixed set of skills or experiences. He's searching for something far more elusive and much more important—the perfect blend of energy, humor, team spirit, and self-confidence to match Southwest's famously offbeat and customer-obsessed culture."[23] From this description came a hiring adage that I've adhered to since I first read it—Hire for Attitude, Train for Skill.

In today's competitive marketplace, when the success or failure of an entire organization rests on the effectiveness of our work teams and when our own professional success is only as good as our weakest employee, I believe we can *teach* skills, but only if we *start* with the right attitude.

They're getting busy out there. Make the best decision you can make, be prepared to correct mistakes, plan to grow your new employee, and place the call. "I'm happy to be able to invite you to join our staff."

Your team has just grown by one!

EXERCISES

-16-

1. **Why not just fake** it? If a team leader has the perfect person in mind for the job, why should or shouldn't she go through the motions of interviewing just to make it look good? Answer thoughtfully and honestly.

    _____
    _____
    _____
    _____
    _____
    _____

2. **Write at least two** questions you might pose to your hiring team to help them in their "personality" assessment of a candidate. What are you trying to help them consider? How would you ask it?

    _____
    _____
    _____
    _____
    _____

3. **You'll need a blank** paper (or Excel Spreadsheet, if you're ambitious) for this one. Create a review sheet you could use to evaluate the many perspectives of each candidate. Make sure it does two things: (1) stays focused on the library's overall mission and goals, and (2) keeps the hiring criteria centered.

    _____
    _____
    _____
    _____
    _____
    _____

4. **What would you do** if you checked with a college and found out that a degree the candidate you'd selected had listed had never been awarded? How would you handle this?

    _____
    _____
    _____
    _____
    _____

5. **Write a brief justification** for your boss explaining why you passed over two qualified candidates with bad attitudes to hire one with a great attitude, but fewer skills.

    _____
    _____
    _____
    _____
    _____

BLENDING

| ## THE INVITATION

Are you jumping-up-and-down excited, just thinking of the day your top candidate first reports to work? At this point in your team-building process, when you're *almost* ready to extend an offer and make someone very, very happy, this is the question I pose to team leaders. Why? Because this is the last chance you'll get to sit back, stare out the window for a while, review all of your accumulated information on this hire, and *be certain* you're making the right decision. Consider a few factors before moving into the invitation:

1. Are you settling? This goes back to the jumping-up-and-down question. While it may be a bit of hyperbole, the point is we often make a crucial mistake at this point and settle for the best of the pack, because we just don't want to face another month or more of searching before getting back to full staff. Big mistake. As I've suggested to bosses many times, remember that you may be about to hire the very best employee your organization has ever had—or your very worst. And whichever it turns out to be, they're staying for thirty years! Picture the candidate's arrival on that first day, and consider your gut feeling. If it's excited anticipation, then move on. If it's prayer, then consider that dreaded "R" word— Repost!!

2. Refolding the flags. In reviewing the interview answers just one more time, was there something the candidate said that you haven't been able to get out of your mind while driving or shaving

10 THINGS EMPLOYERS FORGET WHEN HIRING

From the very beginning of this book, you'll recall an emphasis on how bosses treat people. Hiring is no exception. In order to demonstrate a strong and honest concern for the people you may or may not be adding to your team, remember these tips:

1. **Interviews aren't a one-way street**. In addition to making sure the candidate is right for your team, you need to also be making sure your organization is the right fit for the candidate. Allow—encourage—them to explore you, as well. Don't treat the process like a one-way investigation. In the end, you'll both be better off.

2. **Job postings shouldn't read like an internal processes manual**. Read your job ads carefully before posting them. If they're filled with "bureaucratese" that takes all the life out of the role, rewrite them!

3. **The best candidates have options**. This won't be the only job that your strongest candidates are considering. Others want them too! If you make them go through seven interviews, or treat them poorly, or drag your feet when making a decision, you'll risk losing them to another offer.

4. **The goal of the hiring process is to make the best hires, *not* to make the HR person's job easier.** There's nothing wrong with making your recruiting system efficient, but be sure you're not doing it at the expense of your candidates' experience.

5. **Employees start learning about your culture during the hiring process, not on their first day.** By the time your new hire starts, he or she will have already picked up messages about "how we do things here." If you handle them well, or are slow, unresponsive, or don't do what you say, you'll have said a lot already about your culture.

6. **Candidates will scrutinize your rejection notice, so be careful what you say.** Getting rejected is an emotional experience, especially after going through the stress of the interview process. Say what you mean and don't imply they weren't qualified if that's not why you made your decision. Also, don't tell them you'll reconsider their application in the future—if you really won't.

7. **You may lose your best candidates by making the hurdles to apply too high.** If your application process is simply too onerous, your best potential candidates might just skip it.

8. **It takes only seconds to send an automated response to candidates who didn't get the job.** Don't skip this simple and respectful step and leave candidates waiting forever, if ever, to hear your decision. This is about simple respect and courtesy; it just doesn't take that long to e-mail a form letter.

9. **Truth in advertising pays off down the road.** Don't make the job or the pay sound more glamorous than they are. Remember, you're trying to lay the foundation for a long, honest, and trustworthy relationship on both sides.

10. **Your candidates are human beings, just like you, your sister, your dad, or your best friend.** Enough said.[6]

or blowing your hair? (That's when great leaders think!) Get it answered. There's no rule precluding a follow-up phone call *just to be sure.* "We're still reviewing all of our applicants and getting clarification on some of our questions. You mentioned that you left your last job after just two months, but I'm not sure I noted exactly why. Can you help me understand why you made that decision?" Books on

SUCCESSFUL SALARY NEGOTIATION STARTS IN THE INTERVIEW

How many times have you struggled with the decision about how much to offer long after the interview has ended? Do you find yourself a bit short of information at that point? Try asking one or more of these questions during the interview, so you'll be better prepared to understand your options later.

What would be your next logical move in career progression if you remained with your current employer? How long might it take to get that next promotion?

So, now you know how much of a raise they might have been hoping for and whether or not your offer will fit into their plans.

Remind me again why accepting a position with our company would make sense for you from a career development standpoint. How would you explain this move to a prospective employer five years from now?

Again, this gives you a window into how close a match your offer might be to how the candidate had hoped to grow professionally.

If we were to make you a job offer today, when would you be in a position to either accept or reject it?

The ideal answer is "Right now!" Beware of candidates who suddenly ask for more than twenty-four hours to consider your offer. They may be delaying because they're considering another offer. If you suspect that, don't be shy about asking for more information. You need to know if you'll end up in a financial tug-of-war.

At what point dollar-wise would you accept our job offer and at what point dollar-wise would you reject it?

This is the big question; and that's why salary negotiation is often saved for last. Candidates typically expect to "hear" offers, rather than volunteer numbers themselves. Ideally, candidates will close themselves at lateral moves to their current base salaries. It's more commonly the case that candidates peg an increase in their base pay to a percentage hike—5 percent to 20 percent—depending on their desire for the job. Assuming that any of those assumptions are within your salary range, you'll be safe to extend the offer at this point.

The key to these questions, of course, is to ensure that you retain control of the negotiation until you've had all your most critical questions answered.[7]

positive risk-taking will tell you there's no such thing as 100 percent certainty and that's true. But that doesn't mean you should leave any red flags flying.

3. Check back in with your team. Remember, team building is a constant in a healthy organization. While you won't have *had* to reach consensus on this major decision, you should want to come as close as possible to that goal as you can. Doing so will help two ways. First, it will again demonstrate the value you

place in your other employees' opinions and, secondly, it will give you a chance to consider their hesitation and see if you're satisfied that it can be overcome. Okay, three ways. It will also help them be able to be more welcoming to the candidate who is ultimately chosen.

It's time to move forward, but keep this one guiding principle in mind. "Do not make promises or statements that can be construed as promises, that you cannot or do not intend to keep."[1] Most offers are made over the phone, initially, both so you don't keep the candidate waiting any longer than necessary and so that you can get a quick answer. Often, that call is made as an invitation to come in and discuss the particulars of the job. It's following *that* meeting that you want to get things in writing. Once particulars like salary and starting date have been worked out, make it official by having the candidate sign a letter of acceptance.

"You should consider the fact that you may have only one opportunity to make your offer to a prospective employee. Therefore, make the offer in a friendly, upbeat manner. Indicate to the applicant that you will do everything possible to ensure that she or he will succeed on the job!"[2] That could and should include a discussion about your organization's dedication to ongoing professional training and development. "If at all possible, you want to be prepared to make a follow-up offer after you've made your initial offer. Your follow-up offer should be attractive enough to really give the candidate pause to reflect. In fact, you should attempt, if possible, to offer the prospective employee top dollar. If you invest in high-quality personnel, you'll find that it will really pay off for your business. There is *no* substitute for an effective, conscientious worker."[3] Experts have suggested that the point of bringing on a potentially valuable team member is not the time to pinch pennies. Instead, think of the cost you are *saving* your organization by not making a bad hire.

Let's return for just a moment to an earlier mentioned warning to not make promises you can't keep, which is often a tempting alternative to losing someone you've worked so hard to attract. A top administrator was once offered a position at significantly less than his predecessor had been making. (Remember, public salaries are just that!) At the point of the job offer, he was assured this was just because of a current budget crunch and, to make up for it, he was guaranteed a significant increase after the first year. As you can imagine, that increase never came. What was the result? Trust was probably the first benefit to go out the window. Following closely on its heels was confidence in his value to the organization, excitement about his future in the position, and finally just plain money problems, since he'd budgeted the promised increase into his family's future. And the result of all of that was—you guessed it—another opening just one year later, requiring the search and hiring process to start all over again.

There's a lot of joy that goes into a team leader's opportunity to make that significant phone call, offering a job to someone who is in need of work, income, and the opportunity to make a difference. The moral of this story is simple—be honest. Each and every step you take in this process is furthering your overall goal to build a great team, and each and every step should be considered and implemented with deliberate thought and high integrity. To do so will help ensure your team members deliver the same.

So, back to the phone call that sets your team's growth in motion. The entire negotiation needs to be made, of course, with a full understanding of and respect for your organization's current budget and "internal salary ranges. Offering a new employee the same salary or higher than that of current employees can create problems with morale and retention."[4] With all of this give and take going on, pay attention to how hard you are working at it and "don't gloss over signs of a bad fit. You shouldn't have to work too hard to persuade someone to join you and you shouldn't have to agree to something that would disrupt your standard practices. If a candidate seems to be accepting an offer begrudgingly, you could end up with an employee who remains dissatisfied or continues his or her job search,"[5] even after joining your team.

At the conclusion of your offer meeting, hopefully everyone will be smiling and exhibiting a bit of that jumping-up-and-down excitement that comes with starting the right new job at the right new place. Now it's time to get ready. You—and your team—have a lot to do to prepare for your new team member's arrival, welcome, and ultimate success. It's time to roll out the welcome mat and get back to work!

EXERCISES

-17-

1. **Everyone has seen, heard** of, or worked with a "bad hire." Think back for a moment about an example of this that you can recall and then list as many adverse results that it caused below. What happened? What damage was done? What was the cost, both financially and to the morale and effectiveness of the team? Once your list is completed, read it over and over and remember it when your next opening occurs.

_____
_____
_____
_____
_____

2. **What are at least** five options you can think of to help further delay filling an opening, if you're not completely sold on one applicant and you decide to repost. Think carefully and "out of the box." There are many ways to cover work and assignments, other than to just let tasks go undone. List them.

_____
_____
_____
_____
_____

3. **What are several ways,** before you sit down to negotiate a salary, that you can find out what is "fair" for the position?

_____
_____
_____
_____

4. **Let's say your team** is not really sold on the candidate you have selected. What can you do about that? What should you do? List at least five steps you'd take and the results you'd expect, before you'd be comfortable enough to move forward with the hire.

_____
_____
_____
_____

5. **Draft a form letter** you might create to send to the interviewees who are not chosen for the position. Think carefully about what it should—and shouldn't—say and how it should sound.

_____
_____
_____
_____
_____

BLENDING

| **WELCOME MAT**

Here's another true story someone shared with me once. On his first day at work, an assistant director told me he was led to his office by the director. That's it. Oh, I think there might have been a "Call me if you have any questions" comment on her way out. Hmmmm. On the one hand, this approach demonstrated that she had trust in her new hire and an expectation that he knew what he was doing. That's good, right? Maybe, but only after considering the other hand. Years later, looking back on the impact of that first day (and the coming weeks that were no different), it's easier to see the problems of that approach more clearly. There was no delineation of roles, goals, expectations, pending problems (or solutions), potential pitfalls, or offers of potential support. Clearly, the sink-or-swim approach is a far cry from a welcoming, supportive beginning.

During the first year on most jobs, many leaders spend what I consider to be an inordinate and unnecessary amount of time apologizing for and fixing mistakes that could have easily been avoided—if we'd just had a few heads-up. Our fault? Maybe some of it. But, from their first day forward, I'm now sure to begin each and every first day of *my* team members' work life with the admonition that I will stand by them and help them succeed.

So should you.

And you can start by considering where, when, why, who, how, and watch out. As you work through each phase of this welcome plan, though, keep firmly in mind that "following this orientation, it is hoped that the employee will have a positive attitude, have a feeling of belonging and retain his or her excitement for working!"[8]

REVIEW YOUR "RECIPE" FOR SUCCESS

The addition of a new member to your team is a great time to review for everyone's benefit what you and your team consider the top ingredients for your success. This cultural orientation can help inspire and ground them in the basics of your expectations. If you don't have a "Top 10" list already, consider adopting these guidelines:

1. Clear Goals
2. A Plan (for Continual Improvement)
3. Clear Roles
4. Clear and Frequent Communication
5. Supportive, Beneficial Behaviors
6. Well-Defined Decision Making
7. Balanced Participation
8. Ground Rules
9. Understanding and Awareness of Member Needs
10. Data-Driven Thinking[15]

WHERE – Go and sit in the work space your new employee will be using. Look around and pretend you've been asked to sit there for the next ten years or so. Is the phone working? Does someone need to dust or paint or clean up? I once helped clean out an office that had more than fifteen filthy, dirty coffee cups hidden under the desk! That reminds me, how does the space smell? Next, consider supplies. Is there an updated phone list nearby, with both first and last names? Are there files to provide the necessary history for the project to be assigned, or will the new person have to go hunting for them? Are there friendly faces nearby? If your new team member is assuming a spot previously used by someone with a thicker skin, maybe it's time to move the "Negative Nelly" on their right to someplace else and replace her with one of your team's more positive and upbeat members. Extra touches can go a long

way, too. For new managers, I've often had the team compile an introductory binder containing brief, friendly bio sheets (with pictures) for the entire group. Finding something on her desk the first day that can help prepare her to meet the gang can help your new person feel at home much more quickly.

WHEN – Schedules can be the bane of any employee's existence or they can be an answer to their prayers. What's usually the difference? It's called life. Well before an offer is made, usually during the interview, you should have a candid, honest discussion with the applicant clarifying schedule expectations. With that in place, once your offer has been accepted, it's time to sit down and actually chart out what that will look like.

Plan ahead! No matter what special or unusual schedule requirements come with the job, most can be handled and well managed by an employee who has lots of advance notice. I once heard of a supervisor of a larger department who refused to post schedules more than a week in advance. Who can make adjustments that fast, especially when the care of other family members is involved? Create, share, and honestly review the schedule requirements for your new team member looking at least a full month into the future, then be open about your flexibility to change. Without an inviting sense of honesty, she might just be too afraid for her new job to approach you and, instead, either absenteeism or reduced productivity will likely result.

WHY – Without the ability to refer to an approved, standardized personnel manual as a resource, serious credibility issues will undoubtedly surround the validity of any rules you choose to describe. "A good staff manual is of the greatest importance."[9] Without one, there can be no trust that what is expected today might not change tomorrow. Author Alice Ihrig suggests that, as you might guess, all of the basics be covered in this manual, such as organizational charts, job descriptions, benefits and salary scales, but that it should not ignore other, equally critical elements of the workplace. Union-management relation-

A "HEALTHY" TEAM[16]

While everyone enjoys working in a healthy environment, staff often forget that its creation is everyone's job—not just the team leader's. Perhaps the first team meeting to include the new member would be a great place to review the role everyone plays in maintaining this environment. Sharing and discussing a list, such as this one, might just help the whole group get on board.

THE GOOD HEALTH OF OUR TEAM DEPENDS ON. . .

- Coming to work well rested
- Sharing in one another's successes
- Finding ways to make work interesting and fun
- Assuring our work has meaning and purpose
- Maintaining a sense of (professional) community
- Taking workplace safety seriously
- Limiting access to counterproductive "junk food"
- Being open to change and everyone's ideas
- Staying home when sick
- Laughing a lot at work
- Offering help, when asked
- Resolving differences before they become conflicts
- Respecting and valuing all kinds of diversity
- Developing and using all of our talents

FULGHUM'S GROUND RULES[17]

From Robert Fulghum's bestseller, *All I Ever Really Needed to Know I Learned in Kindergarten*, here are some basic ground rules for life—and suggestions on how they could be applied in a work setting.

- Share everything.
  Team members should attend all meetings and fairly share assignments.
- Play fair.
  Start and end meetings on time, everyone's time is valuable.
- Say you're sorry when you hurt somebody.
  Use discretion when sharing information, especially if it's confidential.
- Clean up your own mess.
  Take responsibility for your own learning, growth and commitment to improve.
- Live a balanced life.
  Give and receive feedback well.
- When you go out into the world, watch out for traffic, hold hands and stick together.
  Be a great team!

ships, for example; training, development and conference attendance and allowances; and even a system's bend towards frequent rotations of staff should be clearly and openly articulated. You're describing the playing field. For all to win, describe it all.

WHO – "The person who started work this morning is, at least attitudinally as close to a 'model employee' as you'll ever get."[10] And nothing can ruin that faster than pairing her or him with a disgruntled, negative, and poisonous colleague. Rather than take that chance, take proactive, strategic steps to assure that your new team member's introduction to your library is effective, nonthreatening, and enlightened. After matching her up with one of your more enthusiastic workers, tell the latter to "think like a tour guide. [Have them] point out the subtle features, such as how co-workers prefer to communicate, how the staff has fun together and how employees respond to one another's problems and crises."[11] With your new hire shadowing someone this open and supportive, the likelihood that she'll return for a *second* day is almost guaranteed.

HOW – Fairly. Teams that succeed do so because of an even and shared respect for one another that shows itself in all they do. One way to achieve this level playing field is to establish ground rules early in the game. "Ground Rules are a code of conduct for the group. [They] answer the question: 'How do we want to work together as a group, in order to be the most productive?'"[12] Imagine the opposite scenario, where you'd begin work with your team by announcing, "Okay, starting today we're all going to work together. We'll make sure no one knows what others want to expect or what makes them work well. We'll trip over each other's input, we'll contradict those who could set us straight and we'll generally run in circles, never really reaching our shared goals." Not a pretty picture, is it? Experts tell us there's really only one basic rule when it comes to setting ground rules—and that's do not set them yourself. While direction from the team leader *can* be useful, especially if the conversation is veering off track, the rules must be created by and agreed to by the entire team or they'll be just a lot of paper with no meaning.

One organization began a major endeavor by having the assembled team spend its first meeting filling out flip chart pages with potential rules, which were eventually honed down to the Top 10. They included, at one point or another, ideas such as *allow for interpretation, don't interrupt, don't always refer to past failures, be willing to consider alternatives, compromise and be kind.* Often, appreciative inquiry is a successful method to use in discussing rules that might initially make some team members uneasy. "Ask participants to go back in memory to one of the best meetings they have ever attended"[13] or one of the best teams on which they've ever served. A review of what made those memories so special can be a strong foundation for building rules that can keep your team effective and enjoyable!

WATCH OUT – There's quicksand in every organization and, inevitably, issues will crop up that the most carefully crafted orientation plan could not have foreseen. There's really only one reliable way to prepare to deal with these issues and questions and that's to stay in very close touch with your new team member for at least his or her first few weeks. I know you're busy, but this will be worth it down the road. "For the first few days (or weeks, at least), meet with the employee for half an hour before going home. Encourage him or her to share impressions and ask questions"[14] that you might not have been able to predict would arise.

EXERCISES

-18-

1. **Think back and remember** the worst *first day on the job* you ever had. Don't just think about what actually happened on that day—but about what the impact of that poor orientation was. Write at least five things that went wrong early on that could be attributed to that day.

_____

_____

_____

_____

_____

2. **Next, think of the** opposite. What was the very best *first day on the job* you ever had? What parts of the day were good and what impact did that have on your performance in your role? List at least five things that went right and their impact.

_____

_____

_____

_____

_____

3. **List ten useful and/or** fun and/or intriguing things you can leave on your new team member's desk, to be found on their first day. What positive impact might each one have?

_____

_____

_____

_____

_____

4. **Think of everywhere you've** worked and all those with whom you've worked and write down the name of a person you'd *never* seat next to a new hire and a person you'd *always* seat next to a new hire. Explain why, in both cases.

_____

_____

_____

_____

5. **List at least ten** very basic ground rules you would like to see your team adopt and apply in meetings and while participating in work groups. Next to each—and this is important—note how you as the leader would support and enforce those rules appreciatively.

_____

_____

_____

_____

BLENDING

| ## CLARITY

On their very first day in my department, I used to review with new librarians the performance evaluation form I'd be using to review them each year. After carefully discussing and explaining the various headings and descriptions, I'd ask them if they had noticed anywhere in the document where it said they had to be really good at playing the piano. When they looked at me like I was crazy, I knew I'd accomplished my goal. They'd remember that odd question and the explanation that followed it—so they'd be clear on what my expectations for their work were and what they were not. No surprises! From the very beginning of their career with you, team members must know, clearly and completely, what will be expected of them in a position and on what performance they'll be judged. Human nature being what it is, most really, honestly want to succeed and will strive to do so. If you don't help them from that very first day, the odds against their and your success just got bigger. Consider this example from an executive consultant's phone call with a client.

He was upset and it showed. I could hear it in his voice. "When I told him I was not happy with his work performance and that I was terminating him, he just stared at me and his face turned white! He actually thought he was performing well in his role." "Tell me about the direction and expectations you gave the employee when you first hired him," I said. "What are you talking about?" he responded? "I just hired him and expected him to do what he was supposed to do. He's been in this industry a long time. He should know what his job is!"[18]

< **MONTH 5** | WEEK THREE | BLENDING >

TEAM CONTRIBUTIONS

- **PRIMARY ROLE:** These team members often initiate and/or oversee the work process to completion. They negotiate desired results, communicate to others, design and/or implement an action plan, assure the quality of the process and product, and complete the task.
- **SECONDARY ROLE:** Often the people in charge, these team members actively support the process and the needs of the primary team members. They ensure everyone is involved in the work, they provide resources and information to help, they give feedback, they offer suggestions, they remove barriers, and, most important, they see that achievement is celebrated.
- **TERTIARY ROLE:** These staff members are usually not part of the primary team, but they support the overall work process. They stay alert and watch for connections, they share relevant ideas, and they ask for clarification that can often disappear without those closest noticing, and they keep everyone on track.[22]

If you can admit seeing a bit of yourself in this example, there's still time to save your new hire. The time is now, on your new team member's first day at work, for just the two of you to sit down and talk. There will be plenty of time in the coming days for team assimilation. Now, it's just between the two of you. It's time to clarify expectations—all of them. If you're wondering where to start, consider these top reasons for employee failure that were identified through a leadership study. "The study found that 26% of new hires fail because they can't accept feedback, 23% because they're unable to understand and manage emotions, 17% because they lack the necessary motivation to excel, 15% because they have the wrong temperament for the job and only 11% because they lack the necessary

technical skills."[19] Knowing this ahead of time is a gold mine for team leaders seeking excellence. Why? Because now that you know why your new hire might fail, you can focus your early training and orientation in those problem areas. Think about how many managers begin training by concentrating almost exclusively on the tasks to be accomplished. They're leaving 89 percent of their new staff members at risk. The best approach is to assimilate these problem areas *along with* the practical tasks, duties, rules, software, and other operational components of the job and watch those failure rates go down.

Starting with a critical discussion of roles and responsibilities (and be certain to include yours in the mix) can give you a unique opportunity to address that touchy issue of accepting feedback. Usually, all members of a team will fall into one of three key roles: primary (usually the team member who actually does all the work), secondary (the leader), and tertiary (everyone else, including all support staff and even dissociated coworkers).[20] Hopefully, your team's channels of support, encouragement, and development are circular, ongoing, supportive, and constructive. Knowing who is who and what can be expected of each, including positive feedback, can better prepare a new employee to hear, accept, and apply the inevitable comments that could otherwise have threatened and frustrated her.

An introduction to corporate culture is another discussion that's often avoided (or forgotten), even though it can play a pivotal role in familiarizing your new hire with her or his expected behavior, professionalism (emotions), temperament, and motivation. There will be plenty of time down the road to instruct your new team member in the intricacies of your computer system or to let her practice opening the combination on her locker. (Admit it: if you're like me, you've actually included both of those in first day meetings, haven't you?) The first day is a very important day both for the employee and your organization. "At this stage, the employee is excited to come to work and wants to like the organization. After all, the candidate has also chosen the employer, and it is a reflection of the candidate's own judgment. This psychological condition of excitement and high commitment makes it a perfect time to orient and train employees, because they will usually be highly motivated to learn the job."[21]

So, hit the high points—and the challenging ones—early on. A foundation of honest, open, personal communication can only result in a future built on openness, support, and clarity.

The next logical step on the road to success rests in the achievement of goals and objectives. What, exactly, do you hope your new employee will accomplish in his first month on the job? Since you should be planning at least three evaluations during his first ninety days, let him take baby steps towards success. Identify one or two goals, relating both to assimilation and tasks, and then examine the results together and celebrate achievement. Following a reasonable orientation period, work together to set annual goals and keep those channels of communication open. A note here about meetings. Don't wait thirty days to sit down and talk. During the first few weeks, it's not overstepping to set aside a few minutes *a day* just to touch base and answer questions. Other foundations of clarification can be done simply and can have immeasurably valuable results. Remember, this is a person in whom you're investing. A lot of time and energy has gone into his arrival at your door. Make him glad he came in by focusing on:

1. TIME MANAGEMENT – Explain when schedules are created, how those decisions are made, and in what way they can be amended or at least influenced. Convince your team member—and yourself—that it's okay to ask for changes that would help him balance his life and work.
2. SUPPORT – Early on, assign a mentor to the new arrival, so there's no chance he'll feel distanced from the group he's trying to join. Select someone whose

THE RULES OF THREE

You have three choices when you hire people.

1. You can hire a winner, somebody who already has the experience in what you're asking them to do. What you need to do with them is be clear on their goals and objectives, and then let them run with the ball.
2. You can hire a potential winner. That is, somebody who, with appropriate training and coaching, you think you can develop into a high performer.
3. The third choice is prayer.

Unfortunately a lot of organizations hire people, then give them some haphazard training and pray that the person hired will become a winner. Great organizations don't leave that to chance. They have a well-oiled performance management system.

There are three parts of managing people's performance.

1. Performance Planning. After everyone is clear on the vision and direction, it's during performance planning that you agree upon the goals and objectives and what you're trying to accomplish.
2. Performance Monitoring and Feedback. Feedback is the breakfast of champions. This is where you invert the pyramid and turn hierarchy upside down on a day-to-day basis. Now, the manager is doing everything he or she can do to help the team member be successful.
3. Performance Evaluation. This is where a manager and direct report sit down and assess the performance of the team member over time. (Ed. Note: And base that evaluation *clearly on Point #1: Goals and Objectives!*)[23]

attitude and performance matches the goals you've just established. Serving as a mentor can be an invigorating experience and can often help spur a longtime employee off the plateau they might have been getting comfortable on.

3. STRATEGY – If you don't have a comprehensive orientation program already established, work with your team to design one. A good system should route the new person around to all the organization's various departments and expose them to the full work cycle, even if some of it falls outside of their own areas. This not only helps paint a comprehensive picture of how the organization works, but it's a great way to meet people and start to find their own place in the group.

4. PLANNING – Have a plan. Help your new team member to have a plan. How do they hope to grow? In what areas would they like more training? What new ideas would they like to try? When you sit down together over the coming weeks, months and (hopefully) years, you'll be able to use that plan as a road map, a report card, and a measurement of your combined, ongoing support of one another.

At this point in the book, I hope you're beginning to really see the vast amount of progress you've made in creating your team and adding a new member to it. After all the consideration and study you put into the position, what your team's currents needs are, and then the recruitment, interview, and selection process, you must agree that your new employee's first days on the job shouldn't be handled with any less thought. It's important for you, as the leader, and the new person to have spent this critical time together laying the groundwork for what will follow. It's almost time now to invite the rest of your group into the process, but not quite. Before you continue to blend your new team together, give your rookie one more thing that can help support them and assure their success. A mentor! Next week, you'll learn why—and how.

EXERCISES

19

1. **Interview your current team** members and ask them to describe their best first days on a job. Ask them to list at least ten things that made it a good day. Next to each, note if you provide the same experience for your new hires.

_____

_____

_____

_____

_____

2. **At this moment in** time, what would you say your top five goals are for the coming year in *your* job? List them and make notes about how—and when—you're planning to "check in" with yourself to see how you're doing.

_____

_____

_____

_____

_____

3. **List at least three** people on your team. Next to each name, note what you think *their* goals are for the coming year. Next, take a few minutes from your hour and go out and talk to them and see if you were right.

_____

_____

_____

_____

_____

4. **How do members of** your team usually get feedback and give it? Is it through the grapevine, via gossip, memos, or voice mails? What are three excellent ways you can focus on to help develop circular, positive communication among your team members so that each can have a chance to improve themselves and help one another to improve?

_____

_____

_____

_____

_____

5. **How often do you** do evaluations? How do you prepare? Consider at least five ways you can make the performance evaluations you present to your team members more useful and effective.

_____

_____

_____

_____

_____

BLENDING

WORKING WITH A NET

Groucho Marx once said that if you're arrested, "a good friend will be trying to bail you out; a best friend will be in the cell next to you."[24] While there is surely a difference between work and one's personal life, there is also a strong parallel to friendship that evolves during a successful and intentional mentorship arrangement, that can result in a feeling of relief for the *new guy* that's tantamount to getting *bailed out,* when needed. While we don't expect to become bosom buddies with our coworkers, there's still an element of human nature that will make it easier for us to turn to someone special for advice, for a reality check, or to just blow off steam. Mentors can fill that need. Mentors can help ease the transition into a clique or tight-knit group. Mentors can make all the difference in the world to your green, nervous, and hopeful new team member. Don't roll your eyes. Using mentors isn't the complicated, expensive, and time-consuming experience many believe it to be. It's also not an underhanded approach to developing a clique or developing tomorrow's teacher's pet. Often, it's as easy as a single introduction and a chance for two coworkers to keep each other out of jail.

"Having a strong mentor during your first few years as a librarian can provide a safety net of advice, encouragement, and caution for a newly minted professional."[25] This step, often overlooked and undervalued, can make that first step inside the door and into the group much easier and much more likely to succeed. That is, after all, your number one goal. As team leader, you must remain focused on doing whatever you can to ensure that each and every person you supervise will succeed. Surprisingly,

WHAT EVERYONE NEEDS AND EXPECTS DURING MENTORSHIP

Mentors Need:

- The option to say yes or no to the assignment
- Clear expectations regarding time commitment and closure
- Good guidelines and training
- Strong third-party (usually leadership) support

Mentees Need:

- Confidentiality
- Opportunity for better performance
- Clear information from their mentor
- Clear expectations regarding time commitment and closure
- Not a second supervisor

Supervisors Need:

- Continual evaluation of how the program is going
- To be included in assessments
- Respect between both parties
- Guidelines to ensure the organization's philosophy is being represented
- Demonstrated growth from both parties
- Not to see the mentor acting in place of a supervisor[31]

of being included.[26] Imagine how much an established and respected team member can help in those early and important achievements. And there's more!

"Mentors provide [new staff] with career-enhancing functions, such as sponsorship, coaching, facilitating exposure and visibility, and offering challenging work or protection, all of which help the [new] person to establish a role in the organization, learn the ropes and prepare for advancement"[27]—or success. Let's face it, no matter how excited you are about this new hire and how much you want them to feel welcomed and to fit in, walking around with the boss all day probably isn't going to accomplish those goals. Remember that teams work because everyone has a role. Now is the time to acknowledge that and get someone else involved.

The number one reason mentoring is often skipped or avoided intentionally: time. But it doesn't have to be an all-or-nothing decision. There are three basic tiers[28] to designing mentoring programs (and any number of individually designed plans you can insert into that list) that can allow your staff to devote a lot or a little of their time to this incredibly useful undertaking.

1. LEVEL 1 – SHORT-TERM ORIENTATION
   Usually lasts for only about six months, with goals including basic orientation to the staff and structure of the facility, expanding the new hire's network of colleagues, and introducing her or him to the promotional process, professional activities, and associations.
2. LEVEL 2 – CAREER ASSISTANCE
   Usually lasts six months to a year, with goals including to help assist the mentee in participating in conferences, committees, and publishing opportunities; and to assist with figuring out the system.
3. LEVEL 3 – LONG-TERM CAREER ADVANCEMENT
   This is the least structured system and can last anywhere from one year to an entire

mentors can also be integral in helping staff to do that, by reaching two of what studies have shown are the top three things employees want out of their work.

If you think that's money, money, and money, you're wrong. Out of a Top 10 list, money actually came in seventh! The number one thing most employees say they want is interesting work. Next comes appreciation, and third, having a feeling

career. Goals might include continuing to further the advancement of the mentee's career by introducing them to other mentors outside the organization and providing counseling and professional support in all aspects of their work.

In summary, then, valuable, effective, and meaningful mentoring can take place anywhere between a couple of cups of coffee to thirty years of weekly lunches, and *everyone* will grow in the process—the new guy, the mentor, and most important, your team!

"Fred doesn't make eye contact with you. He mumbles when he talks. Sometimes, he shows up for work in clothes that you wish he would save for the weekend. Coaching . . . can be one of the most delicate responsibilities a manager ever faces."[29] As with *all* other aspects of achievement that take place within a team, rely on the team for help. Curiously, even with all of this evidence at hand, I've seen more managers than I care to count ignore it completely and forge ahead with a preformulated, hierarchical approach to staff development. I and many other mentoring supporters feel this is a lot more than a logistical mistake; rather, it's one of those forks in the road that can literally make or break our shared professional future.

One expert bluntly suggests that "we better stop being so negative and we'd better start being a whole lot more concerned again about the kind of developmental experience, and the kind of modeling we are doing, and the kind of opportunities that we are giving people to demonstrate their abilities to lead."[30]

It's almost time to push that valuable new hire of yours out the door and into your shared future. Use your team to help ensure a happy ending. Assign a mentor.

MENTORING MADE EASY: Step By Step

During the initial implementation of a program such as mentoring, individuals who ultimately will participate, as well as other staff members, will have questions about how it is going to work. Investing the time up front to design and communicate the program's goals and steps will not only help encourage participation but will also end up with less confusion, suspicion and—worth avoiding at any cost—negativity. Try following these simple steps to get your mentorship program off the ground.

Before the new team member starts work:

- Mentor should meet with the team leader to clarify roles and responsibilities.
- If appropriate, both should jointly review the new person's resume and outline strengths and potential pitfalls.
- The schedule should be adjusted for the new hire's first day, so the mentor's involvement in it is planned and doesn't appear to be an interruption to her or his work.

Initial activities between mentor and mentee:

- Joint meeting with supervisors to clarify roles, intended support, and expectations of both parties.
- Review schedule availability, contact information, and encourage ongoing communication.
- Enjoy lunch and a comprehensive tour of the facility, along with team introductions.
- Proactively initiate contact with new hire frequently, to demonstrate interest and encourage ongoing dialogue.

After a few months of ongoing mentoring:

- Meet together or individually with supervisor to evaluate value of mentorship and improve logistics, if needed.[32]

EXERCISES

20

1. **At some point in** your career, you've had a mentor. Maybe an "official" one and maybe just something that happened on its own. Write down at least five things you are grateful for that came out of that relationship and then reread them and consider how differently your career might have turned out without them.

   _____

   _____

   _____

   _____

2. **If you had a** mentor today, right now, what five things would you like to ask him? These can be practical, task-oriented questions you're not quite sure about or even options for the future. After writing your questions, make a list of at least five people who would make wonderful mentors for you today. Finally, pick the top one and call them or stop by or send an e-mail and just check—they might be more interested than you imagine!

   _____

   _____

   _____

   _____

3. **If you were going** to begin a mentoring program within your team, draft the key points below that would be found on your first mentor meeting agenda. Consider the broad picture—goals and purpose to training and evaluation (theirs and yours).

   _____

   _____

   _____

   _____

   _____

4. **If you had a** new team member joining you tomorrow, which current member of your team would make the best mentor? Why? What support and/or training might she need? Draft your initiation invitation to her below (then save it and use it when next you have the opportunity).

   _____

   _____

   _____

   _____

5. **If you wanted to** get the opinions of peers regarding the value of a mentoring program, as well as some tips as to how to run one well, how could you collect that? Are you part of a larger group? Professional organization? E-mail distribution list for team leaders? Decide what your single best source might be, then send a _real_ e-mail out and ask them!

   _____

   _____

   _____

   _____

FOUNDATIONS

"EVERYTHING" 101

The honeymoon period with our new employees never really lasts as long as we hope it will, does it? Often, when orienting a new hire, bosses find themselves cutting short their good intentions and getting their new person right into work. We start out with a nice, clean, shiny checklist that covers all the bases. Handouts, of course. An article or two, for sure. But then, just as you're sitting down on that second day (the first one was handed over to HR for insurance and tax forms), the phone rings. Bob has called in sick again and there's no one at the reference desk. Well, maybe the new guy can just go cover over lunch. "If you run into any problems or have a question, just give me a call," you suggest. But when they call, you're in a meeting. The next day they're on schedule; you're out of the building. Then, a couple weeks go by. In passing, you check in with another team member about how they're doing. "Seems to be fine," holds you over and assuages your guilt. Crisis averted. All desks covered. When you finally sit down for their ninety-day evaluation four months later, you open the folder and, guess what? "Oops, we never finished this checklist! Did you ever find your locker?"

And that's not the only *basic* that's been missed. If you're really unlucky, this reminder of lost opportunities might present itself another way. It could be the customer who calls, angry, and asks you why you employ people who don't know what they're doing. "I asked for a list of surgery centers and she said 'No, we don't have that, sorry' and hung up." No? She said "No?" The number one cardinal rule of good customer service bites the dust again! No one ever says, "No!" What was she thinking? Obviously, she forgot her

RIGHT ARM TIPS

In the rush to cover desks, start getting some of that backed-up work done (now that you've hired a replacement) and move on—finally—to the next crisis you've been avoiding; have you skipped over some of the very basic training that could have helped your new person succeed? Anyone who has worked a reference desk would give their right arm to have heard some of these gems that, without instruction, can take many months and many painfully unsuccessful experiences to learn:

Accuracy

- Don't ever say something is not available—when it is. If not in your building, then at another site to which the customer can be referred.
- Don't provide outdated information.
- Don't read information incorrectly (such as by reading the wrong line of a chart.) Use a ruler or your finger to make sure you're reading the right line.
- Don't ever answer off the top of your head. Locate—and cite—a source.

Currency

- Don't *assume* information you're providing, such as office holders' names or statistics, are still accurate.
- Check copyright dates and provide them, then ask your customer if they need newer information.

Look it up!

- Even if you know the information requested—and you're absolutely certain about that—look it up anyway and cite your source.

Go with the patron! Don't point!

- Old-time librarians had a saying, "Point with your feet, not with your hands." Saying "over there just behind the 600s" might make sense to you, but once your customer gets "over there," chances are they're still lost.

Keep track of where you searched. (What I would have paid for someone telling me this early on?)

- Carry a notepad or clipboard and mark where you've searched. Often, you'll be interrupted and then you won't have to retrace your steps. Or you might get a similar question before you know it.

Over the phone

- You can't see your customer so you lose one valuable communication tool, body language.
- Ask for clarification.
- Smile. It shows over the phone in your tone of voice and conveys a true intention of wanting to be helpful.[10]

IT'S EASY TO DEVELOP A TRAINING PLAN!

Once you see how easy this is to do with your new team member, you'll likely decide to go back and work with even your long-standing employees and do the same. It's empowering, humbling, and rewarding to think that your team leader really cares about your individual growth, development, and career. What better way to demonstrate this than by working out a plan for each and every member of your team? (Don't forget, when you finish this book, create one for yourself next!)

- **DOCUMENT YOUR PLAN:** As the old saying goes, if you don't have a plan written down, you don't have a plan.
- **AVOID PERFECTION:** The key is to get started. Start simple, but start. Do the best that you can for now. There is no perfect plan.
- **DETERMINE GOALS ONE PERSON AT A TIME:** Don't try to cut corners by adopting them from another program, book, or third cousin. Individual training plans work because they're just that—individual.
- **BE REALISTIC, BUT EXCITING:** A dance coach I once knew used to tell her girls to shoot for the moon, and they'll land among the stars. While your plan's first goal should not, necessarily, be to become director in six months, neither should it be something so generic as to put you both to sleep.
- **GET FEEDBACK:** Use the wealth of experience, knowledge, and concern found in coworkers, supervisors, peers, and mentors to help shape a plan that will make a difference in the real world.
- **BEND:** Examine and adjust the plan on a regular schedule so that outside influences or unavoidable changes can be incorporated, without sending the entire plan off the rails.
- **USE TOUCHSTONES:** Once a week—or a month, whichever works—have the employee write down at least one thing they've learned. Compiled in a journal, those achievements will soon result in motivation, support (especially when the going gets tough), and a constant reminder that it's all worth it.[11]

very basic, *Customer Service 101* training or . . . hmmm . . . did she ever get that?

Don't worry, it's never too late. Never. But it is time to get going, fix this mistake, and, hopefully, never let it happen again. It's time to build a solid foundation upon which the rest of your team development can grow.

New employees need more than a security code to get in the door before opening time; they need to learn the basics of what your organization stands for. Think customer service, the reference interview, telephone etiquette, and the like. And, it's up to you to ensure your new team member gets that—no matter how much the place starts falling down around you. Start with a list of what those basics actually are in your organization. On a cartoon cover page for a school district train-ing manual, an employee is reading the end-signs along some book stacks. One says, "Stuff you need to know." The next says, "Stuff you can do without."[1] To that cartoon, I would add a third stack labeled, "Stuff you can learn over time, but I don't want you to worry about until you have the basics in place." In other words, I'm not giving the employee over to a half-day webinar on medical database searching until they know that "No" is never an answer at our reference desk!

I try to plan my orientation by putting those categories in order—and not skipping over number one. Here is a suggested approach to take in designing this very basic training. Depending on what is available in your organization or state, you could substitute existing policies and guide-lines to better match your needs.

COMPETENCIES

I've never yet seen any employee arrive on the scene of a new job with every single competency needed in place. What are your system's basic skill requirements? Using Ohio's example, our professional organization, the Ohio Library Council (OLC), has an assembled list of skill expectations documented for most library positions.[2] The blanket list, required of all staff no matter what their particular job title is, includes the identified competency, its definition, the skills and behaviors that would be exhibited by someone who holds that competency, and suggested training for those who don't. Examples include:

1. *Adaptability* – ability to learn and apply new skills and remain positive and productive while doing so. (That's worth talking about on the second day, don't you think?)
2. *Communication* – ability to listen to others, respond with appropriate language and be understood.
3. *Customer Service* – the ability to welcome interactions ("No, of course you're not bothering me!"), and to proactively anticipate and address patron *and staff* needs.
4. *Organizational Awareness* – ability to know and understand the goals of the library and appropriately follow the hierarchy.
5. *Personal Responsibility* – the ability to accept responsibility for correcting and learning from mistakes and to continually seek opportunities for learning and training (more on this later this month).

I don't know about you, but when I was first introduced to this gold mine of basics, I inwardly cringed remembering how many times I'd skipped over them during new employee training, especially when I recalled the many ensuing—and completely avoidable—conflicts that arose as a result of my oversight.

How you choose to address these critical issues is, of course, up to you and to your organization's processes. If you don't have any, now's a better time than any to get them established. Sticking with Ohio for another example, the OLC's Reference Division came to the rescue. Now available in an updated (and online) format, it created a simple yet comprehensive road map to basic training called *The Ohio Reference Excellence (ORE) Manual*.[3] Many times, as I trained new staff, I assigned them a thorough review of this resource chapter by chapter, including the requirement that they practice what they'd learned by completing the exercises included. And with the *ORE,* a lot of our very most basic "101" training was addressed. For example, consider the value of a first-day library staffer hearing that "reference work is a process that includes mediation and follow-up. The library's responsibility is to meet information needs—not to simply answer an initial question."[4] Following a bit more elaboration on that key concept, new librarians are given actual examples of how to approach their work specifically by "giving a friendly greeting and using a relaxed, upbeat tone of voice."[5] Or, my personal favorite tips, "Smile! Never say, 'We don't have it.'"[6] After further detailing exactly how to perform this most basic task, a chapter-ending exercise asks them to consider that "no reference interview is complete with an ending. What words can be used to end a reference interview?"[7]

The time you dedicate to this basic training will come back to benefit you a hundred times over. And, most important, it will keep your new hire's feet firmly pointed toward success in their new position, which, of course, is your number one responsibility. The rest of the work has waited already; let it wait a little longer, while you ensure that this new person, in whom you've invested so much time already selecting, interviewing, hiring, and orienting, is truly ready to be the best employee you've ever hired.

With the basics out of the way, what's next? At the risk of sounding like a broken record, you need a plan—a training plan. And you need one for each and every member of your team.

If you're just launching into an eye-roll at the thought of how much time a project like this will take, you can relax. Most of it isn't just *your* job. "One aspect of the learning organization that was clear to the librarians and staff was the need for *all* staff to take a more active interest in learning and in improving the organization. Staff could no longer sit back and wait for others to tell them what to do."[8]

It's time to sit down with your new employee, review the performance standards either written or understood by your organization, and create a plan to fill in the gaps. If this step requires you to create the standards from scratch, keep them simple. By identifying basic concepts such as quality, quantity, timeliness, and cost-effectiveness and applying them to your day-to-day work, you'll have guidelines that can help identify the training and development needs you face. Next, take those basic standards and decide how you'll measure them. For example, ask yourself, "Is there a number or percentage that can be tracked?"[9] or, if not, what factors will allow you to judge if the job element was done well?

Here's a simple example. Pages need to put books away, right? The books need to be put away in the proper order, correct? Finally, pages need to accomplish a reasonable amount of work in a given shift. Your concluding performance standard might be an *employee must sort and shelve approximately one book truck (100) books in one hour, with less than a 3 percent error rate.*

Now they know how hard to work, on what to concentrate, and how their achievements or shortfalls might be viewed by the supervisor. If this isn't something they can accomplish on the first day, now *you've* got the start of a training plan!

Just as you would do when creating a strategic plan for your overall organization, the training plan that you and your new hire outline should be clear, measurable, achievable, and somewhat challenging and exciting! Even if they already have the basics down pat, they should be included, their achievement recognized, and crossed off. As they move through the rest of their learning and development, all their accomplishments and growth should be acknowledged, recognized, and celebrated. You've likely got a long working relationship ahead of you. Lay the foundation, clarify the future, and move into it confidently together.

I know, someone called in sick and there's work to be done. Covering those emergencies will save the day. Continuing this comprehensive orientation and training could save a career!

Build your team right. Start with a plan—and stick to it.

SUGGESTED READING

Noack, Deana. "ORE on the Web" (2000–2008) by Deana Noack Web Design, for the Ohio Library Council, www.olc.org/ore/index .html.

EXERCISES

1. **Think back to some** examples of "ah hah" moments you've had on a new job, when you learned a valuable piece of advice that would have really come in handy to have known from day one.

   _____
   _____
   _____
   _____

2. **Picture that inevitable emergency** that might occur when you're right in the middle of your early training work with a new employee. List at least three alternative solutions you could possibly find—other than giving up on training and sending your rookie out to join the ranks, before she or he is ready.

   _____
   _____
   _____
   _____

3. **List at least five** very basic competencies that are critical to _every_ successful employee in your organization. Spend some time on this. Start with ten to twenty, and then prioritize down to those top five.

   _____
   _____
   _____
   _____
   _____

4. **For each of the** competencies above, write down how you can tell when they've been achieved. In other words, how might you measure success for each?

   _____
   _____
   _____
   _____

5. **You've just created** (in question #4) your first homemade performance standards. Congratulations! Now, assuming your new employee needs skill building in all of them, draft a possible training plan and be specific! Look around for real classes in your area that could help develop these skills. (Remember, you're doing this on your own this time because it's your homework. In the real world, you'd be working on this plan along with your employee, so they'd have buy-in and a voice in their own development.)

   _____
   _____
   _____
   _____
   _____

FOUNDATIONS

THE TORTOISE AND THE HARE

Once upon a time, there was a hare who, boasting how he could run faster than anyone else, was forever teasing tortoise for its slowness. Then, one day [insert here the part of the story you know, where the tortoise continues steadily and the hare has fits of starts and stops]. The hare's last leap was just too late, for the tortoise had beaten him to the winning post. Poor hare! The tortoise smiled . . . "Slowly does it every time!"[12]

Isn't it amazing how many seemingly complicated concepts we seek to learn as professionals turn out to have such a strong basis in the simple lessons we picked up early in life? There's a lot to learn for team members who are seeking success and achievement. Whether they're the new guy in town, like your brand-new hire, or the longtime specialists who know each book in the shelves by heart, development never stops. Or, at least, it shouldn't.

As the team leader, one of your biggest challenges is to get your team to both understand and come to terms with this expectation, without feeling overwhelmed and helpless in the face of an unachievable goal. Enter the tortoise and the hare. Now that we've discussed how to find and orient your new employee, the direction of our team development can begin to shift back to that person as a member of the *entire* group, because that's what happens with true development. It's not possible for one person in a successfully functioning group to grow alone. It's not.

"A major principle of PLCs [Professional Learning Communities] is that people learn more together than if they were on their own. It becomes the team, not the individual that is . . . the main learning unit."[13] So your new employee can exhale now, relax, pull up a chair, and join the gang. From here on everyone's in this growth thing together. And that includes you, as their ever-more-important team builder! Don't jump ahead too fast. There will be plenty of time for course selection, workshop design, articles to read, and tests to take. You have a golden opportunity at this point to reset the cruise control on your team's development—not too *fast,* but to tortoise *steady.* By setting your bar at a continuous improvement level and keeping

< 115 >

THREE TIPS FOR SLOW, BUT STEADY, SUCCESS

Sometimes, the simplest approach to a project can seem the most foreboding. If you and your team are eager for success, you might try leaping ahead too fast to reach it. Have you ever exhausted your training budget after just a few months have gone by? Have you ever noticed that a team member hasn't been to an outside-the-building training session since they started work—more than five years ago? If you can answer "Yes" to either of these questions, these tips can help you learn to set a slow, but steady pace—and stick to it.

1. **WORK WITH THE COMPASS, NOT THE CLOCK:** Delay your gratification but keep your eye closely on your objectives. Most important, don't compare with your peers. Spend more time, instead, evaluating if you are on the right track.

2. **SEE HOW FAR YOU'VE GONE, NOT HOW FAR YOU HAVE TO GO:** Instead of counting down the number of years you've got to go . . . the amount of dollars to reach or the days to your next promotion (*or your team member's*), take a moment to flag down the milestones you've accomplished thus far. Celebrate each one of them.

3. **DON'T DOUBT YOUR BELIEFS OR BELIEVE IN YOUR DOUBTS:** At times, you may be tempted to judge if you should have taken this route instead of that seemingly quick and easy path. Don't. Because although you may be able to find a lot of quick and easy schemes, it's very unlikely you'll find one that sustains. At the end of the day, those who succeed are the ones who persist, never once doubting their belief in the process.[20]

it there, no matter what, you'll be bringing along the Type A's in your group right alongside their more reluctant peers. The tortoise in our story might not have been real, but plenty of people have come after who took the same approach to success, and won.

"Take a look at Steven Spielberg. He was rejected by two top U.S. colleges, famous for their film making program, but ended up learning on the job for years at Universal Studios. Not only did he become one of Hollywood's top movie directors, he was also conferred an honorary doctorate and a seat on the Board of Trustees at the University of Southern California. One of the schools he was once rejected admission to."[14] There are hundreds more stories like his. Maybe the story of your own career could join the list? Mine could! When I tell people I applied for three assistant librarian jobs and didn't get any of them, some are surprised, thinking my career had been easier or more direct. Then, I tell them I finally got a circulation department job and, the next time a reference assistant position opened and I applied, I still didn't get it! I don't think my story is much different from many.

Journalist Jessica Savitch once remarked, "I worked half my life to be an overnight success, and still it took me by surprise!"[15]

So you should exhale now, too, and put your team's future development in perspective. No one expects you or them to skyrocket to the top, breaking records and establishing new paradigms along the way. What is expected, or at least should be, is that you can create a culture of continual growth and improvement, both individually and then collectively, that will support a never-ending expansion of your value to the organization. You can do that one person at a time and then watch the exponential changes that will follow.

In his excellent new book, *Great by Choice*, Jim Collins states, "We cannot predict the future. But we can create it."[16] And then he goes on to tell us how. In one example, he centers on a concept called "Fanatic Discipline" that supports the real-

GREAT PLANS INCLUDE REAL GOALS

While great heaving sighs and considerable eye-rolling often accompany any reflection on the concept of strategic planning—or goal setting—that needn't be true. Goals bring the future to life, usually more efficiently and effectively than would happen without them. Plus, they're easy to set, if you remember to include these basic components.

MAKE A STATEMENT THAT HAS ALL OF THESE PARTS—AND YOU'VE GOT A GOAL!

- **CLARITY:** *I want to be healthier* is not a good goal. *I want to lose twenty pounds by New Year's Eve* is.
- **CHALLENGE:** *I plan to support the future of librarianship* isn't all that challenging, especially since you can wiggle out of it by making a small donation to your library school's alumni group. *I will supervise and help develop at least one practicum student each school year* is. Now, you've got some skin in the game, and the reward when your student gets their first job? Well, that's going to feel a lot better than filing your canceled check.
- **COMMITMENT:** If I set a goal for *my most tech-phobic employee to master Advanced Excel Spreadsheet creation by the end of the year*, we both could be left disappointed and frustrated. But if we talked it over and *she agrees to take the basic course and practice with the collection budget*, we both might see achievement before long. You cannot have commitment without buy-in. Whether it's your board's hope for a new library direction or a staff member's individual goals, involve them before writing something yourself that might as well just line a birdcage.
- **FEEDBACK:** When a child takes her first steps, parents don't usually leave the room and wish her well. They stay nearby, they encourage, they support, and they pick her up when she falls. At several points along the journey, teams and their leaders need to reassess, reevaluate, factor in changes, and sharpen their direction. Goals, like life, don't stand still.
- **ALLOW FOR SUCCESS:** How much time might it take to reach a specific goal? Is special training needed first? How will challenges that arise be dealt with? The whole point of goal setting is to facilitate success. It's a journey, not a destination.[21]

ity that it's now time for you to set a slow but steady pace for your team members'—new and old—ongoing development. Collins paints the picture of two companies, one that sets a benchmark of achievement, modest but worthwhile, and meets it year in and year out. The other company experiences exhilarating, huge profits one year, and then suffers the next from setbacks for which they were unprepared. Sound familiar? Guess who wins? Yep, the tortoise once again.

He compels us again to see the value in planned, consistent strategy and goal setting by sharing a "20 Mile March"[17] story that pits two travelers crossing the country, with widely varying schedules and approaches. Once again, the rabbit loses. Don't take my word for it. I've included this book as a recommended reading at the end of this chapter, and, if you don't avail yourself of any other title I recommend, you shouldn't pass this one up. Its team leadership lessons are based on solid, expansive data and study and its lessons are invaluable to us all. Take the March, as Collins explains, which is "more than a philosophy. It's about having concrete, clear, intelligent and rigorously pursued performance mechanisms that keep you on track. The 20 Mile March creates two types of self-imposed discomfort: (1) the discomfort of unwavering commitment to high performance in difficult conditions and (2) the discomfort of holding back in good conditions."[18]

Reviewing his conditions for a successful march is like rereading this chapter—or any work—on strategy, planning, and goal setting. In other words, this isn't hard stuff. He urges attention to *performance markers* (remember those milestones?), to ensuring benchmarks *are within your control to achieve* (that means realistic and possible), and to having a *Goldilocks time frame* which, again, supports a patient, achievable framework to your plan. "The 20 Mile March imposes order amidst disorder, consistency amidst swirling inconsistency."[19]

That pretty clearly brings us back to that first sinking feeling in the pit of a team leader's stomach when they realize that someone is leaving—again—and they have to start their search process all over. Because that's what will happen, right? Just because we made it through all these weekly lessons and successfully brought our new team member into the fold, still we know it could hap-

pen again tomorrow. And what of it? Just because your new team member is now on board, working with their mentor and beginning to blend into a comfortable rhythm with coworkers, doesn't mean another speed bump isn't just around the corner.

Any decent book on team building has to take an occasional jog away from focusing on the team members and bring the spotlight back to you—the team leader—and your role in keeping the ship afloat. You can do that with a steady, unwavering commitment to excellence that can't be jarred by staff changes, budget cuts, or technological advances. They will continue to come—and you will continue to lead—successfully with patience, a plan, and a promise to stay focused and fearless through change.

That model is your team's ticket to success.

SUGGESTED READING

Collins, Jim. *Great by Choice: Uncertainty, Chaos, and Luck—Why Some Thrive Despite Them All.* New York: HarperCollins, 2011.

EXERCISES

-22-

1. **Think back to a** project or undertaking you've experienced that you can now see you approached like the hare, maybe experiencing great, quick success but, over the long run, not realizing the goals you'd hoped for. List at least five ways you could have slowed down and created a more consistent, stable path.

_____

_____

_____

_____

2. **With a clear, shared** expectation of continued growth, how might your team benefit from seeing each other continually improve? Imagine they see, hear, and learn of each other's success and achievement (from you!). What could that do to the team's future, overall?

_____

_____

_____

_____

3. **We've all worked somewhere** where there was that one person who didn't really care about growth or development. They just wanted to come to work, have everyone leave them alone, and get paid. OK, great. But what happens after several years of that kind of stagnancy? List at least five negative impacts you've seen—or could imagine—that could affect the rest of that person's team.

_____

_____

_____

_____

4. **Think back to a** significant "20 Mile March" your team could experience. Might you move to a new computer system? To a new building? What if you had a significant staff turnover all at once? Chart a slow but steady plan that could get you through a tough time with the goal of positive growth at the end.

_____

_____

_____

_____

_____

5. **Write the name of** each team member down and, next to each, write one clear, feasible, and exciting goal each might adopt, for the betterment of the team. For each goal, note how you could assure clarity, challenge, commitment, feedback, and success.

_____

_____

_____

_____

_____

FOUNDATIONS

| ## CATCHPHRASES

Catchphrases are fun, aren't they? Basically, they're just expressions that become famous only because they're repeated so much in pop culture. A quick and dirty Internet search turns up examples such as *"Git-R-Done!"* *"Yada, yada, yada,"* and my personal favorite, *"He's dead, Jim"*[22] (from *Star Trek*). Recently, in the world of management and team-building, a new favorite catchphrase has become *learning organization.* What's that about? I hope, for your team's sake, you don't consider it just a pop concept, but a true reflection of the culture you're striving to build.

In the two weeks that have likely passed since you began this chapter, there have probably been about a hundred interruptions, crises, and distractions that have tempted you to veer away from your dedication to the continual development of your team. That's normal and to be expected. And that's precisely why, at this point, while you're still preparing for next month's review of *how* to train, you need to take this one last look at why your commitment to growth is so very, very important.

I think you can do that by realizing that this concept is much, much more than a pop phrase—it's the foundation of all you'll do as a team leader in order to ensure success for everyone you're responsible for developing. The *Merriam-Webster Dictionary* lists several definitions of and synonyms for *learning organization,* my favorites being "to cultivate, prepare, foster, seek and further"[23] something—or someone. In a nutshell, that's what building a great team is all about. In layman's terms, it's putting your money where your mouth is.

WHAT'S THE OPPOSITE OF A LEARNING ORGANIZATION?

For a picture that can increase our dedication to fostering a true learning organization, let's imagine what the opposite environment would look like to your team. In it, your team members would feel:

- Lack of appreciation
- No reinforcement of positive development
- Low job satisfaction
- No motivation to improve
- Lack of trust in you, their leader
- Lack of self-confidence in themselves as employees
- A gap between their assignments and career aspirations
- Interpersonal team problems
- Conflict[28]

I'm sure we've all had bosses in the past who promised that helping us reach our goals was their mission, too. Right. If I could see you all, I'd ask how that worked out for you and I can imagine a pretty thin show of successful hands. On the contrary, I've heard horror stories from around the county about promotions denied because they didn't want to lose you, about training skipped because it was the busy season and you were needed on the desk, and about development goals never set because there just wasn't time or money. Looking forward, though, to decisions you'll make as a great team leader, those excuses hopefully sound hollow to you now. You've spent time this month considering the importance of starting learning at the basic level, examining competencies, and developing basic, supportive skills for future growth. You've also had a week to commit to a steady, ongoing, well-organized development plan for each employee. In order to renew, strengthen, and cement your commitment to those worthy ideals,

it might help to peek at what the end result for your team would be.

You would be creating a true *learning organization!* Here's a glimpse[24] of what that healthy and productive workplace would look like to your team. See if this is the kind of leadership you want to offer:

1. Team members would be consistently encouraged to take ownership of their jobs and to strive for personal excellence.
2. Team members would be knowledgeable (because of the thorough, basic training they've received).
3. Team members would clearly understand their job responsibilities.
4. Team members would be involved in ongoing discussions with you about skills essential for their success.
5. Team members would enjoy opportunities for increased responsibility and career advancement.
6. Team members would enjoy honest recognition for their achievements.
7. Team members would trust and know that they could look to you to see a model of continual learning.

Or you could hold your staff back so you wouldn't have openings to fill, you could skip training and save the time and money, and you could ignore individual career analysis and strategies for growth and advancement.

So, ok, it's time to start the re-creation of your team's environment as a true learning organization. What do you do first? In a publication[25] put out by the Pierce County Library System of Tacoma, Washington, a checklist of questions a team leader should ask themselves was suggested. First, make sure there is a clear, shared vision of the organization's success and the role each and every team member plays in it. Next, get all members of the management team to support and model learning. Create individual learning plans and be certain they align with the organization's

< CATCHPHRASES >

SELLING THE LEARNING ORGANIZATION TO THE TEAM

Getting the team leader to commit to actively creating and supporting a learning organization is just step one in a two-step success story. Second, the team members themselves must believe, see, practice, and benefit from this commitment. To overcome their trepidation, try these tips for starters.

- Refer to training not just as an expense but as an investment. As a matter of fact, talk frequently about your need, desire, and determination to continually invest in your team members, both for their benefit and for your organization's. First say it, then mean it.

- Determine appropriate needs. Training is not a one-size-fits-all approach. Get to know your team, listen to their goals and dreams, and commit to work together to reach them.

- Get management on board. If sign-offs are required from above to support and finance your team's development—get them! And make sure your team members know you are not the only one supporting their growth.

- Start out small. Before rolling out a massive training program to the entire team, rehearse it with one or two members, to test it for validity and value. Start from the conversation point where mutual goals are established, then move on to include basic competencies and individual growth.

- Clarify a connection. Some team members may feel that the training they're expected to seek isn't relevant to their job. It's important to help them understand the connection and to see it as an important addition to their professional portfolios.

- Create professional portfolios! Award team members certificates that reflect their training and development achievements and support the creation and maintenance of professional portfolios. Not only do they provide tangible evidence of a learning organization, they also help each person begin to see their own career development more clearly.[29]

goals. Ensure learning is happening at all levels. Get rid of status symbols, like long lunches, fancier furniture for some, and lower expectations for the privileged. Offer a variety of communication and learning tools, so there's sure to be something that appeals to every person. Create an excitement about new ideas, share and acknowledge success, and—most important—admit mistakes at every level. And finally, hold individuals accountable for their own learning.

In a library that had recently suffered financial setbacks, conference allocations were reduced and the overall training budget was cut. A librarian complained that since the organization couldn't foot the bill anymore for her training, she was abandoning her goal of seeking professional certification. In one of those bubble

moments where you can clearly see what you'd like to say floating in a cartoon circle above your head, I couldn't help but hear playground chants of "Nah, nah, nah, nah, nah. I'll show them. I won't learn anything new, keep my skills current or advance my career in any way!" Right. That'll show 'em! What I asked instead was "whose career is this, anyway?" Accountability means taking responsibility for one's success and achievement. If that can be underwritten financially, great. If not, I don't know about you but I'm going to find a way to keep on growing on my own!

While growth can mean a lot of different things to different people, to team leaders it means success. Or, "Create tomorrow, don't maintain yesterday."[26]

< 123 >

This section of *Build a Great Team: One Year to Success* has a distinct purpose. That is to convince you, against all odds and against great temptation, to remain committed wholly to creating a true learning organization for your team. You may have a new team member or you may not. You may have many outstanding performers, or perhaps only a few. You may have a few who teeter, barely balanced with just a toehold on that plateau that can support apathy, inertia, and, worse yet, negativity. Or, more likely, you may have one of each. Everything else that you'll learn and do in your quest to build a great team will rest entirely on development, growth, and success. There is no such thing as a status quo of excellence. You'll read in coming chapters some how-to advice on actually developing staff one at a time, in small groups and in larger settings. You'll get to that.

But let's get back once more to answering, "Why bother?" The next time you get too busy or too stressed or too distracted to stay focused on each and every team member's right to thrive in a learning environment, consider these reasons why bothering is worth it.

A learning organization provides for *superior performance, competitive advantage, great customer relations, improved quality, an understanding of risks, an appreciation of diversity, a commitment to innovation, personal and spiritual well-being, an increased ability to manage change, greater understanding, an energized workforce, expanded boundaries, an engaged internal community, and a sharper awareness and mastery of what the times demand.*[27]

Sounds like a lot more than a catchphrase to me.

EXERCISES

-23-

1. **It's not hard to** understand how employees can view new "initiatives" or catchphrases like *learning organization* suspiciously. We've all been there before when a purported commitment to concepts like strategic planning or shared leadership have gone south. Think back to one such unsuccessful undertaking you've experienced in the workplace and make at least ten notes on why it didn't work.

   _____

   _____

   _____

   _____

2. **Make sure you're convinced,** before you start working on everyone else. List and fully explain at least five ways your team's "learning organization" approach to operating will benefit them. Then list five more ways it will benefit your organization.

   _____

   _____

   _____

   _____

3. **In creating individual training** plans, you'll be asking your team members to identify professional goals—and make sure they're aligned with the organization's overall plan, goals, or objectives. You go first. List your organization's key goals below and, if you can't find them, then come up with new team goals that can work.

   _____

   _____

   _____

   _____

4. **Now, you're convinced and** dedicated to creating and supporting a learning organization environment. In preparation for your introduction of this concept to your team, don't forget the WIIFM rule. What's in it for them? How can you really "sell" it and get everyone on board? List at least ten benefits (keep going, if you can!) that you know of and be open, when sharing them, to adding more. Keep the list posted and handy for all to see.

   _____

   _____

   _____

   _____

5. **Draft an agenda you** might use at your learning organization introductory staff meeting. What do you need to say? How would you introduce the benefits you just listed in your previous answers? What does your team need to hear? Most important, what do *you* need to ask—and listen for?

   _____

   _____

   _____

   _____

FOUNDATIONS

| **PYTHONS AND HIPPOS (OR THE BELL CURVE)**

Don't look for a citation to support this claim, because I couldn't get past all the available videos of these incidents on the Web while I was researching, but trust me when I say that certain snakes have been known to eat mammals as heavy as 100 pounds, up to and including a hippo! Focus, please, instead, on what that snake would have looked like for months afterward, while digestion was taking place. Or just picture a bell curve and you'll get a picture of how your team members will vary in their attitudes toward training and development. Not as effective an image . . . but still a clear picture.

This week's focus is about those team members we've all known or supervised or (unfortunately) maybe been, who aren't interested in any training or development thank-you-very-much, just give me my paycheck and I'll do my job.

News flash. That is not acceptable. Maybe, at one time, it was, but no more. This week's focus is on how you owe it to your other team members, to your organization, and even to these reluctant people to find a way for them to grow at least alongside, if not at the same pace as the others in your group. "Change is not an optional event."[30] And neither is denial of continual growth and development.

Second news flash. The following approaches are at least a bit out-of-date and probably won't work. "Just do your job." "Consider yourself lucky to be working." "Do as I say . . . or else." So the answer lies in-between permitting inertia (at best) or negativity (at worst) and producing results with a stick. It's at moments like this that I'm reminded of the python that swallowed the hippo; or so the story went in a development class I once attended.

PLATEAUING IS NOT AN OPTION!

Let's face it: aside from keeping up with required innovations, which *is* part of the job and *can and should* be required, no one can force someone to grow much further than that. Still, there's a difference between being a vital part and being superfluous—and no team today has room for the latter. Leaders who find themselves with reluctant workshop or conference attendees, take heart! There are other ideas you can introduce to keep staff contributing positively to your team. Consider having them:

■ Create their own personal mission statement, so you can both remain focused on it while searching out development options that "fit."

■ Meet with team members at least annually to consider recommendations from the individual on how they can continue to move towards their goals. Make it clear that you're not the Mom, and the old "waiting for the boss to tell me what to do" is not an excuse for immobility.

■ Redefine the skill set needed for their job each year—and make sure it matches their current capabilities.

■ Interact on some level with others in the same position, so as to keep a flow of ideas and best practices in mind.

■ Set realistic, short-term, attainable annual goals so both you and they can see constant, relevant improvement in job performance (or, at the very least, steady, dependable demonstration of core competencies).

■ Remember that interpersonal performance is just as critical as task performance, as a member of your team. Negativity, unproductive criticism, or consistent complaining are not acceptable forms of team communication.

■ Do not provide, enhance, suggest, or cause problems. Be part of the solution—or get out of the way.

■ Approach everything they do with a positive attitude, certain that what they do does make a difference![36]

I first encountered this snake/bell curve concept while learning about how and where bosses should expend their time and energy, given a large and diverse staff with differing needs, levels of enthusiasm, and commitment. I've found that the same breakdown applies to dealing with change, learning, and motivating all staff towards continual growth. Here's the gist—if you drew a bell curve on a piece of paper, which also might look like a snake that has swallowed a large mammal, you'll notice a pretty even amount of stuff on either side and a big lump in the middle. See how technical this workbook is?

If you consider that to be a representation of your staff, we're told that approximately 60 percent of the staff are the lump in the middle; that is, they're probably going to go along with what-ever training you suggest they take. On the right side of the hippo, you'll find about 15 percent of your staff who go out and look for training, volunteer to learn new things, and eagerly await the next challenge or innovation to conquer. Now you have to look to the left. That represents the other 15 percent who balk at Staff Day, turn up their nose at attending workshops, and put changing habits or learning something new right up there with the (natural) fear of public speaking.

Here's the lesson I was taught. Most bosses make the mistake of spending about 75 percent of their time and energy cajoling, threatening, arguing with and basically wrestling the bottom 15 percent, when they should more productively be concentrating their efforts on supporting those in the middle and congratulating those on the

THE DIFFERENCE BETWEEN A RUT AND THE GRAVE? ABOUT FOUR FEET

A New York writer who covers issues surrounding the workplace offers these suggestions for avoiding—and escaping—that rut which can become the workplace blahs. These are just some ideas for keeping your team members sharp. They can spark great discussions and, inevitably, more suggestions that your group can try.

- **HANG OUT WITH THE RIGHT PEOPLE:** Most studies show even though most people think that if they made more money, they would be happier at their job, it's actually the relationships at your job, at your work that really influence how satisfied you are. That's your coworkers. That's your boss. So a really simple thing that you can do to feel more engaged and excited about your job is to look around at the crowd that you hang out with. Are you hanging around people who are complaining all the time and are whining? Try to surround yourself with people who are more positive, people who are the movers and shakers at work.

- **LIVE IN THE NOW:** A very simple thing you can do is just to try to stay more current in your job. Everyone's probably reading the same daily newspaper, the same industry publication. Break out a little bit beyond your usual reading, read a blog. It's just a way to kind of shake yourself out of your usual routine.

- **STAY IN TOUCH WITH THE BOSS:** You need to be proactive about your own job. (The executive director of Southwest Airlines) said she encourages people to come into her office at any time and talk about their career. She herself will visit *her* boss once a quarter to find out, how am I doing? What are our next projects? What can I be doing better? Don't wait for your annual review to see how you're doing.

- **STAY SHARP; DON'T GET TOO COMFORTABLE:** Something like a quarter of all people ages 35–44 have been on the same job for more than ten years. If you've been doing that, you're probably pretty comfortable and you might be kind of coming in a little bit late every day. Maybe you're wearing more casual clothes. An easy way to get a little bit more engaged . . . think back to when it was your first day of school. You got new supplies. You got new clothes. You showed up right on time. Treat your job that way and you might be a little bit more excited. They seem like small things, but they can really help. One of my favorite mentors used to advise that we treat every day like a job interview![37]

far end. The same can be said of training—with one exception. Don't confuse minimum standards with no standards. I've not seen an organization yet that didn't expect (and reasonably so) at least *some* learning and development from each and every team member. Set those minimums, provide opportunities to meet them, and move on. Simply put, use your considerable energy and motivation where it will do the most good.

What to do with those not meeting your minimum standards? You'll read more about that in a later chapter on discipline because, make no bones about it, what you have there is a performance issue and it needs to be dealt with as such. What should those minimums include? Considering today's staffing shortages and imperative need for cross-training, many places, like the Charlotte Mecklenburg Library, "have moved to a model of 'unified services,' meaning that any staff member at any service point can provide the same level of basic service."[31] That's as good a basic starting point as any.

After taking the word *optional* off the table, then, for at least the very basic training you've worked with your team to outline, how can you actually get everyone on board? Remember, threats are not allowed. How about trying accountability; also not an optional characteristic in a successful team. There's a fairly straightforward mantra to use to introduce and maintain a level of accountability in your team that can produce results, and it comes straight from Oz. "Accountability is a personal choice to rise above one's circumstances and demonstrate the ownership necessary for achieving desired results."[32] Making this easier for everyone to understand is the *Oz Principle:* "See It, Own It, Solve It, and Do It."[33]

Remember what we're talking about this week. You're trying to take those carefully crafted training plans and goals you've developed with new and existing staff and make them come to life. You're trying to establish and perpetuate a true learning organization. Your intentions, skills, and motivation are strong. But you're going to run into some roadblocks. Before you get there, you'll need to establish this expectation of accountability. Once training goals and expectations are in place, who should find the workshops or classes? They should. Who should initiate requests for necessary schedule modifications? They should. And who should speak up when knowledge gaps develop? Right. They should.

Any team leader who approaches implementation by carrying the whole mantle of responsibility for success on her or his shoulders is doomed to frustration at best, and failure at worst. Make sure your team knows they are invested in the game and that the investment is in their own future. The options they face are really quite clear. Today's word, in any industry, is adapt or fail. To pretend otherwise is to lead your team down a path to obsolescence.

"What matters [to libraries today] is responding to customer wants and needs in a timely and efficient manner, even at the expense of letting go of past practices and tools, no matter how cherished or successful."[34] Based on how authors Smith and Pickett tell us to accomplish this, openness to training and ongoing development must and will play a huge role in all of our futures. "The new library should be based on the just-in-time model. Our emphasis must be on flexible, multipurpose space" and a constant "engagement in additional activities."[35] None of that sounds like status quo to me. As team leader, it will be your job to ensure that staff on every inch of the python accept the challenge of growth, assume responsibility for their own learning, and help move the team consistently forward.

Neither change nor development are optional events anymore.

SUGGESTED READING

Connors, Roger, Tom Smith, and Craig Hickman. *The Oz Principle: Getting Results through Individual and Organizational Accountability.* New York: Penguin Group, 2004.

EXERCISES

-24-

1. **Often, those staff members** who lounge in the bottom 15 percent of your motivational, learning curve can do more than exhibit dormant skills—they can actually cause damage to the rest of the team. List at least five serious, negative consequences they can cause and, next to each, what you can do to watch for them and minimize the damage.

_____

_____

_____

2. **In order to ensure** that everyone is at the very least advancing along *minimum standards,* you first have to have those minimums established. If you do already, then look them over and make some notes below on how they can be updated. If you don't yet, draft out a plan below listing each unique position and what you feel minimum growth standards should be for each.

_____

_____

_____

3. **Consider the 60 percent** of your team that are in the middle. They're willing to learn and innovate—as long as you tell them what to do, where, and when. List at least five ideas you could try to move some of the more motivated of that group into the top 15 percent. What support could you give them? What rewards? How could you get your team leaders to help them move up?

_____

_____

_____

_____

4. **Unfortunately, accountability often requires** consequences. Draft a team accountability statement that you can use as the basis for starting a group discussion on expectations. Then send it out to your team (and to your supervisor) for reaction and be sure it's on your next meeting agenda. Together, agree on what each person should be responsible for regarding their own growth, team improvement, and ultimately a better service product for your customers.

_____

_____

_____

_____

5. **How can you, as** a leader, help to steer your team away from ruts they might be approaching? List at least five ways you can recognize the situation as it is developing and, next to each, list at least one action step you can take to get someone back on track and remotivated.

_____

_____

_____

_____

COMMUNICATION AND GROWTH

| ## WATER AND LIGHT BULBS

Can you remember the first book you ever read that truly had an impact on you? I can. It was Helen Keller's *The Story of My Life,* which tells the tale of the amazing deaf mute and her equally incredible teacher. What's interesting to me is that, even after seeing Patty Duke portray both roles and feeling each time that the story was striking a deep chord, it wasn't until I became a boss that I even glimpsed what that experience must have been like.

"The 'miracle' . . . occurs when Sullivan and Keller are at the water pump refilling a pitcher. It is at this moment that Keller makes the intellectual connection between the word Sullivan spells into her hand and the tangible substance splashing from the pump. Keller demonstrates her understating by miraculously whispering 'wah-wah.'"[1] While I would never claim to have taken part in such earth-shattering learning, I have seen the light bulb come on for someone who, while previously struggling with a concept, finally had the veil pulled back to reveal clarity, understanding, and excitement! My realization? It is truly a privilege to be able to teach, develop, and (hopefully) inspire another person. And teach you will!

Here's what your average team leader's "To Do" list might include: budgeting, scheduling, interviewing, paperwork, filing, and organizing. And here's what each and every one of these interactions will include— teaching and coaching. "One of the criteria that leaders are evaluated on is how well they develop others. Managing people in the new millennium is becoming less about command and control and more about development and empowerment."[2] As the leader of your great team, this is not just another hat you will wear, but one you will never take off. So you'd better be sure you understand the importance of this role and how best to put it into action.

For the next four weeks, you'll be focusing on the challenges and rewards of teaching and coaching your team. You can interview them, you can hire them, you can give them assignments till the cows come home, but unless you're continually providing support, development, and coaching along the way, greatness will remain out of your reach. Depending on the task at hand, you'll be providing this important support service in many different ways—person-to-person, in groups of all sizes, through the written word, and by unspoken actions and implications. Because individual learning is always your ultimate goal, start by asking yourself how you could possibly develop a truly great team if you didn't address *all* of your team members' needs, starting with getting to know them one-on-one?

Experts at coach4growth.com suggest that these one-on-one opportunities provide the very foundation for team success and should always be the starting point of any development efforts. They ask, "How much time do you spend with your employees? Now, think about how much dedicated time each employee receives in coaching one on one sessions, focused on *their* individual performance and development? In many cases, the individual attention is not on the high end of the scale. Because of this, individual performance as well as team performance [can become] stagnant and employee morale low."[3]

Formally and informally, scheduled and spontaneous, in classroom settings and while walking down the hall together, opportunities will present themselves for you to turn your undivided attention to one team member at a time. Maybe you've never been a teacher and you're not comfortable with this responsibility. It's really no more complicated than demonstrating that each team member's achievements and challenges are your own, as the team's leader. You may be relieved to hear there is no wrong way to coach for suc-

cess. What's wrong is when you don't take the time to do it.

In an excellent book on training written by Dave Arch, Bob Pike, and Lynn Solem (see the reference in "Suggested Reading" at the end of this section), there are several useful tips and suggestions for making the most of your one-on-one opportunities with team members. They start with basic suggestions that you assess each individual's specific training needs (and they should be part of this), design coaching or training to address those needs, deliver that training, measure its impact, and then stay in touch and follow up, especially focusing on new training needs as they arise. "No matter what the setting," these authors explain, "your training endeavors will be more successful if you build in the four Principles of Adult Learning."[4]

1. Principle 1: Adults Must Be Viewed as Individuals
   Be certain to acknowledge your team members' feelings, values, attitudes, and expectations. Make sure that, during training, their physical and psychological comfort levels are being addressed. Acknowledge their past experiences and existing skills and experiences.
2. Principle 2: Adults Want to Be Involved in Their Own Training
   Involvement can be encouraged many different ways. Talking, for example. Talk to your team members and solicit from them what they see as areas in which they'd like to improve. Involve them by having something they can fill in as you go along. This is why you often get handouts at workshops that have blank lines next to slide images—so you can take notes!
3. Principle 3: What Adults Are Taught Must Be Perceived as Useful
   Obviously, everything you teach new hires is necessary for them to keep the job they just got. But what about existing employees? Make sure they understand

NINE BASIC COACHING STEPS

1. **PUT THE EMPLOYEE AT EASE:** It's always important to start here, and even more so when coaching is a result of poor performance.

2. **FIND OUT WHAT THEY ALREADY KNOW:** So you don't waste time telling them what they already know and so you can build confidence that they already know the basics and are only adding to that.

3. **PRESENT OR DEMONSTRATE:** This is the information portion of training; keep it clear and focused.

4. **REPEAT:** Repetition helps support understanding and encourages retention.

5. **EVALUATE:** Did they understand? Can they apply what you've shared? Can they reiterate the lesson?

6. **GIVE FEEDBACK:** Start with the positive—always—but be honest about what they still might be missing and how they can fill that in.

7. **CORRECT:** Offer more training, suggestions, reinforcement, or whatever is necessary to review the information.

8. **EVALUATE:** Check again. Are they really getting it now?

9. **REWARD:** Give honest, realistic praise or encouragement, so learning will continue.[7]

GREAT COACHING QUESTIONS

The most valuable tool for a coach is asking more and better questions. Your team member is struggling and it's your job to help—to train—to support their growth and learning. In short, to find answers. You can start by asking the right questions.

- **WHAT** do you want to be doing that you're not currently doing?
- **WHAT** areas do you want to strengthen, improve, or develop?
- **WHAT** is most important to you in your life and career?
- **WHAT** are the three most important things you would like to accomplish right now?
- **WHAT** is your action plan to achieve those goals?
- **WHAT** do you need that's preventing you from reaching those goals?
- **HOW** can I best manage you and hold you accountable for these results?
- **HOW** do you want me to approach you if you don't follow through with your commitments?

If you rely on pushing to get someone into action, they won't move unless you're there to push. It's more effective to help them articulate what they want, so they can begin to self-motivate. The real benefit of getting this is that empowering people by tapping into their internal drive doesn't drain your energy.

Pushing for results is exhausting![8]

that there is an accepted requirement and expectation of continued learning and that achieving that is a performance standard. Don't make learning new things optional. All that will accomplish is the creation of a few team *know-it-alls,* who could eventually come to resent the fact that no one else is stepping up to the plate.

4. Principle 4: Adult Learning Must Be Reinforced

Reinforcement can consist of feedback, time and opportunity for practice, or both. You've heard that it's dangerous to assume anything. That's certainly true when it comes to learning. And if the task being taught or the issue being coached isn't important enough to practice, then it will probably also flunk the relevancy test. With scheduled, regular meetings planned with each team member, there will be abundant opportunity to revisit, review, and continually evaluate learning and progress.

This isn't about one hour of training each year. This is about establishing a day-in, day-out coaching and encouraging relationship with each team member, resulting first in individual improvement and, in the end, in overall team success and growth. Make it important. Make it consistent and make it always about them. "The purpose of training is for trainees to leave impressed with themselves, not intimidated by the trainer. They should leave excited about what they now know that they didn't know before—excited about what they can now do that they couldn't do before and with more confidence about using their new knowledge and skills on the job!"[5]

If you're new at team development and, especially, at individual or one-on-one coaching, a great tip is to create your own, personal "coach's manual" to help develop this skill as you go. Creating a great team takes time and dedication, and remember, just when you feel you're making great progress with your existing team members, new ones will come along and join in and you'll be starting all over. You can build your own skills at coaching and be better prepared for each and every encounter if you commit to developing your own teaching skills as you go. The great tip is to have your team members *help you* build this guide. After coaching sessions, ask for your own feedback, as well as giving yours to them. Ask them, specifically, "How would *you* remember this best?"[6] Then make notes on what is working in your approach and how you might increase your own effectiveness. Be open and willing to adapt your teaching style to match what you're hearing from your trainees. After all, the way they would best learn is ultimately the way you want to teach.

You have been given the privilege of helping others succeed. As they do so individually, so too will they excel as a team. If you haven't already seen some of those light bulbs come on, you're in for a rare and valuable treat.

SUGGESTED READING

Arch, Dave, Bob Pike, and Lynn Solem. *One-on-One Training: How to Effectively Train One Person at a Time.* San Francisco: Jossey-Bass Pfeiffer and Creative Training Techniques, 2000.

EXERCISES

25

1. **Think back and recall** a time when you helped a staff member truly understand something that had previously both mystified and frustrated them. Describe what the topic was, how you approached the coaching, and how you felt when you realized you'd been instrumental in making learning happen. Next and most important, note why it mattered. What changed for the staff member and for the workplace?

   _____

   _____

   _____

2. **List the members of** your team and then get out your calendar. If you don't already have this done, pick one day of the month when each of them is normally on schedule and add in a meeting, then send them an invitation (if you use Outlook Calendar, this is easy to do and you can set a "Recurrence" for every month of the year). Even if you have to change some of the meeting dates or adjust the times, once you have a monthly meeting on the schedule for everyone, you're more likely to really do it! Make a note next to each person's name (or put notes in the folders you hopefully keep for each) about topics you might address at your very first monthly meeting. (And don't forget to ask them to help keep that list going!)

   _____

   _____

   _____

3. **Think of the last** time you learned something completely new, something that you had never learned before. What specifically helped you learn it? List the training techniques (demonstration, practice, documentation?) that helped you the most.

   _____

   _____

   _____

4. **Using the above example** again, list the training techniques that helped you the least and, in fact, might have even contributed to slowing your learning and feeling of achievement? Make a mental note to avoid those examples.

   _____

   _____

   _____

   _____

5. **What one skill, either** hard or soft, can you think of that your entire team might benefit from enhancing? Outline at least ten methods, activities, or approaches you could possibly use to teach or coach them to success in this area. Now send an e-mail to your team, outlining your ultimate goal in addressing this area, and explain that one hour of your next team meeting will be dedicated to this issue. Ask them to send you their top three choices, from your list of ten, of preferred methods you should utilize. Give it a real try, get some feedback and—you're on your way! You're a coach—and you've gotten your team involved from the beginning!

   _____

   _____

   _____

COMMUNICATION AND GROWTH

| **EN MASSE**

On his way out the door on my first day and his last, a former boss offered this bit of parting advice: "Be prepared to be met to death." Boy, was he right. Team meetings, staff meetings, planning meetings, disciplinary meetings, hiring meetings, managers' meetings . . . the list went on and on. But as I got better and better at this critical form of group learning, we diverged on one major point. I *liked* them! Contrary to the many one-on-one opportunities you'll have to develop and train your team, these *en masse* gatherings can offer you a unique and invaluable opportunity to strengthen ties, build trust, and develop loyalties that every great team needs. First, though, you have to learn to master the meeting.

James T. Kirk of *Star Trek* fame wasn't a fan. "A meeting," he once said, "is an event where minutes are taken and hours wasted."[9] Not so when a great team leader is at the helm of the ship!

There's hope for meetings! To begin with, great leaders should truly appreciate them as a gift of time, especially these days, that results in your entire team coming together at once! Second, team leaders need to be just that—leaders—and take the time to learn the art of the meeting. "Meetings are a problem [only] when no one is accountable for them."[10] If you're building a great team, it's time to take charge of the gavel. Consider these tips,[11] to begin polishing your technique.

1. Be on time. Start on time. End on time.
2. Prepare for the meeting. Reread the previous meetings' minutes, preferably well before the next one begins. Follow up and be

prepared to have someone update the team on previously assigned tasks. Read all associated documentation.

3. Send any support materials along with the (timed) agenda at least a week before the meeting and create a culture of expected participation. Meaning? Team members will have read what you send them.

4. Don't start a meeting unless you know how and when it will end. Again, have a timed agenda and a plan to stick to it.

5. Meetings are for decisions and distribution of tasks, not for reports. Don't read to attendees.

6. Have a competent chair. Rotate the assignment. Provide training so all are qualified.

7. Share leadership or shift it month to month. Provide training on agenda preparation, facilitation, and any other skills needed for success.

Why bring team members together? All too often, it's simply because it's meeting time. Every third Tuesday at 9:00 a.m. you meet, whether you need to or not? That shouldn't be the answer. Instead, for the dynamic team you're developing, members should be coming together to donate their particular knowledge, experience, and passion to a group stew that will produce a better solution together than would have been possible alone.

There are lots of different ways to lead truly effective meetings. Perhaps, the more unique approach you try, the more intrigued response you might get. One innovative method to consider to achieve a new level of group learning and sharing is called "idea gardening." Jack Ricchiuto, a certified management consultant, explains how this approach to team thinking, exploring, and sharing differs from more traditional brainstorming exercises. "In classic brainstorming, criticism and tangents were always 'forbidden fruit.' By contrast, we regain our original sense of harmony with our creative nature because, in the Idea Garden, there is no forbidden fruit and every

temptation is encouraged."[12] While the group simultaneously discusses ideas, considerations, and variations on those ideas, they benefit from the "open-mindedness, inventiveness, provocation and pragmatism required to grow [truly new and exciting] ideas"[13]—as a team!

Back to reality, how can a team leader create a meeting that does all this and not just get stuck with the same old, same old? Step by step, it's not as hard as it looks.

1. Start your agendas at least one year in advance. Seriously! Put monthly meetings on the calendar in early January for the full year. This sets aside the space, provides plenty of schedule notification, and shouts to the team that meetings matter. Then, create an agenda template, with each page headed with the appropriate day and time for the coming year's meetings. As agenda topics arise— real topics that require the creativity of the combined team to consider—enter them on the agenda.

2. At least one week before each meeting, consult the agenda draft you've been crafting and finalize it with times for each topic. Attach any supportive material to be read and send the agenda out to your team. *Note:* If the template is empty, cancel the meeting. Everyone will appreciate the newly freed hour (no meeting should be more than one hour) and, even more, will appreciate the reality that your team meetings aren't just meant to fill time.

3. Make punctuality a performance issue. No one is so important as to be able to stroll into a meeting late, while others are seated and ready to begin. Respect each other and the work the team does by starting and ending according to the agenda.

4. Have no more items on the agenda than can be adequately covered in the time

BAD MEETINGS ARE YOUR FAULT

You've been there—we all have. The best way to describe a bad meeting can vary from excruciating to infuriating and can leave attendees wavering between frustrated and suicidal. You're the leader, it's time to take responsibility! Run your meetings well and train your staff to do the same, and that valuable time everyone is spending will be well spent instead of wasted.

1. **TREAT THE AGENDA AS A CONTRACT:** Consider it binding and don't casually breach it by veering or letting others veer off topic or away from the timetable. If the team leader stays on point, so will everyone else.

2. **CREATE AND MAINTAIN THE RIGHT ENVIRONMENT:** Good facilitation is subtle. Be prepared to adapt your style and approach, chameleon-like, to the needs of a constantly unfolding and changing situation. Is humor appropriate? Or is it time for a businesslike focus? Respond to the group's need and leave your ego at home.

3. **KNOW AND CARE ABOUT THE TOPIC:** Know enough about the topic to understand the key challenges and dynamics. Care about the issue—that's what can get you over the rough spots.

4. **YOU'RE NOT QUEEN OR KING OF THE WORLD:** Be kind, respectful, open, and fair to all—not just to a hand-picked inner circle of advisors. Earn the trust and respect of the audience.

5. **KNOW THYSELF!:** Have strategies in mind to deal with whatever might come up. Indecision? Conflict? Aversion to change? Don't be surprised, be prepared!

6. **EXPECT THE UNEXPECTED:** Like I said, have a "Plan B" in mind, so deviations can result in good, instead of evil.

7. **LEVEL THE PLAYING FIELD:** Try to eliminate power dynamics that might exist if attendees hold various titles or authority levels. Treat everyone at the meeting as though they're equal in opportunity for input—then make sure you respond to them that way.

8. **WHEN IN DOUBT, ASK THE TEAM!:** No team leader knows innately how to handle every situation. You have a think tank assembled. Ask them! Finding solutions together strengthens buy-in and, more often than not, makes solutions more feasible. Consider, "We seem to have two differing opinions on how these issues can best be handled. How should we proceed?" is much better than "I hear what you're saying and I'll make the decision and let you know."

9. **CELEBRATE PROGRESS:** Simple. Celebrate progress. Share credit or, better yet, give it away.[15]

allowed. Others can be *parked* to a later agenda or, if necessary, a special meeting can be called to resolve timely, critical issues. Consider how governmental bodies often have a first, second, and third reading of important legislation. This process allows for thoughtful responses, background research, and careful insight before important decisions are made. You can introduce a new issue at one meeting, time the initial discussion, and indicate the next review step that you'll take at the next meeting, if needed.

5. Create action minutes, not narratives. Circulate to everyone (or post) the assignments made and the deadlines created. Then make sure you support the assigned work, provide any necessary support or training, and communicate the clear expectation of accomplishment.

COUNTDOWN

Effectively timing a meeting can result in a more efficiently run and productively ended meeting. Consider these suggestions as methods you can use to be certain you stick to your agenda, begin and end on time, demonstrate respect for your attendees and—accomplish something!

- **STAND UP!:** A manufacturer with a large shipping room (library meeting rooms with chairs pushed aside would work just as well) ran all staff meetings with participants standing. Energy levels stayed high, filibusters were cut short, and focus was sharper. Plus, no one wanted the meeting to run over so timing became an art.

- **PROJECT TIME:** Purchase a simple but large clock or project an Internet clock onto the wall and use it to keep to your *timed* agenda. Appoint someone timekeeper at the very beginning and, when they wave their hand, make it mean something.

- **USE A PARKING LOT:** Don't stand in the parking lot for the meeting, but use the concept to *table* off-topic but still relevant ideas and comments. If you park them to the side so you can stay on the agenda, be certain that they appear on the next agenda, so contributors don't just feel like their ideas are being blown off.[16]

("I didn't have time to get to this" won't work, unless you're running a volunteer corps.)

6. Develop leadership to ensure sustainability. In other words, don't hog the microphone. At each interaction of the team, opportunities exist to prepare your team's next leaders. Share, teach, and develop skills within your group that will improve your performance today and guarantee continued achievement for tomorrow.

Even if your team has been at this meeting stuff for a long time, they might be pleasantly surprised if you started the next meeting with a discussion of ground rules going forward. Everyone has a stake in the success of meetings, so everyone needs to share a piece of responsibility for that to occur. For example:

1. Every team member must take an active part in the discussion and activities of the group. Wallflowers are not discouraged, they're unacceptable.
2. Every team member needs to be as knowledgeable as possible about the subject matter. That means reading whatever preparation material is shared and giving it careful thought before arriving.
3. Every team member should strive, during the meeting, to remain group-oriented, open-minded, and focused on solutions—not negativity![14]

Just imagine an organization whose innovative leader announces the introduction of an "R&D Hour." This gathering will bring together anyone interested in examining current challenges, learning more about options, planning growth, and researching and developing real solutions for progress. All ideas and suggestions will be welcomed, considered, and potentially piloted to test for results. Attendance will be by choice, but given the exciting challenges and potential rewards, eventually everyone will want to take part. Everyone has arrived and she's closing the door as a colleague walks by and asks what's going on. "Shhhhh," she responds. "It's a staff meeting. But don't tell anyone."

SUGGESTED READING

Hines, Samantha. *Productivity for Librarians: How to Get More Done in Less Time.* Oxford: Chandos, 2010.

Ricchiuto, Jack. *Collaborative Creativity: Unleashing the Power of Shared Thinking.* Akron: Oak Hill, 1997.

EXERCISES

-26-

1. **List below the last** ten meetings you have attended and next to each, describe one worthwhile thing, decision, assignment, or event that resulted. If you end up with some meetings that accomplished nothing, note why you think that is.

   _____

   _____

   _____

   _____

2. **In brainstorming, everyone is** encouraged to offer thoughts about a topic, but no one else is allowed to comment on them, negatively or positively. Think of the last major discussion topic your team addressed and "idea garden" below—using a _stream of consciousness_ approach. Jot down a thought, then a problem with that thought, or another idea that thought brings up and keep going for as long as you can. In other words, be your own devil's advocate. Finally, read what you wrote and describe three things about the idea gardening approach that might just enhance your team's work.

   _____

   _____

   _____

   _____

3. **Recall or reread your** most recent team meeting agenda and make notes—what was on there that could have come off? What was strictly information sharing, that could have been shared beforehand and didn't really need to be discussed? What creative ideas pertaining to the topics at hand were missed? Now, rewrite the agenda, as if you were having the meeting over (and maybe you should).

   _____

   _____

   _____

   _____

4. **Figure out how you** can either project a clock on the wall of your meeting room or bring in a laptop with a viewable clock or—any other way that you can track time at your next meeting.

   _____

   _____

   _____

   _____

   _____

5. **Create your next team's** meeting agenda template, incorporating as much of this chapter's advice as possible. Make a note that, after the meeting, you'll review what happened carefully before creating the next one.

   _____

   _____

   _____

   _____

COMMUNICATION AND GROWTH

| ## POWER OF THE PEN

There's a story about "a director pitching the concept of the film *Finding Nemo* to John Lasseter, chief creative officer at Pixar. After an hour, the director finally stopped to ask his listener what he thought. Lasseter replied, 'You had me at *fish.*'"[17] This lesson can clearly be applied to writing, as well as speaking. Although writing is one of the most critically valuable tools a leader has to communicate immediate, pending, or long-term information to part-timers, full-timers in other branches, distanced administrators, and even potential new hires, little if any time is ever spent learning how to stop when you've made your point.

It's time to hone your writing skills if you want all of your other efforts and energies to result in a truly great team. Writing matters. For many staff members whose schedules (or titles) keep them apart from your organization's decision makers, you're the translator. You are the conduit on whom they will depend to hear vital, relevant, and understandable news and advice. We've already talked about the many forms of face-to-face communication venues you'll use, from one-on-one to group meetings, but in addition to those, you'll need to write often and write well. When you write well and they read and understand, motivation, confidence, and performance improve.

"The ineptitude of writing is responsible for lost time, lost jobs, lost productivity, and can leave the audience baffled and bored at best, and at worst, making decisions without the benefit of full understanding."[18] It doesn't have to be that way. You know who you are. Beyond this one chapter you can, if you choose, select from innumerable books and classes

IMPROVE YOUR WRITING: STEP BY STEP[23]

When speaking to bosses about skill development, I almost always caution them to approach their development plan in baby steps. There's so much to learn . . . and so little time. Becoming a better writer can and should be accomplished in the same way. Small, incremental improvements, such as these examples, can make a lot of difference in your final draft.

- **UPSTREAM OR DOWN?:** Some writing is like rowing a boat downstream, *with* the prevailing attitude of your team regarding the topic at hand. Some is like rowing upstream, *against* the current. If you're writing instructions to implement roving reference and the majority of your team members are still cautiously fearful about the practice, consider that attitude in how and what you say. If you're writing to tell everyone they just got a raise, be celebratory! If you're writing pink slips, leave out the smiley faces and exclamatory punctuation. In short, adjust the method and mood of your writing to match what's really going on and you're much more likely to have your message be truly heard.

- **CUT, CUT, CUT:** In my first reporter's class as an undergrad, our instructor gave us 300 facts and told us to condense them into a story of no more than 500 words. It was murder! Then, with ten minutes left in the class, as we were just wiping the sweat off our brows, she announced there had just been a major train wreck in the center of town, page one was being changed, and we needed to cut our story to 100 words. Cutting is good. Reread everything you write before you share it, and cross out any unnecessary words, phrases, or (especially) gimmicky additions. Be clear and be brief.

- **LAST SHALL BE FIRST:** Often or, if I'm being honest, almost *every* time someone asks me to review a letter or report, I suggest they move their last paragraph to the top. In writing, they are trying to make their case. So, naturally, they start at the beginning and lead up to the real crux of the matter. Reread your draft again and see if you can't find a paragraph down a bit that really hits the nail on the head—and move it up.

- **CRACK THE BLOCK:** It's a proven fact that just as water won't boil if you watch the pot, a white piece of paper will not fill with words if you only stare at it. Every writer has had writer's block, especially when the news they're writing isn't good. Blogging expert John Murphy[24] solved that problem for me. Ever since reading this advice he offered, I've had no trouble starting everything from a simple memo to a five-part course design. His technique "involves drawing a diagram of the subject in questions. For example, if I'm writing about an industrial power tool, I put that in a circle in the middle of the page. Then, I think about what's related to that topic: features and benefits; which industries are most likely to use the tool; warranties, evidence of durability; testimonials from users, etc. Each of these items goes into another circle tied to the middle like spokes on a wheel. Sometimes, these satellite circles get little moons of their own. Relationships begin to emerge and the form of the writing practically jumps off the page."

to improve your writing skills. What is important for you to realize here and to accept is that, as your team's leader, it matters. One writing specialist explained it this way: "In the fast-moving environment we live in today, those who jump to the top have fantastic communication skills. You've heard the cliché, 'the pen is mightier than the sword.' Well, in business [as well as in leadership], you'd better be able to flourish a pen or else you may just fall on your sword."[19] And, no matter where you feel your skill level is right now, getting *mightier* isn't as hard as you might think.

THREE LITTLE RULES

Remember to consider these questions and you will be writing well.

1. **AUDIENCE:** For whom are you writing? How might they feel about this message? How can you respect their conceptions, while still delivering the message?
2. **INTENT:** Why do you have to write this? What parts do you have to say? Say just those.
3. **MESSAGE:** What do you want the reader to come away with, after reading? Focus on that, clarify that, and tell them that![25]

Let's review your options. There are e-mails, of course. Ubiquitous and relentless, they have unfortunately become the water cooler of the twenty-first century. What about meeting minutes, monthly reports, hiring recommendations, funding requests, disciplinary letters, and letters of recommendation? It's a safe bet you've not only had to write many of each but that, somewhere along the way, you struggled enough to convince yourself you couldn't do it well. Not true. Here's what always surprises me. When asked for writing or editing advice, I often encourage the person to have more confidence in their own abilities, and I try to support the suggestion with a simple tip. No genius here. It's simple. When they tell me "I'm a great talker, but I just can't write," I admonish them to simply grab a pen and jot down what they'd say.

One of the best pieces of writing advice I've ever heard or shared is "Be yourself." Instead of approaching your writing as though it's something complex and academic—and thereby overcomplicating the entire process—just say what you want to say the way you'd say it. "Great writers have always known that they are communicating express, not impress. Ultimately, writers must

impress their readers with their ideas. Not their vocabulary. As you revise your drafts, look for places where you may have chosen fancier words in a conscious or unconscious attempt to impress your reader. Replace those words with words that express your meaning more clearly."[20] Here's a (real-life) example. I can share it because it was a mistake I almost made in my first book, *Be a Great Boss,* in the very first chapter called "The Attitude You Display."

1. (FIRST DRAFT) It's important to note early on in your career as a manager or a boss that the tasks you will inevitably accomplish will be less likely to be impactful than how you perform them will be. If you want to become a successful leader for whom many will hope to work alongside, then re-evaluation of your basic, core psychological application of leadership is critical.
2. (PUBLISHED REVISION) The title of this chapter is no joke. Your attitude is everything. With the right attitude, you can become a great boss. People will WANT to work for you. Staff will turn down better job offers, if it means leaving your library. Your successes will be legendary. With the wrong attitude, you're going to count the days to retirement, like a ten-year-old waiting for summer vacation.[21]

See what I mean?

I'm not going to launch into a full-blown writing course right here, in the middle of this workbook (but my *next* book, "Communicate with Confidence: One Year to Success," will do just that!). What should help to get you started, though, is to remind you once again of why you need to care about your writing. Consider these important implications, suggested by Karl Walinskas.[22]

1. It will have a *visible impact.* Seeing something in writing makes it more

believable and increases recall. It can also provide invaluable legal support.

2. It's been said that unless you have a plan written down, you don't have a plan. Written messages can better *avoid being manipulated and twisted* throughout the chain of command, whether intentionally or unintentionally.

3. Concerns, complaints, and requirements can be transferred often before they reach the person who can respond to them, often resulting in the old telephone game *confusion*. Recorded requests can comfortably make that trip.

4. Funny thing is, when praise is received in private over a cup of coffee, it's nice. When it's posted in black and white in the newsletter—in writing—it's like *giving someone an unexpected bonus.*

5. If you can imagine telling someone how to perform a complex, Boolean information search, you can appreciate how much more valuable the instruction would be written down. Putting something complicated in writing *leads to consistency* during implementation.

EXERCISES

27

1. **Dig out the last** report or meeting minutes you wrote and, in each section with a red pen, mark where you *could* have stopped. Make note of where, when, and how often you write too much.

   _____
   _____
   _____
   _____

2. **List the most useful** five things you've ever learned about being a good writer. Next to each, note where (or from whom) you learned it. Next, think back to the last time you spent any time or energy to learn more. You might want to review where you've benefited in the past and return to that place or format to continue building your writing skills.

   _____
   _____
   _____
   _____

3. **Think about a time** when something you had recorded in writing turned out to be very, very valuable to you and to a specific situation. Describe why you initially wrote it and why it ended up being so important. Note what might have happened differently if you hadn't written it down.

   _____
   _____
   _____
   _____
   _____

4. **List the dates of** the most recent three letters, notes, or e-mails of congratulations or praise you sent to anyone on your team. Right now, before you finish these exercises, write at least two new ones. Then remind yourself to do this more often.

   _____
   _____
   _____
   _____

5. **Think of something you've** been meaning to get around to writing but you just haven't been able to get your head around how to approach it. Try using the "Crack the Block" method described earlier. If it helps, try it again, with something else on your plate that's just waiting to be written.

   _____
   _____
   _____
   _____

COMMUNICATION AND GROWTH

UNSPOKEN

Pssst. Guess what I just heard?

So far, this month has been all about teaching, growth, and communication between you and your team. Whether those interactions take place one-on-one, in meetings, in small groups, or through writing, you've read and (hopefully) accepted the fact that communication is one aspect of your job that is both crucial and vital to your team's greatness. But speaking and writing aren't the only ways messages get sent. Messages, often the wrong ones, have a way of sending themselves. And that is something else critical for team leaders to consider—and to avoid!

Primary on this list of *alternative communications* are things that team members see, hear, feel, and know (or think they know) that you, in all likelihood, never meant to convey. Let's start with what they hear such as, pssst . . . gossip.

Gossip is not just "spreading unverified news."[26] If it were that simple, it wouldn't be as dangerous. Gossipers add "unexpected and [often] astonishing information, valid or not, to the news and often end up seriously violating the privacy of a person or damaging their reputation."[27] And the damage can go even further than that, as if hurting another team member isn't enough.

Think about all the time some people spend gossiping (you're thinking of at least one person in particular right now, aren't you?), then stop and think carefully about *whose* time they are wasting. "The time devoted to gossip is often taken during working hours! It therefore entails a cost to the employer or to taxpayers! Tasks could be accomplished while those

CREATE A "ZERO GOSSIP" TOLERANCE POLICY

"Even if it's not malicious, gossip kills camaraderie and morale. It can wreak havoc on efficiency. Gossip is unproductive, breeds resentment and is a roadblock to effective communication."[36] Wow, those are pretty serious statements! Imagine intentionally allowing *any* single statement or comment to damage or even undo days or months or years of team development work and progress. If you allow gossip within your team, that's exactly what you're doing. Consider, instead, instituting a complete, 100 percent, total ban on gossip. The results may surprise you. Here's how:

- **START AT THE TOP:** The team leader must declare "No more gossip." That person has to persuade everyone that office gossip won't be tolerated, why this is necessary, and that everyone is going to be held accountable.
- **EVEN LISTENERS ARE GUILTY:** You need to make it clear that even listening to gossip is a no-no. What? You can get zapped even if you just stand there and don't say a word? Yes. Gossip cannot exist without someone to tell it to.
- **WELCOME OPEN DISCUSSION:** Leaders have to create the kind of workplace where it's safe for people to voice concerns and ask for clarity and action. One of the reasons gossip is so commonplace is that people can easily justify it. "I can't say that," "I will be fired if I say that," "The last person who said that got in trouble." Banish those excuses—and gossip—by being responsible and responsive.
- **CLEAN THE SLATE:** Responsibly clean up any messes you have already made, so you can start with a clean slate.
- **LOOK FOR THE FACTS:** Start having the scary conversations. The team—and yes, you too—really will benefit. You will quickly gain a well-earned reputation as a straight shooter and a trusted leader.

three persons are joyously gossiping in the toilet. People may be waiting for documents, the chain is slowed."[28] So people are hurt, time is wasted, and customers are left waiting. Allow no time or acceptance of gossip on your team and keep your communication and theirs above board, healthy, and transparent.

As the team leader, the best thing you can do to combat indirect, inaccurate, and unproductive communication is to battle it with the direct stuff, so get comfortable with talking to your team. Invite thoughtful, constructive commentary. Encourage double-checking and fact-seeking in place of wondering or, worse, guessing and, above all, make kindness towards one's teammates every person's paramount goal. As we learned as children in between graham crackers and the playground, healthy teams must always think before they speak.

Here are some additional unspoken but potentially very loud messages sent by actions (or inactions) that might surprise you:

1. YOUR OFFICE IS A TRAIN WRECK – "Everything in your office sends a message, whether you want it to or not. A messy office or desk, for example with disorganized piles of papers, can discourage people from doing business with you. It suggests that you are not conscientious, as people believe that it can be very difficult to function in a messy office, and they may naturally assume that this chaos will be carried through into your projects!"[29] Picture sitting in your boss's office and thinking "I wonder which of those piles contains the report I worked so hard to write?" Don't say you can put your hand

COMFORTABLE COMMUNICATION

Experts offer lots of useful advice to public speakers in order to help them feel more at ease when presenting to a large group. Interestingly, these same ideas can make leaders more comfortable speaking to their own team members, either individually or as a group. Consider trying them!

- **ADD STORIES:** Personalize your presentation by using anecdotes, stories, products, visuals . . . anything you can think of to enhance the message you're sending. If you're hosting a boring session on something required like CPR, for example, hand out "Life Saver" hard candies. For stories, those in which you yourself learned a lesson, show both your humility and human side.

- **USE HUMOR:** Appropriate, non-offensive humor is greatly appreciated, especially when it's used to dilute an otherwise dull topic. It also reminds your team that no one should take themselves too seriously.

- **REHEARSE:** Use a mirror, a spouse, your dog—anything or anyone who can give you honest feedback if you have a difficult message to share and you want to be certain you're being clear.

- **LOOK ALIVE:** Stand up. Move. Gesture. Talking heads went out in the 1970s.

- **USE NAMES:** If you don't already know all your team members' names, learn them. First. Then refer to them personally. I once had a boss who, each time I passed her in the hallway and said "Good morning," would never respond. Either she hadn't had her coffee yet or she didn't know my name. I always suspected the latter.

- **CONNECT:** To ensure that team members know you're speaking to them and not just to hear yourself talk, make eye contact often or call on them for input or questions. Keep your audience involved and they'll hear what you're saying more clearly.

- **BE YOURSELF:** Honest, effective leadership relationships take place with people we know, not with those who pretend to be someone else.[37]

on anything in a second. Even if that were true (and no one believes you), you're still communicating a strong message of disarray at best and ineptitude at worst.

2. YOUR BODY IS TALKING LOUDER THAN YOUR WORDS – While listening to a team member's report, your eyes wander to the computer screen, rather than remaining focused on her. Your arms cross and your foot is jiggling. You open your mouth and use words to say, "'You did a great job with the presentation. I've had phone calls from several people saying how much they enjoyed it.' But your body's sending very different signals. 'Man, is she ever going to leave! There's that e-mail from Juanita I've been waiting for, I have a conference call in ten minutes and Sal wants that preliminary budget from me by four. And now, my stomach's growling!'"[30] You've heard this before, but for some reason it's one of the easiest and first things we forget about communication. Maintain eye contact. Don't cross your arms. Stand. Don't heave great sighs or look around the person. Here are some you may not have heard yet. Hold your hands with the palms down to demonstrate confidence and assertiveness. Shrugging indicates self-doubt and uncertainty. Compressing your lips, even slightly, indicates resistance, negative feelings, or stress. Pursing your lips is definitely out—it means you disagree.[31] Actions *can* speak louder than words, especially when it's your body that's talking!

3. YOU ARE WHAT YOU WEAR – In library school, I had a professor who suggested that staff should all wear lab coats, so we would look more like library scientists. Another boss dipped his toe into the contentious dress code debate more carefully, by simply requiring that the way staff should dress is so that they'd look different from the customers. While some studies have tried to prove that people who dressed more professionally also acted that way, the bottom line is that this is a communication issue that you and your team need to address. "It's a good reminder that leaders should think through dress codes or workplace fashion norms not just in terms of how employees' attire is perceived by others, but how it makes the employees themselves feel, too . . . Clothes may not make the man [or woman?] . . . but they do hold a strange power over their wearers."[32] Like it or not, waiters in sloppy, grease-stained T-shirts *say* something different to customers than do those in crisp white shirts and neat black aprons. What do you say with your dress about leadership?

4. ACTION NOT PLANNING – While what you say, don't say, wear, and how often you shrug *do* say a lot for you and about you, what you actually, finally, really *do* says even more. Inaction, indecision, wavering, uncertainty, and apathy say *fear*, pure and simple. Leaders who reach decisions with their team and then put those decisions into action speak volumes about the confidence and expectations for success they hold for the entire team. Lots of things can get in the way of you taking action. One is somewhat inherent in library people—the pursuit of perfect. "After all, we are a profession that covets the perfect catalog record, believes that we can organize . . . and offer answers to all comers' questions. Pretty nervy!"[33] But when it comes to moving forward, that zeal for perfection can often hold us back. Seek, read, understand, and strive for a *good not perfect* approach to leadership and finally your team will really hear what you're trying to say—that you can take a leap of faith together and either share the riches that result or fix the shortfalls, then move on. "If you or your team is studying something to death—remember that death was not the original goal!"[34]

5. SILENCE IS GOLDEN – How often you pause, wait, ponder, and, most important, listen, speaks volumes about you—more than you could ever say in a multivolume biography. Be a leader who asks the right questions, provides the right details, fills in the gaps, and then listens. Don't listen for gossip or complaints about dress codes or worries about eye rolling . . . listen for the cues that tell you how to inspire and motivate your talented, dedicated, and communicative staff.

One-on-one, in meetings, in small groups, by writing, or even with silence, use the power of communication to help direct, support, and build your team's greatness. "To sharpen your ability to observe others, learn to love silence. If you spend more time making friendly eye contact with people—and less time talking (or pondering what you want to say next)—you begin to see things you might otherwise miss."[35]

SUGGESTED READING

Siess, Judith A., and Jonathan Lorig. *Out Front with Stephen Abram: A Guide for Information Leaders.* Chicago: American Library Association, 2009.

EXERCISES

28

1. **Be honest and think** back to the last time you participated in gossip. List five good things that resulted and five not-so-good things. If the last five were easier to think of than the first five, then list alternatives to repeating the gossip that you could have used. Repeat this exercise one more time, substituting a time recently when you were the *focus* of the gossip. Good? Bad? Alternatives? (Consider repeating this activity in your next team meeting.)

_____

_____

_____

2. **As you prepare to** speak to your team in a meeting or training setting, what five things are you always certain to do in order to have the experience go well? Think carefully. Even if you think you aren't taking steps to prepare, you almost certainly are. Perhaps, after listing them and realizing their value, you can develop them a bit further, or perhaps even add other steps that can build even more confidence.

_____

_____

_____

3. **Look around. Is your** office organized or a wreck? If it's not organized, then please spend an *extra* hour or so this week cleaning it up. Ask for help, if need be. I once worked with a woman who was so good at organizing that branch managers from all around the system would "borrow" her to help get them on track. If you are already in pretty good shape, then go visit a department head or someone else on your team who could use your help and get them straightened out too. There's simply too much to do to work from a point of weakness.

_____

_____

_____

_____

4. **Walk around and look** at your staff. How are they dressed? How are they acting or appearing? Comfortable, confident, professional? Or haphazard, sloppy, maybe even lazy? Don't write a new dress code policy!! They don't work and I don't want to be blamed for that. But do create a spot on your next team meeting agenda to discuss this issue and, together, come to a workable compromise that will keep everyone at their best.

_____

_____

_____

_____

5. **I hope you have** at least fifteen minutes of your hour left. If you don't, try to extend your time, just this one week. Turn off the phone. Kill the volume on the computer (so you can't hear the "you've got mail" beeps) and just enjoy the silence. When you're done, jot down a few notes about what went through your head. Did you come up with a realization or an idea? Were you motivated to try something new? With silence, as with hope, there's never any waste.

_____

_____

_____

_____

RESOLUTIONS

WEEK ONE | ## DEFINING ISSUES

Anyone who has been the parent of a middle schooler knows this story. Or, maybe it's just me. Anyway, it goes like this . . . your child comes rushing in from school, indignant over an event that occurred in which he was the victim. Frogs. This one was about frogs. Apparently, after being missing for some time, the biology lab frog population was found elsewhere in the building (unharmed, I'm happy to say) and he's being blamed! Serious consequences are pending that could keep him out of college, prevent a successful marriage, and otherwise screw up my retirement years. OK, that part was just my imagination. Rushing to the phone, I give the principal an earful and then agree to pause, take a breath, and listen to the other side of the story. Yep, there was another side and it contained a bit of detail (and evidence) I hadn't been privy to before my outburst. Life is like that, right? There are always two sides to every story?

Leading a team involves a lot of detail work: procedures, tasks, skills, schedules, budgets, and on and on but, most important, it involves *people*. To blithely assume that, with your team, problems will simply not occur because everyone will just get along is to ignore all proven human relations knowledge to the contrary. Wherever there are people, there will be conflicts, contrasts, challenges, and disruption of all kinds. Since you are the person they'll turn to for help, this month's lessons will focus on resolution. It's a big and inevitable part of your job as team leader but it doesn't need to be—and shouldn't be—feared. Conflict resolution is really just another way to grow and develop that diverse and rich group of people you call a team.

Still, before you can bring them together, it helps to be able to understand them apart. The bad news is, every single one of them has a different personality. The good news is, every single one of them has a different personality. When you can understand them all, you can help them fit together with more cohesion and peace.

If you haven't yet led your team through a personality assessment event, such as the Myers-Briggs Assessment or the Enneagram Personality Styles Survey, it's time you did. There is immeasurable value in helping diverse people not only get to know one another better but, as a result, to come to understand one another better and to respect their uniqueness. Most exercises around these tools focus on strengths demonstrated by the different types, and that's the best place to start to understand each one. People like to see where they fit and what benefits their new groups bring to the table. But not to be ignored are the areas ripe for development in each category and a recognition of the associated fears each might face. That's truly where you, as the team leader, can find jewels of opportunity to strengthen, grow, and develop your team. For example, one analysis[1] bravely described the unhealthy behaviors a team *might* see within each of the nine Enneagram-defined personality types and then suggested what they could be fearing from their colleagues:

1. REFORMERS – Sometimes self-righteous, intolerant, inflexible, and critical, these team members fear *being condemned* by coworkers.
2. HELPERS – Sometimes resentful, complaining, martyr-like and manipulative, these team members fear *being unloved*.
3. MOTIVATORS – Sometimes competitive, pretentious, deceptive, or vindictive, these team members fear *being rejected*.
4. ARTISTS – Sometimes withdrawn, stubborn, depressed, or moody, these team members fear *being inadequate*.

5. THINKERS – Sometimes superior, distant, intellectually arrogant, or stingy, these team members fear *being threatened*.
6. LOYALISTS – Sometimes mistrustful, controlling, or defensive, these team members fear *being abandoned*.
7. GENERALISTS – Sometimes unfocused, rebellious, manic, or possessive, these team members fear *being deprived*.
8. LEADERS – Sometimes controlling, insensitive, domineering, or aggressive, these team members fear *submitting to others*.
9. PEACEMAKERS – Sometimes apathetic, unassertive, passive aggressive, or stubborn, these team members fear *separation from others*.

Admit it: even though you've likely heard of the many personality type tools and studies out there, you probably hadn't thought of each type being afraid of something before. There is a valuable lesson in this review.

If you can imagine nine different people, one from each of these categories, telling the exact same story differently, then you are starting to get it. If you have a wide representation of personalities on your team—you win! This is not a situation to be feared or avoided—quite the contrary. The only requirement to leading such an intriguing team to success is that you, as their leader, must develop and nurture strong, effective conflict management skills. With that leadership in place, this mosaic of people will find and seek resolutions at every level of their work and the team will move even closer to greatness.

Back to defining the real issue when conflicts occur. Now that you know there can be as many different perspectives involved as there are team members, the need for you to listen openly to every side of the story becomes even more critical. The real picture will lie in there somewhere. They are emotional. You should not be. As everyone comes into the room and gets comfortable

WHY YOU SHOULD SEEK BOTH SIDES OF THE STORY

Aside from the obvious, these reasons to completely understand a conflict before you begin to resolve it should give you pause. With them in mind, the next time you think you see the answer staring you right in the face, you'll take that extra breath, buy yourself some time, and (as they say in library school) do the research!

- **GAIN PERSPECTIVE:** Since each storyteller highlights and omits certain details, you can hear more information overall when you talk to both.

- **UNDERSTAND WHY ONE IS RIGHT:** By eliminating any negative emotions while you hear everyone out, you are less likely to make your mind up before you can actually see the right answer emerge.

- **UNDERSTAND WHY ONE IS WRONG:** Once you've truly listened to both and been able to make a fair decision, you'll be better prepared to respond to the person in the wrong with confidence—and facts.

- **DECONSTRUCT:** In analyzing both sides of a story long enough, you can start to see beyond all the sensationalizing and emotionally loaded claims. As a result, you can start to see what the real issue is and to know how best to approach the resolution.

- **DEVELOP YOUR EMOTIONAL RESILIENCE:** The more command you have over the material, the more at peace you'll be with your final stance. Your position will also be more coherent and, therefore, easier to impart to others.

- **IMPROVE EMPATHY SKILLS:** You'll be able to better understand people, their motivations and—together—your team's ability to find common ground.

Don't jump to conclusions! Hear both sides of every story carefully and with an open mind![4]

STRENGTHEN YOUR STYLE!

Using the nine Enneagram personality styles as examples, here are some very simple ways you can help staff in each group start growing past their limitations. Teams need to invest in an initial personality assessment tool—then use it to continue to grow!

- **REFORMERS:** Change "I should" to "I want to"; respect others' ways of doing things.

- **HELPERS:** Speak up for what you want; learn to say "no."

- **MOTIVATORS:** Appreciate yourself for who you are; focus on what's best for the team.

- **ARTISTS:** Deal with feelings quickly instead of withdrawing; enjoy the moment.

- **THINKERS:** Recognize you don't have to be the smartest; get out of your head and into doing!

- **LOYALISTS:** Take some risks; believe the positive things people say about you.

- **GENERALISTS:** Don't expect others to keep up with your pace; recognize when you have enough to do.

- **LEADERS:** Be concerned about the well-being of others; think before acting.

- **PEACEMAKERS:** Decide on a course of action and do it; ask for what you want.[5]

around the table, review in your mind your role in the process of mediation. Don't lose focus, concentrate on minimizing impact, let go of the past, and focus on what's happening now, search for meaning (and further learning opportunities) in every crisis, and, above all, seek integration of all parties' feelings and needs.[2]

After hearing everyone out, and resolving the real problem at hand, there are more steps you can and should take so that everyone involved learns and grows from the experience. First, document the problem, then look for obstacles, not excuses, and plan a way to remove them before someone stumbles over them again. Convey your confidence in your team and find a way to subtly congratulate them on the growth all experienced and, finally, plan for improvement.[3]

There's one other caveat to consider when you begin to resolve any new conflict within your team. You cannot ignore it. No, it won't go away. No, it's not minor enough to ignore. No, you aren't too busy with other work. A wise mentor once told me that when a leader sees a problem, it's theirs. They need to either resolve it or get it to someone who can, because the alternative can be devastating and its impact long-lasting. Your very first question should always be, "Have you discussed this directly with the other team member involved?" Second, always, should follow, "Have you spoken to your supervisor?" (if there is one besides you).

If the answer to both is yes and the issue remains, then you have no choice but to step in and have everyone start from the beginning.

Just as mistakes can eventually result in great learning, conflict can result in true growth. But only when direction, support, encouragement, and understanding from an open, supportive leader is present. Leaders who respond with moody, knee-jerk, unprofessional responses lead teams down a dangerous and destructive path, often resulting in slow and painful disintegration of trust, motivation, and pride. Start early, stay involved, and see it through—for all of your sakes, but mostly for the continual development of your team.

It's been said that great leaders never waste a crisis. If you start by understanding where each person is coming from and then listen to what they're *really* telling you, resolutions and progress are almost certain to result.

EXERCISES

-29-

1. **Think back to a** time (we've all had at least one!) when you jumped to conclusions and rushed to action before hearing all sides of a story. Describe what action you took, what the result was, and what you *would* have done if you'd taken the time to get the whole story first. What did you learn?

   _____

   _____

   _____

   _____

2. **Now, think of a** time when you applied what you learned in question 1. How did your reaction (speed, decision making, etc.) change and what was *that* result? If you had to provide your team, today, with a list of five things to do when faced with a crisis—before making a decision—what would they be?

   _____

   _____

   _____

   _____

3. **Try to find yourself** in one of the nine Enneagram personality types described this week. Next, make a list of your team members and see if you can guess into which category they belong. Finally, do a bit of research and find a consultant or trainer who can come and lead your team through a personality assessment. Make an appointment to talk and begin planning the event.

   _____

   _____

   _____

   _____

4. **In order to get** permission and, perhaps, funding for your team assessment, you should be able to explain why such an exercise would be helpful. In preparation for providing that explanation, list five benefits to your team that might result and, next to each, mention an incident that went poorly that might have gone better had this understanding been available.

   _____

   _____

   _____

   _____

5. **One of the first** steps you were advised to take when team members rush at you with a conflict to solve for them was to ask them to talk it out themselves. Next was to ask if they'd spoken to their supervisors yet about the incident. Why is that important? List at least five negative results your team could experience if the existing organizational chain of command was ignored—and everyone just ran to you for resolution.

   _____

   _____

   _____

   _____

RESOLUTIONS

| ## COACHING OPTIONS

Now that you know the whole story, what's next? The problem is still out there. Emotions are still running high, feelings are still being hurt, and the health of your team overall is at stake. This is when you become a coach.

Coaching is different than training. It's more holistic, for one thing. For another, it's more personal (professionally personal, not personal personal) and it requires more investment from both parties. Why should a member of your team want to invest energy and effort into working with you as a coach? Because we're all in this together. In times of celebration and in times of conflict, you—as the coach—need to continually remind and demonstrate to your team that resolution is everyone's responsibility. When one of my sons was in third grade, his school came up with the idea to appoint "conflict managers" in each classroom. Peers, they reasoned, would be better able to address issues before they got out of hand, and fellow students, they assumed, would reach out better to colleagues than to superiors. Even with all their good intent, all they really accomplished was dropping a lot of pressure and responsibility on a few, small shoulders. No one felt responsible for keeping the peace anymore. Since it wasn't everyone's job to play nice, it wasn't anyone's job to work out problems. Problems? Let the "conflict managers" deal with it! It all went downhill from there.

Suffice to say, this ill-fated program was short-lived. And so should any similar assumption be on the part of you and your team. Resolution *is* everyone's job. And sometimes coaching is the best way to support that work. Coaching, I'll repeat, is different from training. Good, effective coaching has no beginning and no end. Coaching isn't limited to a special task

INGREDIENTS FOR SUCCESS (OR WHAT CAN GO WRONG)

Coaching takes time. Coaching takes patience. Coaching—successfully—takes a lot of stars all lined up in the right place, at the right time. Lots can go wrong. But the more you know about what's needed to successfully develop someone, the more you can make right from the start. Consider these obstacles, then do your best to remove or improve on them.

- **ABILITY:** The capacity with which we were born that enables us to acquire new skills and knowledge. Note: this varies from team member to team member, as should your approach to coaching and your patience.

- **PRIOR KNOWLEDGE:** Prior knowledge helps the learner acquire additional knowledge or skills more rapidly. A brilliant philosopher or mathematician may not learn as well as a less intellectually gifted carpenter, even if you're trying to coach them on how to be a better carpenter.

- **MOTIVATION:** Are you coaching a team member with a strong desire to achieve something? Or are you working with someone who doesn't care, has no drive, or seems to lack interest in improving their skills? If you answered yes to the later options, you may have some *different* performance coaching to do, before you get to skill sets.

- **CONFIDENCE:** One reason your team member from the above example might lack motivation is because they feel totally inept in their ability to learn. You can address that, too, by taking it slow and celebrating all achievements!

- **MOOD:** While there's not much you can do about personal problems, you can improve your odds of successful coaching by working in an environment that is conducive to a positive experience. The room, and your attitude, should be open, optimistic, and comfortable.

- **ABILITY:** Although we can't alter a person's ability, we can observe and detect her or his strengths and weaknesses, then take additional appropriate steps to improve or eliminate those.[11]

or assignment. Coaching *is* a perpetual, learning relationship that results in more than just resolution—it results in growth. Coaching is more important than being right; it's about making the situation right.

Sometimes, it's harder than other times to help someone out of a jam. If you're coaching your team out of a difficult, contentious situation and you've started by collecting all the facts and hearing all sides of the story, move forward carefully. What's next is finding a healing, positive way to repair damage and move forward stronger. To reach that point, there are a lot of different approaches you can take.

1. Reframe: Actively look for evidence of a more positive way of viewing and discussing the situation. Force all involved to look for the silver lining or, at the very least, something positive they can learn and take away from the situation.

2. Avoid "all or nothing" thinking: Don't place catastrophical interpretations upon actions or results. Seek compromise in every step. The final result should bring your team closer together, not further apart.

3. Identify your team's shared, core values: No matter what external changes occur, remember that you can always, as a team,

COACHING DIFFICULT PEOPLE

Thanks to the wonderful diversity you (hopefully) have within your team, you're going to need to approach some people differently than others when coaching. For those who are a bit more reluctant to respond, try to remember these simple tips.[12]

- **BOUNDARIES:** Establish for yourself clear boundaries and communicate them if necessary. For example, let team members know that you will not accept shouting or profanity in any conversation.
- **DELAY!:** When a conversation is escalating and both team members are frustrated or angry, you are not at a good point to reach a resolution. Agree to come back and talk further at a later time, when the emotional charge has dissipated.
- **ADULT MODE:** Parent behavior (judgmental) gets a child reaction (emotional). Remain an adult and focus on facts. Be the problem solver.
- **BLURTING:** Don't blurt out an answer or solution! Even if you can't help disagreeing with team members, asking questions and listening helps calm everyone down and gives you a better perspective, not to mention time to think.
- **AGREEMENT:** Defuse by finding an area of agreement. Without completely conceding to their point of view, try "I can see your point. . ." or "You're certainly right about that part. . ." and then move on graciously to the area of contention.
- **UNDERSTANDING:** 70 to 90 percent of communication is screened or changed by the person who receives it (you), based on your own personal history. Be certain you understand the issue at hand before moving on to finding resolution.
- **POSITIVES:** Focus on what *can* be done, not what *cannot*. One way to help this is by using the word "and" instead of "but."

fall back on your core values and shared goals.[6]

But coaching isn't always about resolving conflict. More often, it's simply about development. Opportunities for team leaders to work individually with members of the group to help grow, enhance, and deepen their skills are gold mines of learning that lead to great teams. If you're lucky, coaching won't be an occasional activity within your team. It should begin on each employee's first day and continue long after the retirement cake has been cleared away. "It's important to understand that coaching relationships are essentially eternal—they have no finite beginning or end. They have their roots in all the learning that precedes us and they continue long beyond the

time spent together as we continue to draw inspiration from our coaches into the future."[7]

If you didn't realize before that you were in this leadership position for the long haul, you should by now. Just think back to the most influential coach you've had in your career. Even if you're still not working alongside one another, chances are you can still hear their advice—and you still heed all that they taught you. You have that golden opportunity, now, to have that same, long-lasting impact for good with each and every person you supervise.

The benefit to developing these coaching skills isn't just something that will look good on your resume. Finding solutions and keeping your team on track will impact your entire organization in a very significant way. That's why people need bosses. Someone has to keep the group moving forward. "People in today's workforce at every level constantly have to work on the interface of their knowledge, skills, and experience in a changing and somewhat unpredictable environment. Coaching is not just something that engages people's efficiency; it increases individual and organizational effectiveness through changing times. Coaching has a multiplier effect. It enhances the library's assets. The more able the individual is to apply her/his skills dynamically to an every-changing environment, the more valuable he/she is to the organization."[8]

The single most valuable coaching skill any team leader can hone is to develop the control needed to be able to teach the group to fish, and not just invite them to dinner. In other words, support *their* efforts and success in resolving their own issues on their own. This can go well, if done right, or badly, if carried too far. Both results begin with the coach (you) listening to both sides, developing a shared understanding of the issue, and urging the team members to reach an agreeable resolution. If you then support them in developing their abilities to do so and—in fact—in doing so (which means you can't forget about it as soon as they walk out of the office), you've done right and it can go well from there. If however, you simply dump it back into the laps of people who are unequipped to handle the challenge, the problem and damage will likely grow before they get better.

"As much as you want to run a harmonious team, a key to preserving harmony is to step back and let staffers fix their own problems."[9] But they're still going to need a coach in their corner. "You're not supposed to possess all the answers to every problem. If one of your team members regales you with stories of a co-worker's 'obnoxiousness,' it's not up to you to make the obnoxiousness go away. You can't overhaul someone's personality—and you shouldn't try. A smarter response is to tell the employee, 'I understand you find your co-worker difficult. I know you've taken some steps to deal with it. What else can you try?'"[10]

Just don't stop there, either. Coaches don't just get the team ready at practice (training), and then watch them run out onto the field and step out for lunch. They stay involved, supporting, encouraging, backing up, retraining and developing skills, even while the game is taking place. This week's lesson has been all about your role as that coach and how you find the right options to use. If option one is your team and option two is you and you all stay in it together, there can be no better solution.

SUGGESTED READING

Stolovitch, Harold D., and Erica J. Keeps. *Telling Ain't Training.* Baltimore, MD: American Society for Training and Development, 2002.

EXERCISES

-30-

1. **Think for a few** moments about the most effective, professional coach you've ever had. List at least ten ways they impacted your development for the better.

_____
_____
_____
_____
_____

2. **Consider that two team** members have just burst into your office, each yelling about what the other just did. What would you do first? Next? List, in all, your initial five steps of coaching in this situation.

_____
_____
_____
_____
_____
_____

3. **What if you coached** your two team members from question 2 through their issue and found consensus on how they should resolve it. They were in agreement when they left your office but, since then, you've learned that only one of them carried through on his promises. How would you coach the other person now?

_____
_____
_____
_____
_____

4. **Think back to a** time when you stepped in maybe a little too early and "produced" a solution for your team members that didn't work out so well. Note what might have happened if you'd invited—and supported—their own resolution of the issue. Cover both the immediate impact and, perhaps, what other long-term results might have been.

_____
_____
_____
_____
_____

5. **Coaching is hard enough,** but when team members are emotional, it's really tricky. List at least five approaches you should take when someone literally storms into your office. Again, think both about what you could do at that moment and, perhaps, at a later coaching opportunity, once heads have cooled and problems have been resolved.

_____
_____
_____
_____

RESOLUTIONS

| ## POSITIVE DISCIPLINE

Discipline has a bad rep. Done well, its goal, aim, and solution should be success, but largely it's considered a major part of failure. It's your team and it's time to change that image.

When listening, understanding, and coaching won't work, great team leaders know that discipline is the next step in effective growth. Leaders who avoid discipline are sending several clear messages to the team, none of them positive or productive. Staff members are left to wonder which of a number of unpleasant options is the true one. Does the boss just not care? Do they not see or—worse—understand the problem? Or do they understand what's happening and just not have the courage or conviction to have those difficult conversations that can make things right?

Most organizations have disciplinary charts or policies and they have them for a reason. Once all other options have been exhausted and discipline remains the clear, appropriate choice, it should be handled professionally, impersonally, and effectively. If you don't have established steps to follow, it might be time to make a recommendation that they be developed. Discipline policies provide a support system for leaders and employees alike, so both can be certain decisions and actions taken are reasonable, predetermined (not knee-jerk), and appropriate. But any series of steps require an overall understanding of purpose. What's the point? Why discipline? And an even better question might be . . . how do you do it?

Trainer Steve Yacovelli, in designing the Public Library Association's *Turning the Page 2.0* learning modules, crafted an effective and simple concept that, while intended to support advocacy and community needs

TOP FOUR WAYS TO DISCIPLINE WELL

1. **HAVE POLICIES IN PLACE:** Even if you're not looking at impending discipline as potentially becoming a legal issue, it's important to note that courts are increasingly ruling that handbooks and other official communications are implied agreements. Just having personnel policies in place is not enough (although it's critical). Make sure your orientation or annual review practices refer to these policies frequently enough that staff know they are expected to know, understand, and follow them.

2. **WORK ON PREVENTING THE NEED FOR DISCIPLINE:** Hire hard, slow, and for fit with your organization, which will reduce both costly turnover and the need for employee discipline. Make expectations clear before hiring, during orientation, and then through regular, professional feedback and review.

3. **DEAL WITH DISCIPLINE RIGHT AWAY, PRIVATELY AND CONFIDENTIALLY:** Focus on the action, not the employee. Attack the performance, not the performer. Refer to specific, observable behaviors, not generalities or secondhand gossip. In short, respect the individual involved.

4. **TERMINATE HUMANELY:** If firing becomes the only option, do it as humanely as possible. Done properly, it assures the employer will stay out of court and helps the terminated employee get on with their life.[18]

experience. Inconsistent, off-the-cuff, excessive punishment signals a poorly thought out approach to improvement. There's no place for that either. Problem. Solution. Opportunity. With this methodology, both the leader and the team member can be clear, from the moment the office door first closes and the discussions begin, that they're both headed for a positive end to a challenging situation. Here's how it can work.

PROBLEM – As discussed a couple weeks ago, the team leader, by the time of the first disciplinary meeting, should have finished doing her or his homework and should have all the facts of the incident or issue under scrutiny at hand. Now is the time to review the facts objectively, and then clarify the problem. Remembering to keep away from taking or addressing the issue personally, the leader should always begin by clearly outlining the problem *in relation to its effect on individual or organizational performance.* One of the best tools to use to keep this problem review on track is the organization's existing performance evaluation tool. Is the team member being rude or even verbally abusive to coworkers? "It says right here in our evaluation tool that you are expected to have good internal communication skills and to contribute to an effective team. These incidents of verbal outburst are therefore a problem," could be a sample application of this concept.

SOLUTION – Give hope. This is the beginning of the team leader's ability to demonstrate that all is not lost. This isn't a yes-or-no situation. There's a correction available to get the individual back on track. Be clear. Be specific. You're going to have to reevaluate for progress down the road, so don't be nebulous in your expectations for improvement. "A more courteous and respectful response to criticism is required of you going forward." Or "further negative and personally subjective comments by you about your coworkers' abilities or ideas will not be excused." Note, not *expected* but *required.* Not *please don't* but *will not be excused.*

OPPORTUNITY. Now you get to the good part. Here's where you're giving the team member the

assessment, I feel also performs perfectly as a guidepost for disciplining for improvement. It is: "Problem. Solution. Opportunity."[13] What's great about this mantra and about this approach is that it keeps a sharp focus on success. Yelling signals a personal and emotional approach to discipline. There's no place for that as a success-targeted

chance to wrap up your meeting and walk out of your office on a positive note. Rather than grumbling about unfair or unwarranted punishments or ambiguous and unreasonable expectations, together you articulate a clear opportunity for change and success. "You have a chance to improve your attitude and communication skills. The organization will support your attendance at an upcoming training to support that. With your adherence to these reviewed skills, the issue will be behind you." Hopefully, you see the difference in this disciplinary approach from *everyone is mad that you did this, don't do it again,* to *here is the problem we're having, here's what needs to happen to solve it, and here's how you can make this happen.*

Several key benefits can be realized by using this framework:

PUT THIS IN THE PERFORMANCE PLAN

- The performance being improved (be specific).
- Level of performance expected and a note that it must be performed consistently.
- What support, resources, and/or training will be provided to reach and maintain the expected level.
- What feedback will be provided and (specifically) when.
- Consequence options of performance not met.
- Signatures of understanding of staff and management.[19]

1. **The solution is now in the hands of the team member**. Rather than falling back on their emotions and frustrations, you've handed them a path to resolution. The only question remaining is whether or not they'll take it. Sometimes, yes, sometimes, no. One career coach noted that "I frequently encounter otherwise intelligent people who are allowing anger or resentment to kill their careers . . . the [team leader's] next step is to help him recognize certain organizational realities."[14] Problem: you've demonstrated clearly defined expectations for performance. Solution: there is a realistic path to resolution. Opportunity: the team member has the option to elect to take it, in order to succeed. While it remains your job to outline the consequences of their choices, the decision to make those choices is in their hands.

2. **The opportunity can and should be put into writing.** Disciplinary meetings are serious events. Recordings of them should be kept in the employee's personnel file. But that's not where the process should end. When outlining the *opportunity* for resolution, effective team leaders will provide, in writing, what's expected, by when, and what the consequence of inaction will be. Often called performance plans, these documents can leave both parties feeling confident that there is a resolution in sight and what steps must be followed to reach it. Make the plan detailed. Include dates. Set the next meeting the same day, even if it won't take place for months. Half-finished discipline can be worse than no discipline at all because what it demonstrates is a lack of commitment to success. When writing these plans (which are arguably similar to letters of reprimand but much more positive), use an appreciative leadership approach. That is, be certain to highlight the positive elements of the staff member's performance, in addition to addressing the "problem."

3. **The team can trust that discipline will be consistent.** "Absent mitigating circumstances, all employees should be treated alike when it comes to discipline. Although it is necessary to judge each situation on a case-by-case basis,

arbitrariness in the administration of discipline can make an entire disciplinary system totally ineffective."[15] Thus the application of *Problem, Solution, Opportunity* can become a trusted part of your organization's professional culture.

When most new team leaders consider the myriad of challenges, duties, tasks, and leadership elements that go into supervising others, they are often surprised to learn that the most common mistake they can make involves *not* doing something. "The biggest mistake a manager can make is not addressing performance problems quickly enough."[16] While there can be a lot of reasonable explanations for the delay, frequently it's because of the lack of a comfortable approach to take. Where do I start? This is awkward and uncomfortable, how should I approach it? Excuses not to discipline are easy to come by (it's unpleasant, it doesn't work, I'll get sued, my boss won't support me, it's too time consuming)[17] but won't move your team any closer to greatness.

Problem. Solution. Opportunity. And one more word not often associated with discipline. Success.

EXERCISES

31

1. **Think back to a** time when a coworker or you were called into the boss's office and reprimanded for something—and nothing good came of the event. Why? Describe how the reprimand was handled, where it went wrong, and what the outcome was. (Remember, if the outcome was resentment or frustration or embarrassment, you have to count the implications that occurred well down the road.)

   _____
   _____
   _____
   _____

2. **Now think of a** situation going on currently, either within your team or in another organization, that clearly requires discipline. Start by outlining how comprehensive information gathering should occur.

   _____
   _____
   _____
   _____

3. **Next, state the problem** (in terms—of course—of performance, not the personality).

   _____
   _____
   _____
   _____

4. **What solution should be** sought, specifically?

   _____
   _____
   _____
   _____

5. **What opportunities exist for** the leader to aid the employee in resolution? Include a description of any support or training that might be provided.

   _____
   _____
   _____
   _____

6. **Finally, reflect back on** the poorly handled incident in question #1. If the _Problem, Solution, Opportunity_ system could have been applied in that instance, how might the results have been different?

   _____
   _____
   _____
   _____

RESOLUTIONS

| ## THE FINAL CONSEQUENCES (DEALING WITH FIRING)

A workshop speaker[20] recently described a workshop on firing in which everyone entering the room was handed a Q-tip at the door. Puzzled as to the connection, they didn't have long to wait for an explanation. The speaker began by admonishing them to *Quit Taking It Personally* (*Q-TIP*)!

Everything, everything to do with your job as a coach should remain on a professional level at all times, from recruiting to interviewing to selecting to training to coaching to disciplining to firing. When you can accomplish that, you won't need the Q-tip anymore.

Last week, you learned that discipline should always have the goal of success. But sometimes, nothing you try will work. If you presented the options clearly and remembered the key rule of putting your team member's future in *their* hands from the beginning, then there's nothing personal in making that final decision. If you can look in the mirror and say you honestly, intentionally, and sufficiently provided every possible alternative avenue for resolution and your team member has not opted to take advantage of them, then firing is your final consequence. The most common leadership mistake at this point comes from pure avoidance of that unpleasant choice. But avoidance, in a great team, is really not an option at all.

"No one likes to talk about firing people. It's traumatic for all involved. But, ask 100 executives to identify their biggest personnel-related mistake and more than half might say, 'I didn't terminate poor performers soon enough.' The avoidance strategy—waiting too long to act—is the easy way out."[21] But, oh, the damage it can cause! If you've been in management for any time at all, you've seen what can go down with that ship.

FIRING ADVICE FROM AN EXPERT

Heed these words from Ed Rensi, former CEO of McDonald's USA . . . a man with a "team" of thousands from whom to learn.

"I've learned that I needed to hire people very slowly but fire very quickly!

What I've found in many cases is that firing them makes them grateful.

They know it's the wrong fit.

They know they can't do the job.

They're just looking for a way to start down a new path."[25]

1. MORALE – Other team members wonder why they're working so hard, when the person next to them is playing online games (and the team leader knows about it) and nothing is ever done.
2. MOTIVATION – Team members wonder why they should raise their hands and take on a new initiative (and more work), when they're already doing their part and carrying someone else's share as well.
3. PRODUCTIVITY – If other team members, no matter how dedicated, simply cannot pick up the slack for poor performers, then someone isn't getting served and something isn't getting done.
4. REPUTATION – An organization's reputation with its clientele is only as good as the worst interaction they've had. Once you allow a poor employee to send someone away mad, guess what? They probably won't be back.
5. GUILT – Once a team leader has let one person slide because they can't face the uncomfortable option of firing, it won't

be long before they dodge the next big issue before them as well. And the next. Eventually, trains without conductors derail.

And all of that could be avoided by just doing the inarguably hard job of firing a poor employee. "I wanted a happy culture. So I fired all the unhappy people,"[22] a CEO once said. While it isn't that simple most of the time, sometimes it's really pretty clear. He then asked, "How many of you out there have gotten the 'what took you so long?' question from your staff when you finally said goodbye to a teammate who was seemingly always part of the problems instead of the solutions? (I) imagine a whole bunch of hands."[23] Finally, he concluded that there are three types of people who should be fired immediately:

1. THE VICTIMS – "Can you believe what they want us to do now? And, of course, we have no time to do it. I don't get paid enough for this. The boss is clueless!" Victims are people who see problems as occasions for persecution rather than challenges to overcome. Victims aren't looking for opportunities; they are looking for problems. Victims can't innovate.
2. THE NONBELIEVERS – "Why should we work so hard on this? Even if we come up with a good idea, the boss will probably kill it. If she doesn't, the market will. I've seen this a hundred times before." If you are a leader who says your mission is to innovate, but you have a staff that houses nonbelievers, you are either a lousy leader or in denial. Which is it? You deserve the staff you get. Terminate the nonbelievers.
3. THE KNOW-IT-ALLS – "You people obviously don't understand the business we are in. The regulations won't allow these . . . customers won't embrace the change . . . we don't have the money . . .

< THE FINAL CONSEQUENCES (DEALING WITH FIRING) >

DON'T FIRE (THIS WAY)

Here are some cautions to consider when the option of firing seems the only one open to you. Keeping these suggestions in mind can help ensure that your decision and its ramifications keep both you and your organization in the best light. They also lessen the negative impact on your soon-to-be former team member.

- **ON THE SPOT:** Sometimes, awful things happen. When the situation seems dire, or worse, dangerous, refrain from firing someone on the spot. Rather, as long as your policies allow it (and they should), send the person immediately home and tell them not to return back to work until they hear from you. You'll have time then to seek resolution, if possible, and, if not, to take the necessary and required professional steps that lead to termination.
- **PUNITIVE ACTION:** Firing isn't a punishment, it's a result. Make sure you clarify with your employee that if A happens, then B will result. Then clarify that whether or not A happens is entirely up to them. B won't be something you're doing to them, but something they've chosen to have happen.
- **IN A VACUUM:** Consult an HR professional or a lawyer who specializes in labor matters before mailing out that final letter. Why? Because the termination letter needs to say more than just "You're Fired." It should contain a clear, professional summary of what is happening, as of when, and how all remaining matters (such as insurance, last pay, key return, etc.) are to be handled. Confusion is lessened when information this important appears in writing, and the specialists can tell you just what and how to write it.
- **IN PUBLIC:** All personnel matters and, especially, one that has the potential to damage someone's reputation *must* be kept strictly confidential. There are no exceptions to this rule. If anyone in your organization shares information about a firing without your permission, their behavior must be treated as a serious violation of privacy, with discipline resulting.

(and the ever-popular) we tried this once before!" The best innovators are learners, not knowers.

What's the rush? Paul English, a cofounder of Kayak.com, explains that often "bad hires stay put. Eventually, their mis-matched skills or prickly attitudes bring down the rest of the team. As months turn into years, the substandard employee depletes everyone's time and attention. Peers and managers grow to accept the myriad of frustrations that accrue from having such a disruptive, negative or unskilled person on staff."[24] No leader building a great team can allow that to happen.

As reviewed last week, performance evaluations are every team leader's best defense against firing. Conducted effectively, they provide a sound backdrop, a clearly outlined plan, and a realistic record of performance issues, solutions, and, ultimately, consequences.

Still, if termination is the ultimate solution in any staff situation, it's critical that team leaders not neglect addressing the potential impact a firing will have on the surviving team members. Here, as everywhere, communication is the key to moving forward. Staff members should be told just enough about the situation to allay their fears, while not crossing privacy lines. In one library, after several people were fired in quick succession, the remaining employees walked nervously around as if there were targets on their backs. No explanation had been given, no intermediate plans outlined, and, worse, no damage control applied to correct problems left behind.

Consider the impact poor performance by even one member can have on the group. Open yourself to questions, firmly but professionally dodge the inappropriate ones and openly and candidly talk about where you all go—together—from here. Vacuums of information have been known to be filled with gossip, fear, and sometimes even guesswork, none of which can help begin the necessary healing process.

EXERCISES

-32-

1. **Think back to a** situation at work in which someone who needed to be fired was not, at least not for a long time. First, list the damage they caused to the organization. Next, list the damage they caused to the team.

_____
_____
_____
_____
_____

2. **Once that person had** been let go, what was the positive impact to the team and what steps were taken to support a healthy move forward? (If there weren't any, list the ones you wished had been taken and explain why.)

_____
_____
_____
_____
_____

3. **How can "the victims"** bring a team down or inhibit its success? Before resorting to firing, what steps could be taken to change their behavior?

_____
_____
_____
_____
_____

4. **Lots of experts advise** team leaders to "fire fast." When you add a new team member, describe how you handle performance reviews during their probationary period. How many do you have? How critically do you test or examine their growth and development? What would justify firing during probation and how would you handle it?

_____
_____
_____
_____
_____

5. **One of the best** defenses against firing is to hire good matches for your team. List at least five characteristics or attitudes that would be a bad match and, next to each, explain how you can look for that during the hiring process. (It might help to consider why some people have been fired already, if that has happened to your team.)

_____
_____
_____
_____
_____

ACTIONS

WEEK ONE | **MAKING DECISIONS**

Do you have one or two key things you remember from management training? Not that you didn't learn a lot more, but those few concepts have become almost mantras in your memory, often coming out to guide you in difficult situations. Someone once shared with me what she never forgot from a lecture on decision making. It doesn't matter if you end up making a great decision or a terrible one, she said, just make a damn decision! Often, that's easier said than done.

One of the first uncomfortable lessons new leaders often learn is that they're not going to be able to be everyone's friend. Why? Because decisions have to be made. Hopefully, the second lesson they learn is that, depending on how well they guide that decision making, their team can replace friendship with respect, trust, and commitment. Getting there requires, at the very least, a two-step process. "Management experts often say that every decision is really two decisions—who gets to decide and then the actual decision."[1] Teams that have a healthy respect and understanding for the first part of this principle are well on their way to achieving the second.

It's time to talk about including—and involving—your team as intricate and critical decision makers.

If you've been a member of a team at any point, you've undoubtedly experienced being dragged through a lengthy decision-making process, only to learn that the final decision was really a foregone conclusion. Why were you asked to contribute in the first place, then? Good question. Approached correctly, well-managed decision making can both reduce the resentments built from false involvement while building an honest, trusting relationship

WHO GETS TO DECIDE?

The first step in any decision-making process is to decide whether the leader or the entire team will be making the call. Or somewhere in between. Here's a review (from Month 2) of the five optional decision levels from which you can choose. They're worth repeating.

- The team decides and informs the leader.
- The team decides, but the leader will also contribute.
- Within parameters set by the leader, the team decides.
- After soliciting input from the team, the leader decides.
- The leader decides. Period.[11]

at the same time. Plus, decisions can actually get made, too!

Faced with a needed decision, start by considering *how* it should be made and *by whom.* Clearly, some decisions must be handled at the executive or team leadership level. For reasons ranging from confidentiality to legality and beyond, leaders can't and shouldn't involve team members in deciding issues that could result in conflict. You wouldn't ask the team, for example, to decide which of three coworkers should be laid off. Nor should you. For issues that require team input, a variety of opinions and a diversity of insight, however, the team should be invited to participate. While sometimes leaders will need to set parameters, on other occasions options can be left wide open.

A warning: if you ask for a team decision, be ready to support it. There's no surer way to destroy confidence and trust than to second-guess a decision others were invited to make. What if it's the wrong choice? A mentor once suggested that leaders must ask themselves, what's the worst that could happen? Assuming it's not something detrimental to the organization, then a wrong

decision can and should become a unique and valuable learning experience. Decide who gets to decide, then make the situation clear. "Leaders gain respect and credibility with their team members when they are clear—prior to the decision—about who is going to have the final say."[2]

A word of warning about disappointment and communication. Leaders have been known to throw around expressions like *shared leadership,* which is a good thing, without clarifying the continuum on which it rests, which is a bad thing. Lives—and management—are not black and white. Early team discussions must clearly clarify roles, responsibilities, and opportunities for input, so the concept of shared leadership can remain alive and well, while realistic administrative options also remain.

So, how is decision making and its results best assigned and shared? The best rule of thumb is, whenever possible, to keep the team involved and invested and, in the end, to allow credit for success to grow their confidence and allegiance to one another. Coach Bear Bryant put it best when he explained how he shared credit with his teams on the field. "If anything goes bad, I did it. If anything goes semi-good, we did it. If anything goes really good, then you did it."[3] Questions don't often arise out of the hard calls. Layoffs, budget realities, and personnel issues, to name just a few instances, call for swift and inarguable decisions by leaders. But, as often as possible, teams should be involved in choosing options that affect the group, so as to build buy-in, accountability, and pride.

Ownership of the work of the team is critical. "Every worker is a manager. Each of us manages our work tasks, our time and our relationships with colleagues and bosses. It's just the scope of management responsibilities that differs."[4] Broad involvement and investment in decision making can underline this concept and perpetuate the vision that the entire team, not just one or two favorites, owns their work and their success. The expectation that the team will join together in decisions can actually build team strength and individual skills, especially if the calls are hard

INHIBITORS TO TEAM DECISION MAKING

Watch for these resistance tactics, which can come from the team or its leadership, and remove them in order to make joining in group decision making more comfortable and enticing.

- **BLAME STORMING:** Remember Bear Bryant's approach and take the blame, but share (or give away) the credit. Humility can go a long way towards building confidence. A simple "I probably didn't make this clear," or "I should have better explained. . ." can shift guilt and blame onto the broader shoulders of management, where it ultimately belongs, while keeping team members open to remaining engaged.
- **SCORE KEEPING:** When should a team leader effectively take decision-making authority back from the team? After their first mistake, second, third? Don't keep count. Instead, remain focused—as a group—on goals overall and learn from each misstep. Every day is a new chance to succeed.
- **LONG MEMORIES:** Human nature can contribute to making it difficult to erase one's past and escape prior errors and imperfections—in an unhealthy team. Allow trust to be won back for your staff or your team's progress will be forever stalled at its last mistake.
- **PERFECTIONISM:** Don't wait to be *sure* the perfect decision is being made. That's why they invented the word *pilot*! Instead, counsel your team to make the best decision possible at that moment, then reconsider, evaluate, and adjust as time goes on.
- **MANAGEMENT'S JOB:** After centuries of hoarding decision making at the top of hierarchical organizations, it's no surprise that individual team members may struggle with the concept that accountability is shared. That probably won't last much beyond the first success you credit to them, and the first failure you absorb yourself. Share the work, grant the credit, but always be willing to assume ultimate responsibility—then forgive yourself the misstep and move on.[12]

to make. To "stretch employees beyond the scope of their current job and skills . . . to push and test their capabilities, opportunities and experiences"[5] can make each team member's role more challenging. And "top performers most frequently cited challenging and meaningful work as the most frequently sought after aspect of the job!"[6]

Be sure to prepare your team before handing stressful decision making over to them. As a group, preemptive discussions about how decisions are made and what's needed to make the best ones can set your team up for success. Often, at the point the decision is needed, it's too late to start from scratch building the appropriate skills. In an ongoing manner, though, review as a group the process of gathering facts, applying logic, considering experience or history, clarifying a desired outcome, considering effects, and applying resources. With a firm process in mind and the confidence they can apply shared values at each juncture,[7] your team will build confidence in their own abilities.

In addition to meeting day-to-day challenges with strong, reasoned decisions, there are many other benefits that will result from this sharing of power and direction. Among them, leaders who manage inclusively will build stronger teams along the way. Adopting one model of strong teams whose cornerstones are trust, purpose, accountability, and commitment,[8] just look how effective decision making can account for each:

1. TRUST – Leaders are clear so as to not mislead team members into thinking they'll decide everything together. Each understands that, when appropriate,

they'll be asked to participate and their input will be valued.

2. PURPOSE – Using preestablished, shared decision-making processes, the team will focus each decision on identified goals and objectives, rather than personal or emotional considerations.

3. ACCOUNTABILITY – By not fearing negative consequences that might result, and knowing their team leader will assume responsibility and not pass the buck, a strong sense of ownership will ensure accountability.

4. COMMITMENT – With focused goals, clear roles, and adequate support and preparation for decision making, team members will join in support of one another and grow in their shared commitment.

The best news is that this process is self-perpetuating, with nothing but continued growth of the team as an ultimate result. And on and on. In fact, "the deeper and richer the relationships among [the team members], the more 'intelligent' the decisions made."[9] One expert put it this way, "I am often asked by management students and middle managers, 'How can we free up the organization and make the changes you talk about if we are not at the top?' I reply, 'You can begin where you are, whatever your job. You can bring new insight, new leadership to your team. With the return of a more fluid, circular view of the world, the days of the Lone Ranger are over. The day of partnership is upon us.'"[10]

Keeping everyone involved sounds like a good decision for any team.

EXERCISES

-33-

1. **It shouldn't be hard** to think back to a decision you've made that met with a lot of resistance and bad reaction. Begin here by describing as many steps as possible that went into your making that decision.

   _____
   _____
   _____
   _____

2. **How could the decision** making process have been handled differently? Could others have been involved? Were too many people involved? List at least three things you'd do differently, considering what you've just read about decision making.

   _____
   _____
   _____
   _____

3. **Whether you've found yourself** in this situation yet or not, describe a decision that might need to be made that *should not* involve anyone but the team's leader—you. First, explain why. Then describe how you would explain their exclusion to the team.

   _____
   _____
   _____
   _____
   _____

4. **If, after completing question** #3, a team member asks "So, you didn't really mean it when you said our team used shared decision making?" how would you clarify what makes this decision unique and why you are justified—and required—to make it yourself?

   _____
   _____
   _____
   _____

5. **Think of an issue** that's coming down the road that will require decisions the team should make. Outline the presentation you'll make to the group to begin the discussion on how the issue and decision should be approached. Will you set parameters? If so, what will they be? When the issue arises, see if using this answer will help you and your team.

   _____
   _____
   _____
   _____

ACTIONS

| ## UNDERSTANDING VIEWPOINTS

Firm, immutable concepts are easier to understand, aren't they? Like, for example, diagramming sentences. Many schools don't even teach this anymore but we library types enjoyed it, most of us, especially when the final, complicated diagram filled the entire blackboard. And geometry, with all those angles that always equaled the same number of total degrees, those were fun too. But, in management or in math, it's the introduction of variables that cause commotion. Unless, of course, you understand them.

This month is all about considering the many, dissimilar, sometimes conflicting but always meaningful contributions your team members make to the whole. Since we're talking people and not right angles, good leaders need to know there *will* be variables and they'll need to be considered, supported, and blended for success. In a human resources lecture once, author and university administrator Richard Rubin outlined four basic variables[13] that invariably impact your team members' commitment to the group.

1. PERSONAL CHARACTERISTICS – Inescapable and influential, our personality types define who we are but can still be understood and managed in a way that brings out the best we have to offer. We've already taken an in-depth look at how our personalities can be described—and understood.
2. ROLE-RELATED CHARACTERISTICS – Any support staff member who has been second-guessed or (worse) thrown under the bus when the boss second-guesses a decision they've made can tell you that your position within the organizational hierarchy matters.

THE FIVE BIGGEST TRAPS TO AVOID WHEN LEADING A DIVERSE TEAM

To be a great leader, concentrate on motivating and retaining all the diverse members of your team, so that the final mosaic is rich in background, attitude, and understanding of your community. You'll find differences varying from race to ethnicity, gender, age, sexual preference, lifestyle, physical and mental challenges, geographic origin, education, personality, values, experience and socio-economic status. The more differences, the better, as long as they're led effectively towards team goals. At all costs, avoid stumbling over these common traps:

1. **Not Valuing Differences:** When leaders see differences as an advantage, they seek diversity in their teams and work hard to get different perspectives and opinions on the table. This encourages individuality, while promoting teamwork.

2. **Failure to Create an Inclusive Environment:** By being open to new ideas, listening to different perspectives, and encouraging creative problem solving, leaders can encourage the involvement of all team members. Try challenging the group with questions like "What other ways can we spin this idea?" or "Who can suggest something totally radical to what we've done in the past?"

3. **Stereotyping:** Avoid associating any behaviors, talents, or lack of ability with any particular group. All women are not emotional and all Asians are not good at math. Assuming these and other stereotypes makes the team leader guilty of prejudice and, further, does not acknowledge the uniqueness of each individual.

4. **Not Modeling the Expected Behaviors:** Demonstrate the behaviors you want your team members to show. Show respect for differences, develop trust, and promote everyone's value.

5. **Failure to Coach:** Encourage each team member towards higher levels of performance and growth. Encourage team members to coach one another. As coaching becomes part of the environment, new members to the team have access to and can build mentor relationships, further strengthening the team and the organization overall.[16]

Important to note when assembling a functional team, these divisions also need to be kept in perspective, clarified, and optimized.

3. STRUCTURAL CHARACTERISTICS – What if we have a union? Often, in management discussions, options available to non-union shops aren't as easy to implement for those in a more structured environment. Teams can work in both settings, though, once boundaries are understood and respected.

4. WORK EXPERIENCE – Unless your team members fell off the turnip truck onto the reference desk, they've likely had other jobs and experiences, the impact of which follows them wherever they go. On the plus side, this builds a richness into library staffs that's rare in other organizations. The trick is to allow the best lessons to be applied, while minimizing the potential implications of contrary practices and habits.

Already, that's a lot of variables for a team leader to keep in mind when blending a group of individuals into a high-performance team. And, there are more to come. Rubin goes on to suggest that where someone is in their own career can play a role in their motivation, skills, and, of

COMMITMENT TO LEADING DIVERSITY

- **MODEL THE WAY:** Clarify your personal values. Align them with your organization's values. If you cannot, you may be in the wrong job. Finally, ensure you and your team's actions support those values.

- **INSPIRE A SHARED TEAM VISION:** Imagine an exciting future; support both individual and shared aspirations.

- **CHALLENGE THE PROCESS:** Seek innovative ways to change, grow, and improve.

- **ENABLE EVERYONE TO ACT:** Foster collaboration at every opportunity. Share power and discretion.

- **ENCOURAGE THE HEART:** Show appreciation and celebrate victories.[17]

course, attitude. If they're at a very early stage, their commitment may be quite high, but their skill levels are still forming. He recommends that leaders treat staff very well at this stage, since career-long impressions and energies can easily be rerouted into resentment and frustration if the employee isn't supported. At an entry or initiation stage, usually one to three years into their career, high turnover often results from uninteresting, unchallenging, or un-fun work being assigned.

After all, who wants to stay at a boring, non-challenging job? After the first three years and up until about fifteen, the career development stage provides team leaders with strong, contributing staff they'll want to nurture, develop, and keep. At the entrenchment level, anywhere from fifteen years to retirement, if plateauing can be avoided, quality leaders and mentors can develop and contribute significantly to the team's success. In order to keep your team on a path to greatness, remembering where they're from, where they fit in your organization, and at what stage their career is all matter—not only to them, but to you as well.

There's one other major impact on individuals that they unconsciously bring to the team table that you, as the team leader, need to understand and blend into your shared success, and that is a generational background and the characteristics and work habits associated with it. While it would be foolhardy and inaccurate to say these qualities apply evenly to each and every individual, they've still been upheld by enough repeated studies to demonstrate a real and important impact on the workplace. Covering the years 1920 to the present, today's workforce has been categorized by sociologists into one of four major categories of generational impact. They all bring value. They all have challenges. Working together at their best, they'll make an incredible team. Here are some ways to help them contribute the most to your team:

1920 – 1945
Traditionalists[14] or Builders[15]

Motivated by duty and loyalty, assure them that what they do will contribute positively to the organization, both honoring its past and those who built it and building a stronger foundation for the future.

1946 – 1964
Baby Boomers

Optimistic and rule challengers, support their career development and show them that both their status and impact can continue to increase.

1965 – 1980
The Busters or Generation X

Self-reliant and technologically engaged, communicate to them what a great impact the team's successful reaching of organizational goals will have on them.

1978 – 2000
The Bridgers or Generation Y

Achievement-oriented and techno-driven, they care about the social and environmental issues surrounding everything and want to find a way to contribute. Invite them to help move your organization into twenty-first-century awareness and global awareness.

If you don't remember anything else about these unique groups and the ones that will inevitably follow, as history and society continue to develop, remember this: people are different. While you all need to get behind the team as a whole and move it towards common goals, everyone will be coming at their assignments and commitments from different positions, backgrounds, societal implications, job titles, and values. Remember also: this is a good thing. The diversity you blend will grow in value and potential impact every single time you bring in someone new. Welcome that diversity. Recognize and respect it and work to bring all of your team's energies and contributions together, for an incredibly positive impact.

EXERCISES

-34-

1. **Describe a grandparent's work** history, then your own. What differences do you see? Explain how you think an individual's approach to work is shaped by their generation. Comment on all four generational groups discussed.

_____

_____

_____

_____

2. **Think of a time** when someone representing significant diversity of any kind joined a team to which you belonged. List the positive ways the team responded and the not-so-positive. What might have been an ideal way to initiate this new person into the group?

_____

_____

_____

_____

3. **Where you currently work,** describe how an entry-level worker, a new supervisor, a mid-level manager, and an administrator might respond to an incident such as a TV reporter asking for an interview. What about these differences would be important to keep in mind, if you'd just welcomed each person to a team you were leading?

_____

_____

_____

_____

_____

4. **There were two great** questions posed in "The Five Biggest Traps to Avoid When Leading a Diverse Team." My favorite is "Who can suggest something totally radical to what we've done in the past?" I like this because it helps you meet one of the most frequent roadblocks to creativity ("We've always done it this way") head-on but with a positive approach. Think of an upcoming change facing your team that has a strong history. If you asked this question, describe how you might blend new, creative ideas, while still respecting past actions.

_____

_____

_____

_____

5. **Are you certain you** are already modeling an appreciation and celebration of all the diversity on your team? How are you doing that already? What else can you do in the future?

_____

_____

_____

_____

ACTIONS

WEEK THREE | **DE-MYSTIFYING DELEGATION**

With an understanding now that your team members bring various personality styles, viewpoints, backgrounds, skills, and motivation levels to the table, the obvious question is—what are you going to do with all that? Hopefully, the answer is: use it! All of it! How? By giving everyone something meaningful, challenging, and rewarding to do. This doesn't translate to letting the full-timers pick out the new books and have the part-timers put the stickers on. Or letting the longtime employee present the book discussion while the new hire makes the coffee. Or (you know this has all happened; you've seen it!) asking the *librarian* to attend the conference, while the *assistant* stays behind to cover the desk—year after year after year.

Your team has a lot of work to do. There's no shortage of opportunities for achievement that everyone can share. Share them. Watch each person's sense of reward, accomplishment, and ownership grow. Your options to smart delegation are plentiful and ignoring them can be equally hazardous. However you manage it, be sure not to make these mistakes:

1. **Do everything yourself**. If there's time in-between all the work that will pile up, you can almost watch pride and motivation slide away when the boss requires that every final decision comes to her. Team members begin, rightly so, to question their purpose and value when the message seems to be they're not good enough to be trusted with the work.

2. **Work exclusively with a clique**. Picture the TV show *Glee* without the music. Or, picture your high school class, with the

WHEN MICROMANAGEMENT IS NOT A DIRTY WORD

A job needs to be done. You are responsible to see that it is accomplished. You make the assignment and it is completed. Excellent. But what about when that doesn't happen? If you step in effectively and offer support, encouragement, and (if necessary) discipline, you're doing your job. Or are you micromanaging? The distinction will depend upon *how* you handle the follow-up that's part of your job and if it's the right time to do so. Here are some times when *proper* micromanagement (also known as coaching) is appropriate.

- **A STRATEGY IS CHANGING:** Until your team members understand and adopt a new procedure or service, it's the team leader's job to make sure it's being properly implemented. This has also been (appropriately) called training.

- **STAFF IS NEW:** This could be the leader, or it could be the team member. Either could use advice and/or mentoring when placed in a new environment or faced with new assignments. Appropriate micromanagement should always include the admonishment that "I will work closely with you for a while, but my expectation is that my level of interaction and review will become less and less over time." That will be good news to you both.

- **A PROJECT LINGERS:** Too often, things simply don't get done. As the leader and with others likely impacted by the delay, you can't afford to wait too long to find out why and to correct the situation. Sometimes, you'll discover barriers you can remove. Of course, in some unfortunate cases, the team member simply isn't doing their job.

- **A COMPLAINT IS REGISTERED:** As a leader, when you hear of a problem, you own it. It's your responsibility to investigate the matter and set it on the path to correction. "I don't want to interfere or I'd be micromanaging" is a cop-out and a crutch. The entire team benefits (not to mention customers) when conflicts are resolved.

- **RESULTS ARE DISAPPOINTING:** Certain outcomes are expected and it's up to the leader to ensure they're delivered. If they are not, questions can be asked and answers found to get the project back on track. Staying out of it at this juncture is not an option.[21]

jocks, the freaks, the geeks, or the band-nerds running the show. Neither picture, most likely, warms the soul. Leaders who hand-select a couple of favorite staff members and then delegate all the best assignments to them cause alienation of other team members at best and high turnover at worst. It's disrespectful and unprofessional to treat people anything other than equally. Plus, think of all that talent you're wasting!

3. **Wait for volunteers.** A point here: waiting for volunteers (bad) is different from asking for volunteers (often, good). Most teams seek, need, and thrive with

direction. Most assignments benefit from a match to the right person with the right skills. Growth can be enhanced and encouraged by getting someone to stretch a bit and try something new they've not done before. That's hard to do when tasks are left jumbled on the table, for anyone to pick or not pick as they choose. Perhaps instead try an approach like this: "I'll be assigning someone to this task on Monday, unless someone would like to volunteer for it first."

Easy as delegation may sound, it requires strategy, knowledge of your team, and a dedication to both their and your organization's overall success. "Delegating effectively is very difficult, and few managers excel at it. However, the ones who do are able to reduce their workload and provide opportunities for growth and challenge for their subordinates. Given the importance of effective time management and employee development to managerial success, delegation is something that managers should do"[18] and do strategically (by planning ahead)!

Reduce your workload? Now there's a benefit that goes above and beyond developing your team and meeting goals and that can actually free up more of your time to lead. In one library, no less than four master's-degreed librarians read prepublication reviews in shared journals and marked titles recommended for purchase. Finally, the department head, also with an advanced degree, as well as many years of experience, compared the list to collection development budget options and inked her approval. Then, last, the branch manager received and *reread* the entire publications, making her own selections, some of which matched those carefully reached already and a few new titles thrown in for good measure. Orders were then typed by the assistants.

Do you see opportunities for delegation and a more effective distribution of workload here? What if, in order to increase everyone's commitment to maintaining the overall collection, each employee, degreed or not, was given a section of the collection to maintain? With only certain sections of the journal to read, they could, perhaps, spend the additional time weeding and marketing their collection areas, or (even better) serving customers. The trust demonstrated by the manager would not only build pride and skill throughout the team, it would also free up more of *her* time for developing the group in other ways. That's using the power of delegation for good, instead of evil.

Many leaders avoid delegation because of its close relationship to micromanaging. In so doing, they lose more than they gain. If it's true that no one wants a micromanager at the helm, it's

TIPS FOR DELEGATING SUCCESS

1. Decide *what* to delegate. First and foremost, don't ever delegate something you're unwilling to do yourself. Do everything once, at least, to demonstrate you are a part of the team and to earn others' respect.

2. Pick the right people, matching the task to the employee—playing to your team's strengths and weaknesses positions them better to succeed.

3. Communicate clearly—if you need something done by tomorrow at 5:00 p.m., don't ask that it be completed *soon*. Specify expectations, deadlines, and what help is available. Give your team all the information they need to reach their goal.

4. Check in. Checking in is the friendly cousin of micromanaging. You can and should allow flexibility in the management and execution of a task, but you'll still need to periodically verify that the work is getting done. Even better than you checking in with them is requiring them to check in with you! Keep staff on the right track, answer questions that might arise, and provide support and help where needed. Don't just assign and run.

5. Share in rewards and give credit away. Assume responsibility for mistakes (your shoulders are broader), give praise for accomplishment, and, most importantly, say thank you, whether for a job well done or just at the end of the day as part of your "Good–bye."[22]

also true that no one wants a ship that never sails anywhere. Here's the simplest distinction to keep in mind: while the team leader remains responsible for the *attainment* of goals, delegation allows for a sharing of their *achievement*.[19] If you want to try the benefits of delegation and avoid all the possible downsides, try turning to communication as your key to success. Try asking the team member to summarize back to you, on an established timetable, a description of the results as they develop.[20] That way, as long as you're being kept in the loop and are seeing the results you need to see, no further intervention from you will be needed.

Remember also that, if and when you do begin to notice an unacceptable lag, *don't take the project away and finish it yourself*. If you've built enough lag time into the original deadline, you can and should use the extra time as a learning opportunity, training, supporting, and helping your team member to learn as they go and develop new and valuable skills. Humans learn from making mistakes—and then correcting them. To be shut out of the correction process, humiliated by failure, and frustrated by lost opportunities to shine, what else could we expect to result but belittled, unappreciated, and undervalued people whose allegiance to the team grows weaker by the day?

To review then, share the work and give away the praise. Support the work by keeping tabs on progress and addressing speed bumps. Leadership and follow-up, when done right, are called development. When done wrong, they're called micromanagement. Don't avoid the former to escape the latter.

Take that extra time you just freed up from delegating and consider what *else* you can do to help build your great team!

EXERCISES

-35-

1. **List the names of** each person on your team, including yourself, and note beside each one what work has been delegated to each. Is there a way to spread the assignments more equitably? Even if each has the same workload, does everyone have at least one task to accomplish that's challenging, new, and motivating? Consider your list and what options there are to improving the delegation.

_____
_____
_____
_____

2. **Looking at the list** again, concentrate on what you do. Are there any tasks you could delegate to someone else, perhaps to help develop their skills in a certain area? Select at least one activity and pick someone to reassign it to, then list the training or support you could offer them to achieve it.

_____
_____
_____
_____

3. **What if you introduce** a new project in a team meeting and no one volunteers to head it up? How can you change your group's culture so that they might be more eager to take on a new assignment?

_____
_____
_____
_____
_____

4. **Assume a team member** is responsible for a major project and milestone deadlines are not being met. List at least five things you could do or say that could be considered micromanaging if they were done wrong, but won't be because you'll do them right. Explain how you'll do it.

_____
_____
_____
_____
_____

5. **Going back to your** team list from question 1, write next to each name a _potential_ skill or strength each has that you might develop and nurture, when the right assignment comes along. Then, watch for them!

_____
_____
_____
_____
_____

ACTIONS

WEEK FOUR | **BUILDING CONFIDENCE**

Even in the most well-balanced, diverse teams, there can remain one major stumbling block that can replace action with inaction (at best) and with antipathy (at worst.) That roadblock is confidence, or the lack thereof. With all the work leaders do to build, retain, and develop their team members, how is it that this critical component can be overlooked? Some might argue that what we lack we have the most trouble teaching. And for all their titles and offices and position, few leaders clearly possess or demonstrate the confidence to fail. But that can be fixed.

First, we remove fear, both theirs and ours. What are we afraid of? Usually, it's as simple as failure, but it can be as complicated as embarrassment, loss of respect, or just plain being wrong. After a lengthy lecture once on setting the bar high on performance standards within a team, one attendee asked how, if she'd already made a lot of mistakes and modeled the wrong behavior, could she now turn around and tell her staff to behave differently? If you have that situation within your team, you're in luck.

One of the strongest actions you can take to reduce fear and build confidence is to put yourself and your own weaknesses out there for everyone to see and, while they're watching, show them the corrections as well. If the boss can fail, repair damage, and move on, then everyone can! This simple and honest process can all but eliminate what one author refers to as "fear based decision making,"[23] which unfortunately can run rampant in libraries. There are plenty of hallmarks of such a risk-adverse environment, and you don't want to see any of them surrounding and influencing your team. In these situations, change is abhorred, value is determined by

YOU'LL WISH YOU HADN'T SAID THIS: CONVERSATIONS THAT DAMAGE CONFIDENCE

I wish I had never made most of these comments, but over the years I have, and you probably have too. Here are some alternative, confidence-building options to offer.

- Following, *"who would like to volunteer"* — *"you were supposed to be done last week.":* Volunteering often involves taking on something new and something additional. Did you allow for extra time to accomplish this, along with the team member's other work? Did you agree on a reasonable deadline? Did you check in or ask for updates intermittently, so as to be sure progress was on schedule? Consider "I'm sorry you didn't have the time to complete this yet; let's work out the issues you're facing and come up with a time we both feel is adequate to wrap it up. How can I help?"

- Following, *"who would like to try this"* — *"that's not the way we've done it.":* The word *try* implies give it a shot, attempt something new, or test an idea. Let them try and don't limit their actions to past attempts. This is where new ideas and the confidence to offer them can be developed. Consider "That's a unique approach we haven't taken before. Let's test the theory out on paper and then pilot your ideas and evaluate the outcome."

- Following, *"please fill this position"* — *"I don't like your selection.":* Before shooting down a conclusion, consider all the steps it took to get there. Did you monitor them, even from afar? When a hiring process is drifting off track, rather than completely negate your team member's autonomy, try "Let's review the selection process you're using and compare it to the final skills we're seeking. I just want to make sure we're both on the same page as to the outcome needed."

- Following, *"how can we approach this"* — *"you're wrong.":* Count the hands that go up the very first time you ask for honest reactions and feedback, then count the hands the next time, after you've jumped to your own conclusion without really listening—openly. Consider "I hadn't thought of that approach before. Help me understand what you're trying to achieve."

- Following *"please give me your feedback"* — *"that's not for you to say.":* Don't ask for feedback if the source is an inappropriate one. If they are not, then ask and be open to the response. Consider "I'll have to make the final decision here but your input and ideas are certainly going to be helpful to me." Or, don't ask.

how long something has been done that way, and new ideas are met by bosses with a love it or hate it response.[24] If you think this describes a pretty risky place to do business, you'd be right. The only thing staff in this team can be confident of is that they'll likely get their head bitten off if they ask questions, their new ideas will make them the butt of jokes, and raising their hand to volunteer couldn't possibly end well.

One of the challenges to becoming a great team leader in our discipline is to rise to this level of big-picture thinking. It's easy, day to day, to get stuck on the interview questions you're writing or the meeting agenda you're crafting or the time cards you're reviewing, all of which are *also* important leadership tasks. But step back. Your success will be in direct correlation to the confidence with which your team approaches all of the other work you've jointly identified and taken on. If they see you avoiding risks too, and just routinely churning out your "task" duties, then the bar of expectation

HOW TO BUILD TRUST

Longtime, successful manager and mentor Cathy Monnin provided this list of simple steps to build invaluable trust between all members of your team.

- Tell the truth as kindly as possible.
- Keep promises.
- Listen well and don't interrupt.
- Ask honest questions.
- Don't just know parts of the truth—get the whole story.
- Ask your team for help.
- Allow legitimate testing of boundaries.
- Deal with problems!
- Provide honest, effective, and quick feedback.
- Be consistent.
- Provide *real* opportunities to step up and lead.[29]

just fell. Take chances! Create an environment that not only tolerates risk and innovation but celebrates it! Support the staff in success and in failure and, with each, you'll build confidence that will carry the entire group forward. You're removing the fear, so what's next?

Next, you build passion. "The ideal of passion is the sense that what we do is important. It is the state of mind that somehow we are providing a service to the public that is beyond the normal realm of customer service in the retail world or other service industries. In our line of work, the interactions we have with our patrons can change their lives—forever."[25] Little can work to strengthen a sense of camaraderie more than a shared passion or zeal for goals. Staff who believe that coworkers share their dedication are more confident to step up their game, due to the shared commitment they all feel. When an entire team is working towards the same end, each individual

can be more confident that their contributions and ideas will be more roundly welcomed.

Then, you seize opportunities. If you raise your hand first, going out on a limb to excel, chances are your confident team will be right behind you. One library leader's visionary initiatives would have been shot down in neighboring libraries faster than his e-mail moved, but on his home court, he had the enthusiasm and support of his team at his back. Why? Because, following his example, they'd learned that the potential value of success for the organization far outweighed the potential of a simple failure. Failures could be corrected. Opportunities, untaken, could be lost forever. Their successes and their progress grew exponentially, as their confidence to grasp opportunity continued to increase.

Always, you invite ideas. The best example of an organization that welcomes ideas from every level of the team is the one that had its staff room walls painted in dry erase paint. Staff members were invited to jot down anything that could improve processes, increase service, or otherwise better the workflow. Its leader explained, "I have to make sure I give employees freedom and latitude and make sure I don't shut them down . . . with a wrong word, a wrong tone in a meeting. I tell my managers, 'Try to have an open mind every day you come to work—how can you do it better and make it better?' If you want to keep an open, innovative culture, you have to see the ideas!"[26] How confident would your team feel about the value you see in them if you told them they could write suggestions for improvements on the wall (ok, you could post a bulletin board, too)?

Finally, you build trust. And trust—in almost any situation—builds confidence. With confidence developed and continually growing, your team will be able to utilize their various backgrounds, skills, interests, passions, experiences, and knowledge to begin to build lasting success. Safe in their own place in the group, they'll become accountable for its growth and effectiveness. And accountability, as a benefit of confidence, can begin to help all the individual elements of your great team truly gel. By "rising above our circumstances and doing whatever it takes to achieve the results we desire,"[27] the definition of accountability, problems, challenges, and shortcomings will be solved, not avoided. Consider the differences found … that separates accountable from nonaccountable staff.[28] Once a problem is detected or an opportunity is spotted:

1. Confident, accountable team members will see it, own it, solve it, do it!
2. Lacking in confidence that the team will have their back, the rest will wait and see, cover their tail, ask someone to tell them what to do, point fingers, deny it's their job, or just plain ignore the issue.

When is the last time you took a risk? Have you told anyone you're working through this book? Or are you afraid they'll question your reasons for doing so or, worse, the likelihood that you or your team can ever improve? Successful risk-taking is often vision-led, which means it is undertaken in order to leap over the mundane, limited success of day-to-day labor in order to find exciting, motivating options and alternatives. There's a lot a leader needs in her or his arsenal in order to take these leaps. What you'll find if you try it is that you and your team can grow and reach together, as long as you're all equally confident that the whole is stronger than its parts.

EXERCISES

36

1. **Think back to a** time when a supervisor showed confidence in you. Describe the results of that encounter. Did you learn a new skill, take a new chance or grow in some way? Describe both how that confidence made you feel and what the result was.

_____

_____

_____

_____

2. **Next, think of a** time when you reported to someone who seemed to have no confidence in you. Do the same analysis. How did that make you feel and how did it affect your work performance and output?

_____

_____

_____

_____

3. **List at least ten** ways you can *demonstrate* to a member of your team that you have confidence in them and that you expect great things! Don't stop short of ten; the number of options is actually limitless.

_____

_____

_____

_____

_____

4. **Next, think of one** team member with whom you can start. This might be someone new or someone who hasn't "stepped up" yet. Using your list of ten options from the question above, select at least three and make some notes about exactly how and when you can get started. Then do it!

_____

_____

_____

_____

_____

5. **Your team cannot ever** have confidence in you unless they trust you. Referring to the sidebar this week entitled "How to Build Trust," note below some very specific things you can do—and when you can do them—to be sure you're putting these important activities into action.

_____

_____

_____

_____

_____

PLANNING AND STRATEGY

There was once a class of library school students taking a management class. First, the students read a chapter on strategic planning from their highly academic text, then they heard a lecture on the importance of planning, its value as a management function, and the positive impact it has on the entire organization. Finally, they were assigned to visit a library and ask the director about her or his plan. One paper came back quoting this response, "Plan!? A Strategic Plan?! Are you kidding? Our budget has been cut, our staff has been reduced, technology costs are skyrocketing! I don't have time to plan—I'm just trying to keep the doors open!"[1]

Ouch. This resulted in what might be called an embarrassing teaching moment. Oddly enough, it served to be perhaps the *best* argument for strategic planning they'd heard thus far. Think about it. The budgets have been cut—so from where do you take the money? Staffing levels are down—so what service innovations are needed and how will cross-training be achieved? How will stress be handled? Technology costs are skyrocketing—so what's the plan to control them, find lucrative, alternative financing or collaborations? Answers to those questions could result in a plan that could demonstrate leadership at its best, rather than panic, which is leadership at its worst. (A coworker of mine from years ago used to swear that in secret swearing-in ceremonies, new managers were forced to repeat the mantra, *When in danger or in doubt, run in circles, scream and shout.* Given the example of this particular director, it's hard to argue with that.)

Let's get the eye-rolling out of the way early. I get it. Most people don't trust, value, or certainly look forward to strategic planning. Given the

VOICES FOR PLANNING

"Failing to plan is planning to fail."
—Winston Churchill

"The best way to predict the future is to create it."
—Anonymous

"Would you tell me, please, which way I ought to go from here?"

"That depends a good deal on where you want to get to."

"I don't much care where," said Alice

"Then it doesn't matter which way you go," said the Cat.
—Alice and The Cat[9]

DOES YOUR MISSION PASS THIS TEST?

Once you've created a mission statement, consider whether it meets these challenges:

Is it you? (Does it reflect your library's personality?)

Is it true? (Or is it so far-fetched that no one will ever buy it?)

Does it make sense? (Seems like an obvious question, but one often missed.)

Is it inspiring? (Will anyone read past it—to the vision, values, and goals?)

Is it exciting? (If not, maybe your organization isn't, either?)

Would it make a good epitaph? (Should your library cease to exist?)[10]

opportunity to volunteer to contribute, they'd probably prefer to weed the entire collection (even around corners) or wash the sticky stuff off picture books. Good leaders can change that impression. Good *team* leaders must change that impression. Why? Because, in the words of the great Yogi Berra, "If you don't know where you're going, you will wind up somewhere else."[2] You have embarked on a journey to take your team to greatness. Tell me, how will you know when you've made it?

For many team leaders, opportunities do not abound that have a direct impact on their organization's strategic planning process. Great leaders should change that, too. Volunteer to take part so that, from the outset of the process, you can develop a clear and motivating understanding of and belief in your library's purpose and goals and then you can return to your team and get them on that same path to success. Throughout this coming month, team leaders will learn how to truly focus the varied skills, energies, viewpoints, and contributions of their team members into specific actions that contribute to overall success. There's no other place to start this journey than with a strong, clear organizational (or, at least, a team) strategic plan. Start today, if possible, to convince your colleagues one is needed, if for no other reason than you want to be known for more than just opening your doors every morning. Lose the excuses.

By understanding the pieces and parts of a strategic plan better, you will be in a stronger position to help you adopt a plan that your team can then use as a springboard to your own success. Planning does *not* have to be a tedious, vague, and frustrating waste of time. Here are some answers to have ready for the eye rollers among you.

CHALLENGE: MISSION STATEMENTS ARE JUST A BUNCH OF WORDS
ANSWER: "If you are prepared to lead followers who are willing to be led, then a mission statement can prove vital to get everyone on the

same page, with a shared understanding."[3] That doesn't sound worthless to me. To put it simply, if you're going to the grocery store to get milk, you have a lot to decide. What kind of milk? What price will you pay and why? How will you get to the store? How will you decide if you like the store enough to return? But you've started off right, at least. "You need to know why you're going. That's your mission statement."[4]

One of the reasons people get lost early in the strategic planning process is because most organizations tend to overcomplicate things at this very first step—articulating the mission. How many mission statements have you read that look more like entries (and winners) in the Annual Compound Sentence Award? The reason is because people often confuse descriptions of work with purpose. Take the Becton, Dickinson and Company firm, for example. They could have crammed everything they do into their mission statement and had it read like this: *We manufacture efficient and reliable medical supplies, including infusion therapy devices, pre-fillable drug delivery systems and surgical blades, as well as conduct medical research.* Instead, their precise and compelling mission statement is "*To help all people live healthy lives.*"[5] They condensed the what into why (remember . . . you need to know why you're going to the store).

Understand, promote, and support your mission statement or "risk wandering 'off mission' and wasting time and resources trying to achieve things which are at best peripheral and at worst irrelevant."[6] Who has the time or money for that?

CHALLENGE: ISN'T EVERY ORGANIZATION'S VISION SIMPLY TO SUCCEED?
ANSWER: Yes, but as the world changes, so should your focus on exactly how you plan to do that. "Legend states that when Cortes led an expedition into Mexico, he burned his ships once everything was offloaded. He wanted his men to be focused on succeeding, not on the option of quitting."[7] What ships could your organization

burn in order to keep everyone focused on future success? Our shopper could have poured every other possible beverage down the drain before setting out, keeping his family focused on the project of finding milk. There are libraries out there, I'm sure, that have plenty of old baggage they could lose to clear the way for today's success stories. Consider a library whose vision might be: *We will save the taxpayer every dollar possible.* Looks like their debate over whether or not to use self-checkout machines, instead of replacing staff, might be an easy one to argue. Or, how about a library vision that claims: *We'll try anything to improve customer service.* How far would you get in one of their management meetings, arguing to keep the old card catalog, rather than provide more expansive, rapid, and far-reaching online options for searching?

After answering the *why* in your mission, your vision will tell you "*what it will look like when you get there.*"[8]

CHALLENGE: VALUES SOUND GREAT, BUT HOW DO WE GET PEOPLE TO BELIEVE WE HAVE THEM?
ANSWER: That's simple. You put your money where your mouth is. Many years ago, a library management team was reviewing their stated values. When they got to *we support literacy*, a debate began about what exactly that meant? They bought books. They visited schools where reading was taught. Finally someone volunteered that they allow adult reading tutors to use their meeting rooms. There was silence for a moment after that comment, while all present realized that they also offered meeting room use to jugglers,

WHAT IS MISSION, REALLY?

Mission does not define how one operates, but simply why.[11]

gardeners, and snake exhibits. They decided to do something to demonstrate their values.

Within a year, more than a dozen staff members from that library were actually working as literacy volunteers—on library time! Their training expenses and the time they spent tutoring were being covered by the library, and they were donating by doing class prep on their own time. Now, that's a real value. Values can show themselves in literally hundreds of ways. Look around your building and see if what you read (stated values) and what you hear match up. Is *we value people* contradicted by DO NOT LOITER or NO CHILDREN ALLOWED signs? Is *we're dedicated to service* demonstrated by empty staff desks and a lack of eye contact? Values discussions can and should be opportunities to grade yourselves on whether or not you're living up to your own promises.

Once your organization has embraced, considered, and identified the critical cornerstones of mission, vision, and values, you are ready to move on to the creation of a road map—or plan—for everyone's success.

EXERCISES

-37-

1. **Write as long and** complete a description as you can of exactly what your team does. Then, condense it down into a single, clear mission statement (even if your library already has one, it's useful to try to create your own). Make sure it answers the question "Why do you exist?"

   _____

   _____

   _____

   _____

2. **Review your mission statement** from question #1 and answer the question, "In five years, how will you know that you've been successful?" Then, condense that answer down to a succinct vision statement.

   _____

   _____

   _____

   _____

3. **Values are next.** If your team was stranded on a desert island with absolutely nothing around them, then someone dropped off enough supplies to build, open, and operate a library, on what principles would you stand? What about your work would really, really matter (intellectual freedom, cost savings, wealth of users)? Think this through, then list what you think your team's values would be.

   _____

   _____

   _____

   _____

4. **You're off the desert** island now and you're back in the real world. What _are_ your team's values today? If they exist, use that list. If not, write what you perceive them to be. Then, next to each value, write how anyone can tell. How do your values show?

   _____

   _____

   _____

   _____

5. **Next week, you'll be** learning about a simple, straightforward way to do strategic planning. The purpose of this chapter will be to make you more open to and excited about the process. So let's get all the negativity out of your system now. Write down every bad thing you can think of about strategic planning. Include what you've heard, what you've experienced in the past, and what you imagine. Finally, forget all that. And prepare for next week's lesson with an open mind!

   _____

   _____

   _____

   _____

PLANNING AND STRATEGY

WEEK TWO | ## PAINLESS PLANNING

Painless childbirth may be an oxymoron, but painless planning is true—and possible.

So, picture this. The game is about to start; the stadium is full of thousands of screaming fans. Both teams, one in red uniforms and one in green, pour out of their respective tunnels and onto the sidelines. They gather in a huge huddle, jumping up and down and chanting to get their blood boiling, then the whistle blows and all of them rush onto the field at once, charging at one another, running up and down the field while wondering, where's the ball?

If you consider the organizational design of a football team, you've got the owner at the top, then a head coach, then *team* coaches (defense, offense, special, you get the picture), then the individual players. Clearly, the strategy described above isn't going to get them very far towards their goals. But wait a minute; they don't have any goals yet. No wonder the teams will fail. Just like the individuals you supervise, every person on a team wants to be successful at what they do. They may understand the overall mission (to present the best athletic performance and spectacle?) and they may buy into the team's vision (to be the most sought-after ticket in the league), and they may even share the values of athleticism, sportsmanship, and power, but they're still lacking the framework that will get them there.

Sound strategy begins with established, articulated goals. Before *your* team can become great, it needs to fully grasp what the goals are and what their particular role is in achieving them. That's success.

Moving off the field now and into your library, everyone involved in its operation has a specific and distinct role to play in creating a successful plan. This is where mistake number one in the process often takes place. Organizations will often allow the highest level of participants (in a library, that's the board) create the whole plan from start to finish. It's not surprising that when they then hand that finished product off to those who will implement it, little happens. Imagine you are a circulation clerk and your supervisor hands you a three-pound binder (which was the result of old-fashioned plans) and announced, "We have to add 30 percent more card holders. Now, let's get to it." Feeling both disgruntled for not being asked for input and frustrated by the plan's inability to understand your job, you might wonder how exactly you're supposed to do that from your position behind the circulation desk. The answer, most often, was to ignore the whole thing and keep doing what you've always done. The response, even more frequently, was nothing. No follow-up to the plan or tracking of its success resulted in even its creators ignoring the gaps they created and the lack of direction the plan provided. The final result was no success for anyone and a final score of zero to zero.

Let's start again. Without veering off into a seminar on strategic planning here, there are some basic concepts that can be cleared up that can demonstrate the simplicity and value of a well-done plan. This is where everyone gets involved—at the right time! Simply put, those at the top (the library board) set the goals; those who manage the work (the supervisors or team leaders) identify what needs to happen (measureable objectives); and then the players (your team members) contribute how they can make the right things happen. Now, your team has its own plan to follow, in support of the library's overall strategy!

The process starts with a reality check, in response to "three primary questions. What seems to be happening? What possibilities are presented? What is the organization going to do about it?"[12] A word of warning: if you do not involve your board at this juncture, you'll risk losing their support for everything you do from here on. One library began its strategic planning process the usual way, by involving community, staff, and team leaders in assessing the current environment, establishing targets of performance, and then deciding how they'd be achieved. Each month, after presenting an update on the plan's progress, staff noticed a growing disinterest from the board members they were addressing. Finally, they came right out and asked if there was something wrong with their report? One board member responded, "Go ahead and do what you want, this isn't our plan anyway, it's yours."[13] That red flag meant they needed a different approach. If leaders need the support (financial and otherwise) of their boards, and they do, then the direction set must come from those decision makers.

Staff may not like that. But opening and clearly identifying a staff member's role as supporting the direction set by the governing board is a necessity. Everyone will get their turn in developing the rest of the plan and, ultimately, if the board's idea of success doesn't match an individual's, then it's time they examined if they're expending their professional energies in the right place.

Returning to our sports metaphor for a moment, the owners, as the team's governing body, have a job to do. Frequently, goal setting begins with a familiar process called SWOT analysis, which is a review of existing Strengths, Weaknesses, Opportunities and Threats facing the organization. By working through exercises to identify those realities and discussing what they tell you, themes emerge that develop into goals. For example, our team's goal-setting process might result in this:

1. STRENGTHS – Our fans love us, we make a lot of money, our players are excellent.
2. WEAKNESSES – We haven't won a championship in years; many players have left.
3. OPPORTUNITIES – Football is starting to appeal to a younger age group, and

WHY PLANNERS ARE MOVING AWAY FROM SWOT

The (SWOT) focus on weaknesses and threats is derived from a warfare mentality, where some win and others lose. This focus on problems is limited in its effectiveness. Many studies have shown negative consequences to this style of thinking, including:

- Problem-solving is often driven more by a desire for relief than by results.
- Problem-solving can be depressing for all involved.
- Sometimes, it can appear that the cure is worse than the disease.
- Most difficult, challenging situations are not solvable because, in fact, they are not problems.[19]

WHAT SWOT AND SOAR GIVE US

- **S:** STRENGTHS
- **W:** WEAKNESSES
- **O:** OPPORTUNITIES
- **T:** THREATS

- **S:** STORIES OF SUCCESS
- **O:** OPPORTUNITIES AVAILABLE TO US
- **A:** ASPIRATIONS FOR THE FUTURE
- **R:** RESOURCES AVAILABLE AND NEEDED TO ATTAIN OUR ASPIRATIONS[20]

potential television and marketing opportunities are growing.

4. THREATS – Other activities are vying for our community's recreational dollars, and the stadium itself is crumbling.

With just this minimal list of realities to consider, the owners might end up looking at a list of themes that may well impact the coming two years. (No plan, in this century, should be created to cover more time than this. Too much is changing too fast to keep it relevant!)

THEMES – younger fans, stadium, revenue, winning, rosters, competition

Now, it's time to remember that strategic planning means saying "No!" Successful goals say "*what*" your organization is going to really do (not just hope they can do) in the time frame you've adopted for your plan. Rather than craft each of these themes into *goals* that will exceed the organization's time and money within the 1–2 year planning period, the owners (or board) need to park some of them for future consideration and

select two or three "*yes*" goals, or top priorities. Resulting goals might include:

1. GOAL 1 – We will commit to building a talented team.
(This could result in more fans of ALL ages gaining interest and could also contribute to winning more championships.)
2. GOAL 2 – We will modernize to create an appealing arena.
(This could also impact increased ticket sales and, as a result, more interest in television coverage—and revenue.)

GOALS TO SAVE FOR THE FUTURE – In coming years, based on our growing success and expanded fan base, we could consider ticket price increases as a means of further increasing revenue and supporting even more expensive players and, thereby, championships.

A final word is needed here on an emerging—and more positive—method of getting to this point. If you try using appreciative inquiry as an approach, you could find your organization can SOAR. Organizational specialist Maureen Sullivan calls the SOAR method of analysis "appreciative inquiry meets SWOT."[14] Let's look at what both of those concepts mean.

"Appreciative Inquiry is grounded by two deceptively simple concepts: *What you seek, you find more of* and *people commit to what they help create.*"[15] Simply put, it's a more positive way to have everyone involved look at everything. So what about our new acronym? According to supporters of the SOAR process, "SWOT has a strong potential to slow down, or even halt, forward momentum during the strategic analysis process."[16] Based on the structure of the SWOT model, half of the time will be spent focused on negatives (weaknesses and threats). SOAR, on the other hand, directs thoughtful reflection on Strengths, Opportunities, *Aspirations, and Results.* "The basic idea of SOAR is to build organizations around what works, rather than trying to fix what doesn't, thus attempting to create more of what is already working."[17] In order to be sure that nothing is missed, however, many experts suggest "that an organization consider a hybrid approach . . . and just use both!"[18]

Regardless of the methodology your organization or team selects, the energy behind it is what is going to matter the most. Why? Because next week, it's your team's turn to shine. The job of identifying real, meaningful objectives falls next to the management level (the board's work is done) and it's the team leaders who will continue to set the course. Next, you'll consider how your team will be directed by the mission, vision, values, and goals considered so far in the planning process. Now, it's your turn to contribute and, with this framework behind you, you can identify and begin to pursue success.

SUGGESTED READING

Stavros, Jacqueline M., Gina Hinrichs, and Sue Annis Hammond. *The Thin Book of SOAR: Building Strength-Based Strategy*. Thin Book, 2009.

EXERCISES

-38-

Performing a SWOT or SOAR analysis doesn't have to be boring or challenging; it should be fun! Try exercises first here on your own. You'll be amazed how the results can grow in value and revelation when you do them with a group—and add discussion! Try them soon with your team or, better yet, with your entire library the next time planning takes place.

1. **To identify your organization's** strengths, consider all the services, resources, and programs you provide and answer this question first. "We get the most compliments when we _____." Now, with the programs you've just listed describe each in one- or two-word phrases. Finally, blend like phrases together, eliminate duplication, and you've got a list of *themes* that represent your strengths.

   _____

   _____

   _____

2. **To identify your organization's** weaknesses, answer this question first. "There's a lot more we could do, if only we could _____. " Follow the same steps as above. Create a list of one- or two-word phrases, eliminate duplication, and you'll have a list of themes representing your weaknesses.

   _____

   _____

   _____

3. **To identify your organization's** opportunities, answer this question first. "If we can take advantage of _____, we could really improve what we do!" (Repeat all the follow-up steps, too, and you'll have your list of opportunities.)

   _____

   _____

   _____

4. **To identify threats to** your organization, answer this question first. "We'd better be ready to react to _____, in order to be certain our organization isn't harmed." (Repeat final steps.)

   _____

   _____

   _____

5. **Finally, start practicing on** how to introduce the additional components of SOAR, by adding stories of success, aspirations for the future, and resources available. (The strongest approach might just be a combination of SWOT and SOAR techniques!) Try completing these sentences:
   "Let me tell you a story about how our library impacted a customer I know of." (In a room full of planners, this will be an even more effective and inspirational exercise!)
   "What I really hope to do is make sure that within the next two years, we can _____."
   "There's almost no way we could avoid success, even if we tried, because we have _____, _____, and _____!"

   _____

   _____

   _____

   _____

PLANNING AND STRATEGY

WEEK THREE | **TEAM PLANNING**

Finally, it's now time for team leaders to step up to the plate. Your board has set the direction by identifying your goals for the coming year or two. Now, it's up to you to chart your team members' success in attaining those goals. In the planning process, the next step—and your next assignment—is to work with the leadership team to identify measurable objectives. We can take a look back at our football teams and see that this part can be fun, too!

If you recall, when we last saw our heroes, they'd just emerged from their individual stadium tunnels and had all charged onto the field in one big mess of uniforms and mayhem. Perhaps they had a vague understanding of a primary goal—to win the game—but their individual team leaders had given them very little else to go on. Objectives would help out here.

In strategic planning processes I run, I begin with a planning retreat for board members only and it results in the creation of clear goals (no more than two or three for a two-year plan). Next, I facilitate a leaders' retreat for supervisors, team leaders, and middle managers, during which we study those goals and create the objectives that will help achieve them. Why involve leaders at this point? Because this is where the plan becomes operational—and you are the ones who know the possibilities—and limits—of those operations.

Soon, every staff member will become involved. That process will be discussed next week, when performance plans are examined. But right now, the plan hasn't developed that far. So while the players continue to bounce around on the field, firing up the fans, the coaches and managers should be getting together on the sidelines. "I know," one might suggest. "I can

CONSIDER OBJECTIVES FROM EVERY PERSPECTIVE

While the original Balanced Scorecard model of strategic planning encourages consideration of four basic perspectives of operation, libraries add one more—stuff (that's not the official term but it's clear enough). So, when reviewing your objectives to make sure they're SMART, be sure to compare them to all of these considerations, so they can have a real chance of being successful.

- **LEARNING AND GROWTH PERSPECTIVE:** In order for the objective to be reached, is there any special training or development needed by staff?
- **BUSINESS PROCESS PERSPECTIVE:** In order for the objective to be reached, does the structure or operation of the organization have to do or provide anything special?
- **CUSTOMER PERSPECTIVE:** In order for the objective to be reached, what customer considerations should be made?
- **FINANCIAL PERSPECTIVE:** In order for the objective to be reached, what costs will be incurred and need to be planned for?
- **"STUFF" (OR RESOURCES) PERSPECTIVE:** In order for the objective to be reached, what "stuff" (books, programs, services) will need to be provided?[22]

tell which of these players can run, throw, and catch the best, so I'll coach the offense and we will score the points." Another might offer, "Since I have experience with blocking and tackling, I'll get players good at that together and I'll coach the defense." And, finally, leaders will be identified to concentrate on the remaining special teams, so that a focus can be placed on the role they'll play in the event. Leaders are in place, and now it's time for action.

Objectives should be two things, at least. One, they must be actionable (that is, they should state what will happen in action terms, not philosophical ones) and, second, they should be SMART (Specific, Measurable, Attainable, Realistic and Timely). Objectives can be created using a painless, three-step process. Remember, we started by having the ultimate governing group (board or owners) identify *what* is to be accomplished. Managers, who know the operation, the staff, and the true potentials, now work to identify *how* success will happen.

STEP ONE – In order to answer the question "How?" a management group should separate into as many smaller teams as there are goals, and

each should be assigned one goal to study. Before you're finished, everyone will have a chance to chime in on all topics, but starting out in small groups generates opportunities for thoughtful, extensive consideration. Discussions should take place at this time, focused on a singular goal, to identify how it can be made to succeed.

It's time next to appreciate the overlap that should and does occur when goals are right on target. If each group shares their list aloud and flip chart pages get filled up, discussion among the entire team will then be able to identify—and group—like ideas. This is the point when everyone gets a voice. Finally, a true, streamlined list will emerge of objectives (milestones) that need to be reached under each goal.

STEP TWO – What comes next is critical and often overlooked. In the early days of strategic planning, teams would just type up everything they have right now, punch in three holes, and their binder would be done. "Let's add bookmobiles!" might have resulted in cheers of excitement at the thought of those circulation figures rising. But wait. Who is going to drive the vehicle? Can insurance be afforded? Might a special collection

WRITE ACTIONABLE OBJECTIVES!

The easiest way to write actionable objectives is to be certain to start them with action verbs! The more inspirational and exciting, the better!

Make sure to articulate your objectives like these examples:

To have (blank) by (date).

To be (blank) by (date).

To become (blank) by (date).

To achieve (blank) by (date).

To grow (blank) by (date).

To introduce (blank) by (date).

To master (blank) by (date).[23]

---

multiple measures just add confusion and result in ambiguity and conflict. But planning experts disagree.

"Imagine entering the cockpit of a jet airplane and observing that there is only a single instrument. How would you feel about flying on that plane after the following discussion with the pilot?

1. Q: I'm surprised to see you operating the plane with only a single instrument. What does it measure?
2. A: Airspeed, I'm really working on airspeed in this flight.
3. Q: That's good. Airspeed certainly seems important. But what about altitude? Wouldn't an altimeter be helpful?
4. A: I worked on altitude for the last few flights and I've gotten pretty good on altitude. Now I have to concentrate on proper air speed.
5. Q: But I notice you don't even have a fuel gauge. Wouldn't that be useful?
6. A: Fuel is important, but I can't concentrate on doing too many things well at the same time.[21]

be needed? Do you need a garage? Before being adopted, objectives need to be considered against the *balanced perspectives* within an organization. A main feature of a specialized model of strategic planning called the Balanced Scorecard, this step can help identify even more duplication, highlight special needs to be put into place, and, most important, introduce true measures of success that can be used through the life of the plan. In short, *perspectives* equal reality.

Mix your planners up into five new teams at this juncture. Each team should next examine the drafted objectives and consider them in light of the operational, financial, customer, staff, and resource needs that can ensure success. The result: likely, a few more highly focused and critical objectives will emerge to be added to the pack. Without this step, great ideas often remain just that. With this added analysis, great ideas come true because, in planning, you thought of everything. Some might think that all of these

Now, substitute that bookmobile your library decided to buy. *How* can you add bookmobile service and make it successful? Should you just concentrate on the route or where it will go? Or should you also measure (and plan for) its collection budget, driver, training, insurance, marketing, and Internet connectivity? By considering the objective in relation to the whole organization, from each perspective, you're likely to catch important, supporting objectives that will also have to be attained.

STEP THREE – Make sure your final objectives are SMART! You're not done writing them until you send them back into small groups to be examined one last time to identify these measures. What needs to be checked is this: are they *specific, measurable, attainable, realistic, and timely?* If not, rewrite them until they are.

Now you have strong goals that come from the very top—a direction! And you have realistic, carefully crafted *how* steps that will lead you to fulfilling those goals. *Plus*, you have ways to measure your progress along the way, or to notice your lack thereof and therefore gain the opportunity to make adjustments during the life of your plan.

Next week, every single member of every single team in your organization will have a chance to have their voice and input heard, and the result will be to chart your library's future, as well as your team's, and the work of those who contribute to it.

EXERCISES

-39-

1. **In order to practice** writing actionable, SMART objectives, let's work with the fictional *goal* an individual might have to *live a long life*. Make a list of as many things as you can think of that need to occur in order to make that happen. Concentrate on *how* you'll be able to live a long life. So approach this exercise as though you're trying to find as many answers as you can to this comment: "In order to live a long life, I will have to _____."

   _____

   _____

   _____

2. **Hopefully, you'll have created** a long list of objectives. For example, you have listed *eat right, get exercise, reduce stress*. Now make sure each objective is SMART. Make each one *specific*. (Not just *eat right*, but *eat healthy, balanced foods*).

   _____

   _____

   _____

3. **Make sure each objective** is *measurable*. (Not just *eat healthy, balanced foods* but *eat healthy foods at least six days a week*).

   _____

   _____

   _____

   _____

4. **Make sure each objective** is *attainable*. (Okay, try *eat healthy, balanced foods at least five days a week*).

   _____

   _____

   _____

   _____

5. **Make sure each objective** is *realistic*. (Maybe, *make sure to eat healthy, balanced foods for most of the meals I eat at least five days a week*).

   _____

   _____

   _____

   _____

6. **Make sure each objective** is *timely*. You've already got that covered.

   _____

   _____

   _____

   _____

Now, you're ready to make the work of your team SMART, too!

PLANNING AND STRATEGY

WEEK FOUR | ## STRATEGIC CAREERS

If you're lucky and you're working in an intentional environment, your library or organization has already outlined overarching guidelines of mission, vision, values, and planning for you to implement. If it hasn't, you now know how to create these invaluable guideposts for your team. Do that first. Because, next, it's time for you to help develop real performance goals for each and every member of your team.

I don't know why, but even outstanding employees always seem to dread that annual evaluation appointment with the boss. Don't they? Maybe it's because not all leaders adhere to the restriction that evaluations should never contain surprises, so they're expecting to be caught off guard by something awful. Or maybe it's an aversion to the last part of the meeting, because that's when the employee and supervisor should be setting goals for the coming year. What's not clear is whether those goals are dreaded because of the challenge—or the futility—they represent. If it's the latter, what a shame. And what a lost opportunity for team leaders.

Always remember, what most people want from their jobs is "the satisfaction of knowing they did a good job and that it was appreciated. The key, then, to motivating is to figure out what they want from work"[24] and then help your team members achieve it! You've reached the point in the planning process where the people who actually *do* the work need to take action. What better way to make sure their efforts are worthwhile than by setting *real, purposeful* goals with them, so they can watch their contributions make a real difference.

TURN IDEAS INTO REALITY

By using your organization's strategic plan to craft real, usable, and valuable contributions from team members, true employee involvement can occur. At the next opportunity, wrap up your evaluation meetings with a goal-setting session that starts with you *listening* to how your employee wants to contribute! Then turn your staff members' hopes, aspirations, and ideas into initiatives that support the whole. Here's what happened when this took place at BIC Corporation.

- When Ray Winter took over running BIC in 1991, he saw immediately that lack of improvement was due to poor employee-management relations.
- He focused on developing a strategy to increase employee involvement in the company to remedy this.
- Employees' concept of *involvement,* he found, was vague at best.
- In one unit, this was not the case. In it, involvement meant letting the staff come up with their own ideas to improve performance.
- Most importantly, in that successful unit, staff ideas were acted on!
- With this direct involvement coming from the employees themselves, leaders found their outstanding performance could be both managed and measured!

Strategic planning may begin with broad concepts such as mission and vision—but they should end with real plans for action from the front line. Your teams' ideas could just be your organization's road map to success![27]

Consider how planning often used to work. A small team, usually made up of managers, got together in a back room and hashed out what everyone was going to do for the next several years. They then handed their finished document over to the staff—the people who were expected to actually do the work—with little or no effort made to consider those individuals' career aspirations, special talents, ideas, or input. "They want us to have more story hours? We can barely staff the ones we have now!" "What? I'm supposed to provide more evening staff coverage? With whom? Nobody wants to work on Sundays!" "Raise circulation by 30 percent a year? Are they kidding? How am I supposed to do that from behind the reference desk?" And on and on.

Quickly, whatever excitement or anticipation *might* have been building for the release of the new plan can be replaced by contempt, frustration, and futility, based on comments and impressions such as these. Why? Because nobody asked them. And you, as the team leader, aren't faring much better. Left with quotas and mandates to fill that could possibly have very little basis in reality, your chances of team success aren't looking much better. So turn things around at this point in your planning process and invite your team members themselves to identify the actions they want, need, and are qualified to take to bring the plan to fruition. "Performance, health and happiness are grounded in the skillful management of energy."[25] If you're new at this, you can get some good advice from the Career Success for Newbies site,[26] which suggests some of the following tips:

1. Be clear with the team member. Don't allow expectations to be misunderstood by wording them too vaguely. The actions they're planning to take must contribute to a stated team or organizational objective that will be measured. You're past the conceptual stage here, so be specific and clear.
2. Share expectations. Define how the team member will be evaluated in detail, so they understand completely how detailed their performance should be.

3. Build trust. Although the plan your team is supporting may cover multiple years, the process of achieving its goals should build on a day-to-day relationship between you and your staff. If you continually check in with them, support them, and help remove obstacles to their success, they will come to trust that you're in this together.

4. Provide what they need. If further training or education is required in order to meet individual goals, don't leave getting that training up to each individual. Involve them in selecting appropriate support but then be sure to provide the essential tools—time and money—to really get what they need. I once had a supervisor who told me that, after I'd attended a few Excel training classes, I'd be put in charge of annual statistics. The report deadlines came long before the training materialized and my goals of success were even longer in coming.

5. Communicate. Often. Just as performance evaluation conversations should never *only* come along once a year, neither should review and support of progress. Set up a frequent and dependable meeting schedule, even for brief appointments, just to check in and ensure your ongoing support.

So, back to the strategic plan itself. All the pieces are coming together now. You have big-picture direction from your governing board, specific, measurable objectives set by leadership, and action steps added by team members. With everything so linear and interconnected, everyone involved can be assured of their role, their support, and that, in the end, your plan will really mean something. A far cry from strategic planning models of old, this method allows leaders of each team within the organization to feel and be

WHAT NOT TO DO WHEN REACHING FOR GOALS

- Overcommit your time and energy.
- Say yes, when you want to say no.
- Allow your "have to" list to overshadow your "want to" list.
- Let external influences make decisions for you.
- Expect others to make you feel good.
- Compare yourself and your accomplishments to others.
- Stress over things you can't control or change.
- Focus on problems and not solutions.
- Blame others.
- Not ask for help when you need it.[28]

a real part of the picture. Ownership and cohesion of efforts build a strong base for a culture of camaraderie and achievement. But, that's just one side of your library's culture. It's the visible, we-wrote-this-down-on-paper side. What's more, every single one of your team members and, hopefully, you have a clear performance plan to follow, ensuring that their efforts and growth for the coming year will be clear and attainable.

Next month, we'll examine what *else* you can do to build a strong culture within your team. Some of it you'll be able to see and the rest will contribute to a feeling of respect, productivity, and the right kind of motivation.

SUGGESTED READING

Loehr, Jim, and Tony Schwartz. *The Power of Full Engagement: Managing Energy, Not Time, Is the Key to High Performance and Personal Renewal.* New York: Free, 2003.

Robinson, Alan G., and Dean M. Schroeder. *Ideas Are Free: How the Idea Revolution Is Liberating People and Transforming Organizations.* San Francisco: Berrett-Koehler, 2006.

EXERCISES

40

Before you help create meaningful goals for your team members, start with one for yourself. With goals and objectives already created to give you direction, fit yourself and your own ambitions into the mix and create your own performance plan.

1. **Make a two-year "Strategic Career"** plan for yourself. With an understanding of your organization's stated goals and objectives (or ones that you wrote with your team, if your organization hasn't done so), create at least three goals of your own that would both support the overall plan and meet your personal and professional hopes and dreams.

    _____

    _____

    _____

2. **For each of your** career goals, which tell you *what* you hope to accomplish, list two or three objectives under each that demonstrate *how* you'll do just that.

    _____

    _____

    _____

3. **Go back and review** all of your objectives, to make sure they're SMART.

    _____

    _____

    _____

4. **Now it's time for** action! Under each objective, list no fewer than three steps or actions you'll need to take to achieve the objectives and reach your goals.

    _____

    _____

    _____

5. **Finally, add a milestone's** measuring device to your calendar. Pick dates (monthly, quarterly, whatever you're comfortable with) and, on those dates, go back and review, revise, tweak, and update your plan.

    _____

    _____

    _____

    _____

6. **Don't forget to take** time to stop and congratulate yourself on your successes along the way!

    _____

    _____

    _____

    _____

Now you're ready to help each member of your team do the same!

TEAM ENVIRONMENT

WEEK ONE | ## WINNING CULTURE

> *The only thing of real importance that leaders do is create and manage culture. If you do not manage culture, it manages you.*
>
> —Peter Drucker[1]

Because we are, after all, a part of the animal kingdom, it's not unfair to begin a discussion about team culture with an analogy to puppies. They're adorable. Climbing all over each other in the puppy crate, each animal has started life with exuberance and an openness to learning. Two of them end up going to different homes. For one, the atmosphere is quiet, serene, and peaceful. Raised by some pretty nice DINKS (double income, no kids), they know when they'll eat, go out, get attention, and rest. Life is orderly and predictable and they're happy with that. For the other, chaos abounds. Six kids, keeping all hours, music blaring, sometimes they eat, sometimes the Little League games take precedence and dinner is forgotten. The neighbor kids are omnipresent and, often, aggressive and teasing. Fear, uncertainty, and distrust become the watchwords of the day.

So far, your team studies have focused on some pretty tangible issues. Hiring, interview questions, meeting agendas, discipline charts, and the like have painted the *visible* picture of your team's environment. But before you can be really ready to move the group to greatness, you must consider those *invisible* components that make up the atmosphere, the ethos . . . the *culture* in which we all operate. Like our friends Clifford and Cujo, your team members will be affected by the environment you create and manage. If you listen to Peter Drucker's advice from today's opening quote, you'll realize the incredibly large part you play in running that show.

So, what is culture? "Asking a person to describe his or her workplace culture is like asking a fish to describe water. The fish isn't even aware of his environment because he is swimming in it and is completely oblivious

A PEEK INTO ZAPPOS'S CULTURE

Known for its unique corporate culture, the online shoe and clothing retailer Zappos has been described as having five unique signposts of their culture. Try adapting these to your team!

1. **Treat everyone like family.** In other words, value each member as you would someone important to you because they are! An analyst visiting Zappos was surprised when an employee drove all the way out to the airport to pick him up. Why did they go to so much trouble for just one visitor? "We treat all of our customers as family. If you had a family member in town, wouldn't you pick them up?"

2. **Hire for a cultural fit.** Because Zappos values a culture that reflects fun and a little weirdness, they ask interviewees, "On a scale of 1 to 10, how weird are you?" It's not the number that's important but how people react to it. What's important to remember is that once you determine what your brand stands for, hiring for cultural fit will ensure that each team member passionately demonstrates your team brand through all they say and do.

3. **Trust your team.** Zappos gives a simple directive, "Wow the customer," then allows all team members to do so any way they can think of. One salesperson sold flip-flops to a customer planning a tropical vacation, then sent her a postcard that read "Have a great trip!" No scripts here, just the guidelines of courtesy, common sense, and the desire to treat everyone as family.

4. **Share everything.** Any team member can tell any customer anything about how the team works. All information (statistics, sales records, etc.) is shared openly and no one is monitored or hampered in what they're allowed to say.

5. **Have fun!** Quoting a former GE executive, Zappos's management agrees that "employees shouldn't feel that it's wrong to appear to be having fun at the risk of their superiors thinking they're not serious enough." Why? Because Zappos focuses its culture on what it's selling—happiness![5]

to its presence or importance."[2] For team leaders, however, the option to remain in this state of oblivion is not on the table.

Let's keep it simple. Culture is what's considered normal. People *consider* something to be normal if it reflects what they see happen, hear about, and come to believe. In some organizations, for example, even if a brand-new clerk shows exceptional skills and motivation, she simply will still not be promoted into a management position until she's climbed up through several promotions. It's just not done. It's not normal. That's not exactly a culture of motivation and growth. Culture is learned and pretty quickly. It wouldn't take long for that exceptional clerk to quit even applying for the job she's really meant for. After just a few punishing rejections, she'll either settle back in to her *place* or she'll leave. Consider, if her amazing performance had been rewarded by a quick and major promotion, how motivated other staff would be to jump-start their careers! It would be worth it! You'd have a culture of limitless opportunity!

What if the current team culture is unhealthy? Then it's up to you to work on correcting it and fast. One study illustrated the impact of culture as it might relate to a dress code—written or assumed. If everyone wears suits and ties, for example, consider how awkward a new team member would be made to feel if he showed up in khakis and a golf shirt. "So, why is this important? Who cares how you dress? You care, or you should. People like to belong, and they trust others who they see as belonging."[3] That's another

HOW DOES YOUR TEAM REPRESENT ITS CULTURE?

Consider these simple demonstrations of culture and how your team is affected by them.

LANGUAGE

Job titles—do your team's titles keep them in their place within a hierarchy or motivate them to soar and excel?

DECISION MAKING

When you ask for input for decision making, are you met with a "why bother, you never listen to us anyway" eye roll or with eagerness at the invitation to contribute?

SYMBOLS

Do your team members proudly wear clothing embossed with your organization's logo or reluctantly do so only when it's mandated?

LEGENDS

Do stories about people who don't even work there anymore still influence how your team behaves, just because that's how the legend used to do it?

ACTIONS

Does your team really believe you support their development or do they expect to not get that internal promotion because nobody ever does?[6]

---

way cultures—positive or negative—perpetuate themselves. If your team's current culture hangs on unhealthy or unproductive habits and practices, it's up to you as the team leader to correct those before everyone is wearing the same tie and it's too late to get them to change.

Let's substitute two brand-new staff members for our puppies (I know this analogy is a stretch, but just bear with me) and see how important creating a healthy team culture can be. Employee one gets a job right out of school at a busy, professional reference desk in a library that is home to several advanced degreed staff members. It's a competitive, challenging, and not for the faint of heart sort of place. The other person goes to a small village library that's set in a quaint historical storefront, where every afternoon the staff makes tea for one of the neighborhood's elderly residents. All other staff there have been around for almost thirty years and the only thing that's changed has been the book titles. Some of them.

Will these two contradictory cultures matter to our rookies? Let's keep imagining. The first person, who landed at the busier place, has always been somewhat shy and has never had a lot of self-confidence. She or he is certainly capable and got all top grades in those in-depth reference classes, but she prefers working in-depth, one-on-one with her customers, and one at a time. The staff and demanding customers will likely, then, chew her up and spit her out. Her only success will be escaping successfully to her car at 5:30 and she'll spend most of her energy keeping her resume polished. Our second hero is a Type A multitasker who loves a challenge and welcomes all tough questions—the bigger and more frequent the better! Change is his middle name. He thrives on examining the process and streamlining it, so there's more time to add new, innovative tasks to his list. If he doesn't die of boredom in the village, they'll probably tar, feather, and run him out of town.

Culture controls how you feel at work. Comfortable? Challenged? Supported? Scared? Clumsy? Unappreciated? Underutilized? Frustrated? Angry? As the team leader, it probably isn't hard to pick the words out of that list that you want your team to feel. So how do you accomplish that?

First, you recognize how important a healthy culture is. You talk about it. You identify it. You define it around the group's values. Then you put your money where your mouth is and you make it so. In the next few weeks, you'll consider how to identify what your team values. You'll learn to see how those values—and their resulting culture—are part of who you all are, even without lifting a finger. And finally you'll consider action, intentions, and practices that can keep your team culturally fit. These aren't just empty words. Ignored, as Drucker said, culture can manage you and your team, and not necessarily for the better. But, with strong leadership in place, you can reap the benefits of a healthy culture and create an environment where everyone can flourish.

1. You can attract talent! The best people want more than a salary and good benefits. They want an environment they can enjoy and succeed in.
2. You can retain talent! How likely is your staff to stay if they don't enjoy where they are?
3. You can engage your team! Engagement creates greater productivity, which can impact your organization in innumerable ways.
4. You can create energy that builds momentum! Energy is contagious and will build on itself, reinforcing the culture and the attractiveness of your team.
5. You can change people's view of work! Would you rather see work as drudgery or a joy? Which do you think your team members would prefer? Which will bring you closer to the greatness you seek?
6. You'll create synergy! When people have the opportunity to communicate and get to know each other better, they will find new connections. These connections will lead to new ideas and new ideas will lead to greater productivity—and a greater team.[4]

EXERCISES

-41-

1. **Culture is made up** of behavioral descriptors or constants that team members *believe* are true or are normal. List ten descriptors or terms that your team would probably use to describe its *normal* culture.

   _____
   _____
   _____
   _____

2. **People believe things are** normal because actions support those beliefs. Next to each of the ten descriptors you just listed, add at least one action that supports it and keeps people believing that it really is part of the culture. For example, if you'd listed *honesty,* the action that supports that might be that staff members who are caught lying are fired.

   _____
   _____
   _____
   _____

3. **Let's test these beliefs.** Circle the descriptors that you believe actually *do* reflect the culture of your organization, and then list next to each the values they represent that drive the group.

   _____
   _____
   _____
   _____
   _____

4. **Now, look at the** ones you didn't circle. These are the cultural descriptors that people might think are true—but they are not a real match to your team's values. List five reasons why staff members come to believe that a certain characteristic is part of a culture, when it really isn't.

   _____
   _____
   _____
   _____
   _____

5. **Finally, look hard at** those five reasons and note next to each as many ideas as you can think of to make the misconceptions stop. What *action* can be taken to ensure that true culture does reflect real team values—and how can you correct the misconceptions floating around out there?

   _____
   _____
   _____
   _____
   _____

TEAM ENVIRONMENT

WEEK TWO | **VALUING VALUES**

We've all heard these refrains lately, and each time they're spoken, they can easily make team leaders cringe. *Everything has changed around here! I can't keep up these days, everything is different! This isn't the job I signed up for, the whole place is different! I didn't go to school for this, everything . . . everything has changed!* These comments often reflect a sense of panic, chaos, and uncertainty that can derail even the most strategic team plan for success.

The truth is, *everything* has not changed. Your values, in all likelihood, are the same as they were when your library opened its doors. Leaders who believe this, profess this, and center their team on this reality can help everyone weather any real changes that come along. By making certain that your team's culture is based firmly on its values, you can together weather any period of change, and still emerge as strong or stronger than you were before.

Here's a simplistic—but applicable—comparison to consider. In a happy, healthy marriage, the two people involved likely start out sharing critical values. Loyalty, love, support, caring, and strength might be included in that list. Fast-forward through about twenty years and consider the changes they might experience. Death of parents, financial crises, housing emergencies, layoffs, the marriage—and divorce—of children, and frightening medical diagnoses are just a few possibilities. How in the world could they weather those changes and remain strong? You guessed it. By relying on their loyalty, love, support, caring, strength. By relying on their values!

How does that relate to your team and your workplace? When I started in libraries in the 1980s, our work was based largely on the values of

HIRING? LOOK FOR THESE TOP TEN VALUES

Identifying these "Top 10 Values Employers Seek" can be accomplished by asking the right questions. Consider these examples when you create your next interview.

1. **Strong Work Ethic:** Tell me about a time when you exceeded your normal work hours on your own time in order to complete an important task.
2. **Dependability:** How does your dependability show?
3. **Positive Attitude:** At a time when your other team members were really feeling down about something, how did you model a positive attitude?
4. **Adaptability:** Describe a major change to which you had to adapt—that required that you do things very differently—how did you adapt?
5. **Honesty:** Give an example of a time when it was very difficult to be honest, but you were. Why?
6. **Self-Motivated:** How have you demonstrated initiative in the past year?
7. **Desire to Grow and Learn:** Describe the past year's development. What have you done, specifically, to continue growing and learning?
8. **Confidence:** What does your self-confidence look like in the workplace?
9. **Professional:** Things happen between individuals working closely together that can often be taken personally. Tell us about one that happened recently and describe how you avoided taking it personally by remaining professional.
10. **Loyalty:** How have you backed up your boss or your organization recently?[16]

freedom, community, service, and respect. Over the past quarter-century we've changed the way we work, we've changed the tools with which we work, we've changed the types of people that we try to hire, we've changed the way we fund much of what we do, and we've changed our understanding of what our communities expect and need from us. What hasn't changed? Right. We still base everything, every day on freedom, community, service, and respect. This is a very critical point that is often overlooked and, on the contrary, should be remembered every day—to help steer us through the unrelenting sea of changes we have and will continue to face.

Many people doze during the first hour or so of strategic planning. For them, the *mission, vision, and values* part of the discussion is tantamount to the first few episodes of a new *American Idol* season. Sort of important, yes, but wake me when we get to the good part. That's why so many teams

lack the strength that values can provide to keep the ship steady through the rapids. Statistics and studies have proven this concept to be true. In his newest book, *Great By Choice*, noted author Jim Collins and his staff researched thousands of companies they dubbed "10Xers."[7] They called them this because the levels of success these companies reached "beat their industries' averages by at least 10 times."[8] And guess what? In spite of all of the changes, demands, and shifts of what went on around them, they succeeded because they never changed what really drove them internally.

Collins debunked the assumption that "radical change on the outside required radical change on the inside. The 10X cases changed *less* in reaction to their changing world than the comparison cases. Just because our environment is rocked by dramatic change does not mean that you should inflict radical change upon yourself!"[9] Team leaders who can keep their staff aware of and focused

THREE CORE VALUES TO HAVE

CHARACTER

Ethical integrity; an emphasis on seeking solutions, not casting blame; welcoming and accepting honest communication—including differences of opinion; doing the "right thing."

COMPETENCE

An entrepreneurial spirit that seeks to innovate; creativity; decisiveness; initiative for self-growth; leadership; flexibility; consistent application of best practices.

COMMITMENT

Loyalty to the team and the organization; zeal in representing the team and the organization; responsibility; encouraging and empowering others to succeed; pledge to do what we promise and helping others do the same.[17]

on their critical shared values can keep the panic and fear of change at bay.

For leaders who are sold, then, on how their team can benefit from the strength that comes from shared values, the next step is to answer . . . what are those values? Consider them in terms of everyone's contribution to your team's success:

1. Organizational Values: Hopefully, your organization already has—and keeps current—stated mission, vision, and values statements as part of its strategic planning and management system. If they exist, you have a strong base on which to build your team's plans and against which to measure your team's success. You can make decisions, allocate resources, and take action, following a path that directly supports the purpose of your library. In the rare cases where that foundation

doesn't already exist, it's a good idea to see if you can initiate a process to create it. Yours won't be the only team flying blind if there's not a stated overarching direction to follow.

2. Team Values: Whether your organization provides strong direction or not, successful team leaders still need to lead their group in discussion to consider and articulate team values, from which true goals can be established. Stated team values can incorporate everything from shared decision making to effective delegation, open communication, respect for diversity, or motivational options. Once agreed upon, these values can be the rock that steadies the team through their uncertain future.

3. Leadership Values: Regarding the effective running of the team, what should leaders value? Again, the potential list is endless. Fairness, respect, encouragement, support, training, professionalism, and coaching are the most common winners in this category. Be sure before establishing your list you ask your team what they value in a leader.

4. Personal Values: As the leader, it's often your interpersonal skills that can set you apart as someone who seeks team success over personal achievement. Oddly, what many leaders miss is the fact that the former actually leads to the latter. Remember, though, that "neglecting the interpersonal aspect of the job can leave you hamstrung by miscommunication and substandard team performance!"[10] Consider how you set goals, communicate expectations, manage projects, motivate team members, watch for team opportunities, and solve problems, just to name a view options.[11]

Here's a final focus point for team leaders. When you're faced with a lot to consider, such as the articulation of a concept as critical as values from an organizational, group, individual, and management perspective, sometimes the view can get cloudy. Here's a two-part focus to consider. Strictly from the point of view of team leadership, two values stand out as, arguably, the most critical to promote. With these two understood by your team and demonstrated relentlessly by actions, your group's stability will be enhanced beyond measure.

Trust. "When all is said and done, no matter how far an individual gets, they almost always come crashing down if they are not trustworthy. When this happens, it's major. Careers end."[12] Model, promise, and deliver trustworthy leadership at all times. How can this show? "Never be dishonest or lie. Never fail to make your team aware of the truth. Do what you say you're going to do, when you say you're going to do it."[13]

Integrity. "Some people . . . will tell you (with a wink) that these days, nice guys finish last. If that's what you've been hearing, may we respectfully suggest you're running with the wrong crowd?"[14] Team members with the benefit of having leaders with high integrity have confidence that the group will "stay the course. Consistency is the mark of a person who is not impacted by changes outside . . . but who is inseparably connected to his or her inner, moral values."[15]

Knowing *everything* won't change will help your team adjust to whatever does.

SUGGESTED READING

Collins, Jim. *Great by Choice: Uncertainty, Chaos, and Luck—Why Some Thrive Despite Them All.* New York: HarperCollins, 2011.

EXERCISES

-42-

Use these exercises to self-examine five of the core team leaders' values described this week.

If you feel shortcomings in any are in evidence, design your own next steps to work on improving them! A key to remember—try to answer these questions from the perspective of your *team's* view of your leadership.

1. **First, reread the definition** of *character* from "Three Core Values to Have." Then list at least five ways you demonstrate character as a value.

   _____

   _____

   _____

2. **Next, reread the definition** of *competence* from "Three Core Values to Have." Then list at least five ways you demonstrate competence as a value.

   _____

   _____

   _____

3. **Then reread the definition** of *commitment* from "Three Core Values to Have." Then list at least five ways you demonstrate commitment as a value.

   _____

   _____

   _____

   _____

4. **What have you done** lately to instill and earn the trust of your team?

   _____

   _____

   _____

   _____

5. **If your team members** were asked to explain why they consider you a leader of high integrity, how might they support that conclusion?

   _____

   _____

   _____

   _____

6. **This week's lesson was** all about why values are important. If you believe that everything impacting your team will continue to change—except values—summarize here how you can use that reality to your team's benefit.

   _____

   _____

   _____

   _____

   _____

TEAM ENVIRONMENT

WEEK THREE | ## LANGUAGE, LEGENDS, MYTHS, AND REALITY

There was a director I've been told about who could always be found professing his dedication to shared leadership. In lectures, at conferences, and during staff meetings, he always began and ended his comments by expressing heartfelt thanks for all the help his staff provided him in making the tough decisions. They were all in this together, he'd proclaim, and he couldn't do it without them. In reality, he was rarely even in the building, and when he was, his door was closed (except to his inner circle) and he'd let his assistant answer (read: screen) all his calls. At one point, he even issued an edict that, if any staff members wanted to speak to him, they'd have to do it through their manager. *No one* could contact him directly. True story.

You can't talk a culture into being. You have to make it so with your actions.

What, then, is cultural reality? If you think about it, over the past two chapters you've been considering this question from two diametrically opposed viewpoints. First, you read that culture is what people *believe* to be true about the workplace. That doesn't sound like much of a firm foundation, does it? Then, you read that there *really is* a foundation to culture—and that it is a set of values. So, which is it? Concepts and opinions or real, solid values? If today is the day you plan to begin cultivating a professional, respectful culture in which your team can thrive, you need to make sure that what they hear and what they see are one and the same. Actions, not mythology, speak the loudest.

BRING CULTURE ALIVE

If values = actions = culture, consider what actions you can take or support to build the healthy culture you want to surround your team.

- **We value ideas:** Have regularly scheduled meetings, with agendas created to always include time for brainstorming and idea-sharing. Report regularly on ideas that were implemented and celebrate their success!

- **We value diversity:** Train hiring supervisors how to legally and responsibly screen applicants with an openness to diversifying the staff. When reviewing interviewing or hiring recommendations, ask what diversity considerations were made.

- **We value respect:** Challenge inappropriate behavior, language, and disrespectful treatment of team members swiftly and consistently. Don't look the other way or make excuses for outbursts. No, "blowing off steam" at a coworker is not allowed in a respectful culture.

- **We value professionalism:** Define and then enforce the trappings of a professional team. That might mean tackling the often challenging issues of dress code, manners, punctuality, and gossip. While these issues are easy and often preferable to ignore, doing so can result in the opposite culture that you seek.

- **We value innovation:** Don't slink away from needed change, even if it means replacing an outdated but comfortable activity with a new, more relevant service. Sure, he loves leading the mystery book discussion group and has been doing it for many years, but look how few people are still coming. What other more current and appealing service could he be doing?

- **We value a healthy culture:** Have your team describe what that means and what it will require, then hold them to that expectation. Make contrary behavior a performance issue and deal with poor performance accordingly.

"Simply describing a desirable outcome won't make it happen."[18] Effective leaders bring values to life every day. Culture is born of what really happens. At best, what happens will reflect your team's values, not contradict them. Remember, "you don't create culture. Culture happens. It's the by-product of consistent behavior. If you encourage people to share, and you give them the freedom to share, then sharing will be built into your culture. If you reward trust, then trust will be built into your culture."[19] Although contributions to developing culture can come from anywhere, it's the leader, with the power of reward and punishment, who sets the tone.

To accomplish that, all you have to do is rewrite history. "Every company has its own language, its own version of its own history (its myths), and its own heroes and villains (its legends), both historical and contemporary."[20] If you start today, and if your team is with you, together you can make your language, legends, and myths tell your *real* story.

Here's a language example. Let's talk job titles. "What is it with the library profession and our obsession with individual titles? Is it insecurity? Fear? Elitism? Maybe the focus on titles is not entirely our fault?"[21] Maybe it wasn't originally but, now, today, you can change that *language* barrier to a healthy team culture by "what each person brings to the table,"[22] not by how many (or which) Roman numerals follow their title. I heard of a library once in which assistants were not allowed to answer reference questions because they were all assigned to the circulation depart-

REWRITE THE LEGENDS

Legends you may not be so crazy about may have formed your team's current culture, but you can change that! All you have to do is update them with real, positive actions that match the culture you're seeking. You change culture with stories. Try this:

- Do dramatic, story-worthy things that represent the culture you want to create. Then let other people tell stories about it. (If you're trying to create a more employee-focused culture, instead of making a bride work the day before her wedding, give her the week off.)

- Find other people who do story-worthy things that represent the culture you want to create. Then tell stories about them. (If you're trying to create a culture based on open communication, give awards at monthly staff meetings for team members who proactively shared information that improved service by sending their team members "heads up" e-mails or phone calls.)

We live by stories. We tell them, repeat them, listen to them carefully, and act in accordance with them.[25]

ment. Even a simple inquiry, such as "Where are the cookbooks?" had to be referred to a librarian, because you needed a master's degree for that title. If you're thinking that might make a bit of sense, you need to know that every single nonfiction book was in the basement of this facility. Every one. Not a cookbook to be found on the first floor. It's hard to support a culture in which what you're called determines your ability to point out the stairs.

Legends always remind me of playing telephone because, as the years go by, they resemble less and less the actual person credited with so

strongly impacting the culture. Whether they're pictured as heroes or villains (and that can fluctuate, based on the teller of the story), folklore surrounding their achievements, disasters, or antics can guide, predict, and prevent more progress than the individual themselves ever could. If you're considering attempting to discredit old legends, save your breath. More productively, create new ones and tell their stories over and over until your culture begins to shift around the new reality. When team members do something significant that supports your newly realized value system, reward them, celebrate them, and give their achievements a place in the new legends of your culture. Before long, attempts to reawaken those names of old will be met with . . . "Who?"

A recent article in *U.S. News*[23] offered some excellent examples of workplace myths, and it's pretty clear how each one can have a clear impact on the culture of your team's environment.

1. *If your boss is unfair or hostile, you might have legal recourse.* This is only true if the behavior is due to your race, gender, religion, or other protected class. Otherwise, being a jerk is not illegal.
2. *HR has to keep things confidential if you request it.* There are cases where HR is required to report things (such as concerns about harassment or illegal behavior) no matter how vehemently the employee requests confidentiality.
3. *You can't get unemployment benefits if you're fired.* In most states, being fired for poor performance won't generally make you ineligible for unemployment benefits.
4. *If you disagree with a performance review, you should refuse to sign it.* Refusing to sign has no practical purpose and will just get you labeled as adversarial and difficult.
5. *Salaries are set fairly.* Salaries vary for all sorts of reasons. Maybe one person was a better negotiator than the other when being hired, or maybe the job market was tighter.

Communication is your best arsenal here. In attempting to re-create a mythless culture (otherwise known as honest), "practice pro-active information sharing and create forums"[24] in which questions or rumors can be openly addressed. Openly inquire, at every opportunity, "What are you hearing? Are there any questions or crazy answers out there that we can dispel?" What might happen if you opened your team meeting by asking "What's the craziest rumor you've heard this week?" By showing your willingness to hear—and respond honestly—to such early myth building, you might just be starting your own, current-day legend of the team leader who really cared what everyone thought.

Imagine the cultural impact of that!?

EXERCISES

43

Use this opportunity to both examine your team's culture and determine how you can impact it for the better.

1. **Describe an element of** your team's culture that's driven by language or terminology. For example, do you only call a small portion of your team "professionals"? First, list the negative impact the language has. How does it affect your team's morale and motivation? Think hard. You will certainly find at least one example of troublesome *cultural language*.

    _____

    _____

    _____

2. **How can you change** the language you've described so that it has a stronger, more positive effect? What new terms or words or titles could you use—and what difference might that make?

    _____

    _____

    _____

3. **Describe an element of** your team's culture that's tied to a legend—someone or something that may or may not have happened long ago—that still has a deleterious effect on the group. Hopefully, you also have positive legends, but for this exercise, we're looking for opportunities for positive change, so think of a damaging one.

    _____

    _____

    _____

4. **How can you change** the negative impact of that story? Maybe talk openly about it and bring some reality into the picture? Consider the time period and perspective of hindsight? Maybe think of a more positive legend that you can bring in to slowly begin to replace it? (This could even include inviting a retired team member back to tell some new, motivational stories to take its place. For example, how did the brave team members of "old" get through their initial trepidation about computerization?)

    _____

    _____

    _____

5. **Describe an element of** your team's culture that's built on an out-and-out myth. How is it still thriving and holding back your team's progress? What makes it so strong?

    _____

    _____

    _____

6. **How can you change** the perception or understanding of that myth and why would you bother? What positive cultural change just might come about if it were debunked?

    _____

    _____

    _____

    _____

TEAM ENVIRONMENT

HOME SWEET HOME (ENVIRONMENT AND SYMBOLS)

She turned down an intriguing, high-profile, high-paying job offer once based solely on the condition of the work space she was shown during the interview tour. The hiring team was dumbfounded. After searching high and low, they couldn't believe their good luck at finding such a perfect candidate. And she said *No*? Why? The candidate told me afterward it was simple. The work space was unhealthy. The messes she saw in office after office warned her to stay away from an organization that was screaming unprofessional, afraid of change, and lacking in leadership. After spending several weeks now considering all the factors, real and legendary, that can affect culture, it's time to close with a touch of reality. What does your team's work space say? Or scream?

Symbols or artifacts play an important role in culture, and in the workplace the primary physical symbol to be dealt with is the work space itself. Look around. Check the condition, arrangement, and functionality of the places in which your team is expected to work. If you can offer your visitor a chair without first cleaning it off, if you can pour a cup of coffee without first retrieving and washing abandoned cups, and if you can put your hand on last month's invoices without holding a séance, then this week's work will probably make you feel pretty good. But if you're like the rest of us, read on. You can do a lot to improve your team's culture through symbols!

For a lot of team leaders, time spent concentrating on the more serious, service-related issues leaves little time left over for something as innocuous as a messy desk. With that approach as a guide, before you can say "I know it's here somewhere," the team's entire environment can look like your teenage son's bedroom. If you're still thinking, "So what? I have more important things to think about," consider this. "The design of office interiors can have a deep consequence on the mood and production of employees! Keeping a well-maintained workplace is significant in regards to health and safety . . . and can actually impact welfare and efficiency."[26] With your team starting out on its quest for greatness, which do you think will move them along faster . . . organized, supportive, inspiring, and comfortable spaces to call their own or dusty, chaotic, uncomfortable, and unwelcoming ones? Don't be ready to ignore the trappings of environment on your team's culture, and don't be afraid to start making changes right now. Unlike arguing with that teenager, improvements won't be as difficult to negotiate or to see put into action.

Samantha Hines, author of *Productivity for Librarians*, offers plenty of reasons for team leaders to request and require healthy work spaces. "Having a pleasant physical space to work can aid in motivation. Keeping things clean, organized and relaxing can save time. In addition, a tidy work area can prevent procrastination."[27] Still, explaining why the work environment matters can seem like a cakewalk, you may be thinking, compared to actually making improvements happen. Hines suggests one method that, because of its simplicity, might provide a good place to start when conveying expectations to your team: use TRAF.[28]

T – Toss it out. *If you'll not likely need it again, get rid of it.*

R – Refer it. *If someone else might need it, give it to them.*

A – Act on it. *Do whatever it represents, then toss it out.*

F – File it. *If it's too early to do the first three options, it only takes a few seconds to file it away. You'll know where*

WORK SPACE ENHANCEMENTS TO CONSIDER

Providing a culture in which people can do their best work sometimes means retooling the physical space. If possible, try some of these tips to make your team's work areas more productivity-friendly.

- **PROVIDE QUIET SPACE SOMEWHERE:** Creative thinkers often need solitude, so be sure there is someplace available so that, when needed, they can block out distractions.
- **OFFER AN INFORMAL GATHERING SPOT:** Employers often see water-cooler chats and break-time conversations as wasted productivity, but they're actually some of the main conduits of office communication and innovation. Make sure your team has access to spaces that encourage networking.
- **KEEP EMPLOYEES COMFORTABLE:** A controversial 2004 study showed that keeping an office at 77 degrees, versus 68 degrees, made employees 46 percent more productive! The underlying idea is clear—comfortable employees are more productive.[34]

it is (not on your desk or in piles on the floor) when you do need it.

Or, as one colleague more succinctly, if inelegantly, put it, "When in doubt, throw it out."[29]

In case you're beginning to drift, perhaps it's time for another true story. The director's requests for a cleanup of the work room had gone unanswered for so long that he gave up. If they wanted to work in that mess, let them. There was nothing specific enough about their behavior in the evaluation form to support disciplinary action, and besides, these *you're a slob* conversations

THE HEALTHY WORKPLACE

How can an office or team work room be healthy? It can be clean, livable, useable, attractive, comfortable, and free of pests, mold, or dust, just to name a few descriptors. What impact might that have on your team?

A Healthy Workplace Will:

- Improve employee health outcomes
- Make it easier to attract and retain qualified employees
- Lower absenteeism
- Reduce health benefit costs
- Enhance morale
- Reduce risk of injury
- Improve job performance[35]

were becoming more and more uncomfortable and awkward. And, truly, they were outstanding employees—if you just kept your eyes closed in their office. The since-retired director told me that it wasn't until he was trying to fill some open positions on his team that he finally realized how wrong he'd been to give up.

No one would take the jobs. After just one look at the mess they'd be inheriting, they ran the other way. It was too much. It was too daunting. It was too overwhelming. It seemed that candidate after candidate just couldn't picture themselves succeeding in that environment. Following a serious intervention, the room was re-outfitted with only the necessary supplies, furniture, and equipment. And it was beyond clean. The next candidate offered the job accepted on the spot. Why? *He could picture success in the space.* "People act out the roles in which they are placed. We

match our expectations of behavior to the surroundings in which that behavior occurs."[30]

By now, you should be sold. While much that affects your team's culture is too ephemeral to actually touch, here's something that isn't. Here's a chance to show them their value and your respect for it. Here's your chance to not just ask them to be great, but to treat them and their work as though they already are. So where do you start? You start with yourself.

"If you are looking to reinvent your workplace into a productive, balanced place to be, you will have to start with your own work habits. You will need to be the one that sets the example and the tone for the workplace. As silly as it may sound, your attitude and aptitude for productive work will do more to guide your team than your words ever will."[31] In the 1950s, lots of moms used to say *Do as I say, not as I do.* That didn't work then and it doesn't work now.

And setting a professional tone for your team won't be the only benefit of you, as the leader, reorganizing your approach to what you do. You'll also benefit by becoming more productive in your own right and, in all likelihood, actually feeling and acting more positively.[32]

Whether you like—or intend—it or not, "your office is a reflection of your capabilities. Even though a messy desk isn't a sign of a character flaw, it does tend to give others the impression that the job is too much for you to handle, you can't make decisions, you are not doing the job, or all of the above."[33]

None of which are the cultural symbols of a great team or leadership environment.

SUGGESTED READING

Hines, Samantha. *Productivity for Librarians: How to Get More Done in Less Time.* Oxford: Chandos, 2010.

EXERCISES

1. **Take a long, good,** honest look around your office. Think about what you see and what it tells others about you. Find at least five "symbols" of your work area that you could improve. Make notes of how you'll do it and what positive, potential impact that will have on the message you're contributing to your team's culture.

_____
_____
_____
_____
_____
_____

2. **Repeat question 1 for** the work space(s) your team members use.

_____
_____
_____
_____
_____
_____

3. **Repeat question 1 for** the public space(s) your team members use.

_____
_____
_____
_____
_____
_____

4. **Repeat question 1 for** the meeting/thinking/collaborating space(s) you and your team members use.

_____
_____
_____
_____
_____
_____

5. **Repeat question 1 for** the social or relaxation space(s) you and your team members use.

_____
_____
_____
_____
_____
_____

For each of the above steps, don't forget the most important part. _Think_ about the group's culture and how it is impacted by symbols. That will help you continue to focus on the value of a healthy environment!

INTENTIONAL SUCCESS

| ## BE A NEW LEADER, EVEN IF YOU'RE NOT

Congratulations!
Today is your day.
You're off to Great Places!
You're off and away!
You have brains in your head.
You have feet in your shoes
You can steer yourself
Any direction you choose.
You're on your own. And you know what you know.
And YOU are the guy who'll decide where to go![1]

—Dr. Seuss

Wow. If you look back through this book's table of contents and consider all you've read about team building so far, it can seem a bit overwhelming! Recruiting, Narrowing, Interviewing, Blending, Learning, Communication, Resolutions, Actions, Planning, and Culture . . . where do you start? Perhaps, before you began this yearlong development journey, you thought most of your time would be spent focused on time cards or schedules or weeding collections? Now I hope you know, if you remember nothing else, that's it's really all about people.

With the opportunity, privilege, and responsibility of leading your team members through the days, weeks, and years of their careers, your *real* job—the important part—is all about those people who depend on you to help them be great. So where *do* you start? In this final month of the book, you'll get some tips on how to sort through all of these roles and challenges and focus on the right parts at the right times. There are things you can do today to position your team well for the long term. There are other actions to take and consider in order to move productively from year to year. And certainly, there's a lot you can do today—to be ready for tomorrow.

ADVICE TO NEW LEADERS

BE. DO. LEARN.

- **BE:** Be authentic, be credible, and be able to value the dignity of those who work with you.
- **DO:** Focus on two fundamental sets of tasks: coping with complexity and coping with change. Both involve deciding what needs to be done, developing the capacity to get it done, and ensuring that it is done.
- **LEARN:** To lead effectively, you must face each day as an active learner. The rate of change today requires that each of us become a frantic learner. Leaders respond to change by learning something.[6]

EVERY DAY, A POSITIVE FOCUS

Organizational development consultant Maureen Sullivan offers these methods of staying positive, which is part of the "promise of appreciative inquiry" she advocates. Whether facing long- or short-term goals and challenges, apply these to keep strength and success as your team's overall focus.

- Begin *any* planned or unplanned change with an exploration of the best of what is. Focus on strengths, values, sources of pride, and your best experiences.
- Drop the *devil's advocate* approach in favor of the *angel's advocate* one.
- Involve the whole team in identifying the core elements or values that give life to the organization. This set of values can then be translated into a set of behaviors for the team to practice.
- Close meetings and other activities with a discussion (and celebration) of what worked well.
- Introduce, support, and perpetuate learning and development plans.
- Remain always mindful of the language used by the team. Words are powerful and convey reality.
- Expect the best performance and assume that everyone has the best intentions. It's always a good place to start.[7]

This final month of the book will give you a chance to catch your breath and to set some priorities. One thing's for sure. You can't do it all at once. You can't even do most of it every single day. But you *can* move consistently forward and develop your team's success intentionally, passionately, and decisively. And you *can* succeed! We'll start with some generalities, first, during this week's hour, then move on to some more specific actions you can take to chart long- and short-term achievements. As with anything else in life, it's best to start simply. Shared in an online blog[2] about team leadership, these steps can prepare you well for everything that will come after them.

1. Recognize that you are not alone!
2. Keep the end in mind and practice patience—daily.
3. Consider setbacks as opportunities.
4. Persevere with confidence.
5. Keep learning.

Realize first that you need to set some clear goals for yourself. One, I hope, will be to continue

your hourly commitment to continuing to develop your skills as a leader. One of the best ways to do this is to create your own, personal development plan. With this plan outlined and in place, you can move forward to implement what you've learned in this book for the benefit of your team. While facing challenges in real life, you often hear about people getting the advice to take care of themselves first. Without strength in leadership, even the most well-meaning, well-intentioned team can go astray.

"It's never too soon or too late to pull together your own personal leadership development plan. Whether you are just out of school and beginning your career or whether you are a seasoned veteran, a *plan* can pull everything together for you."[3] It's the twenty-first century. What is required today to keep, grow, and lead a strong team is different than it was not so many years ago. Hopefully, this book has helped you to clarify what needs to happen within your team. Start first by determining what *you* need to do to make it so.

According to a study by the American Management Association, modern-day leaders can't go far wrong by concentrating their efforts on developing today's critical skills, called "the Four C's. Skills such as these—critical thinking and problem solving, communication, collaboration and creativity and innovation, will become even more important as the years go by."[4] Maybe another workbook is in order.

If you've developed—and I hope you have—the valuable skill of setting aside weekly time for your own growth, don't let that go to waste once you've finished this book. Instead, write your own plan for the coming year. In this week's exercises, you'll see how. Once you've completed your own, personal leadership development plan, pick one of the topics you've selected in which to grow and, very simply, break it down into twelve subsections. Then take each one of those subsections and (at a rate of one a week) consider:

1. Week 1: What strengths do I already have in this area, on which I can build?
2. Week 2: What aspects of this topic leave me room for development?
3. Week 3: What resources can I use to achieve that development?
4. Week 4: How can I apply what I've learned to support my team better?

Month after month, you can continue the development habit you've started and, year after year, you can add new areas in which to grow. Remember, "there is no right or wrong way to use your Personal Leadership Development Plan, once it's created. The only 'wrong way' is not to create one at all."[5]

EXERCISES

-45-

Follow these steps to see how easy it can be to create your own personal leadership plan.[8]

    If you chart your own ongoing development first, it's going to be easier to work with your team on goal-setting and building the skills needed to reach those goals.

1. **CLARIFY YOUR VISION AND VALUES** – What is most important to you? What principles and ideals do you most cherish? List them all here, and then identify your top three. Expand a bit on what those top three professional values mean to you.

    _____
    _____
    _____

2. **DESCRIBE YOUR GOALS** – Think about what your goals are in terms of five levels: *individual (self-improvement), interpersonal (relationship-improvement), team (for organizational impact), community (to be a force for good), and professional (have a positive impact on your library)*. For each goal you listed, under each heading, answer: Why is it important? What benefit will be achieved by your reaching it?

    _____
    _____
    _____

3. **TAKE ACTION** – Next to each goal, write what you have to do to reach it. Include changes you might need to make. What challenging assignments might you undertake? What mentoring and support will you seek? What additional training might you need? Considering the coming year as your plan period, put a completion date next to each action.

    _____
    _____
    _____
    _____

4. **TRACK YOUR PROGRESS** – For each goal, note how you'll know when it's been achieved and when you will know. (Don't forget to transfer these "checkup" dates to your daily work calendar, so you can keep tabs on your progress.)

    _____
    _____
    _____
    _____

5. **PLAN TO GET HELP** – It's out there. Use it. The stronger you can make yourself, the stronger and more successful you can make your team! List names next to each goal of specific people and the date by which you'll talk to each person to enlist their help with reaching your goals.

    _____
    _____
    _____
    _____

In the next weeks, you'll move on to setting goals (long- and short-term) for your team!

INTENTIONAL SUCCESS

| ## THIS TIME, NEXT YEAR (SETTING LONG-TERM GOALS)

Usually, somewhere in one's fifties, the concept of short- and long-term goals becomes glaringly apparent. OK, so we can't go without sleep any longer, eat anything and everything we're offered, and worry about money tomorrow. Life begins to clarify the reality that it's time to set some goals. Long term—maybe it's time to concentrate on getting healthy. Short term—not smoking and a little exercise probably wouldn't hurt. There's a professional parallel to this kind of thinking.

If you've worked your way through this book over the past year, your head is probably swimming with concepts, challenges, ideas, and maybe even fears. Communication, hiring, discipline, salaries, job titles, mentoring, and on and on. To bring it all together, it's time to narrow a few things down.

If this book was about theory, multiple options for moving forward could be introduced at this point. But it's not. This book is designed to be a practical, applicable, usable tool for making teams great. As such, the most succinct and intentional step to be recommended at this point, when a leader is ready to begin a new, development focus, is to start with fine-tuning something you may have been using for years—a performance evaluation.

Often misunderstood and all too frequently misused, this tool can help you clear the cobwebs and sharpen a focus between you and every single member of your team regarding what actually does come next. And, most important, what everyone's expected contribution to that *next* really is. "The need to understand each person's role, how that role is translated into a job designation, and how it relates to the goals of the larger organization"[9] is

HELPING OTHERS LOOK AHEAD

It's not easy to look too far down the road. Great team leaders can help their team members develop their long-term goals by setting the stage through action and inspiration. So that your team members are open to and ready for future planning, consider these steps to drawing a positive long-term picture of the future.

- ESTABLISH AND COMMUNICATE A CLEAR VISION
- STIMULATE TEAM MEMBERS TO DEVELOP NEW SKILLS
- HELP TEAM MEMBERS TO OVERCOME MISTAKES AND FAILURES
- LEAD BY EXAMPLE
- SHARE AND CELEBRATE ALL SUCCESSES
- EMBRACE CHANGE[14]

a critical element of the accountability that must follow. There are books by the hundreds on how to conduct staff evaluations. Forms can be found on the Internet. Advice can be found at the water cooler. Horror stories abound almost everywhere.

For the positive, motivational purposes of your first step in team greatness, keep your focus sharp. Great evaluations involve analyzing, questioning, listening, and planning. If there are poor performance issues to be dealt with, handle them effectively, efficiently, and without rancor. Focus on the future. Focus on your plan for greatness. Where do you start? Once again, you start at the beginning, with mission.

One development tool explains it this way: "As you may be aware, most organizations have a mission statement. The purpose of this statement is to communicate to the public what the organization is committed to doing."[10] With mission clarity in hand, you and your team members can move forward, assessing opportunities for the group and for each person, and identifying a course of long-term goals to motivate, encourage, and ensure success. Motivation is another by-product of focus that can be a welcome and valuable asset to have on your side, as you begin leading your team forward.

According to development experts Schrieber and Shannon,[11] the cycle of motivation can follow many steps: commitment (which is clarified with a stated mission), reinforcement (that's your support, training, and encouragement), achievement (good news for your library), recognition (which spurs the cycle around again), more motivation, and a growth of involvement in the team. Look back to the starting point. Clarify mission with each person, then set those long-term goals that set their feet on the path.

You'll need a few other supplies as you start this team journey. Each will bring you closer to the crossroads, where you can begin to set short-term goals or milestones for progress. One important tool you can't ignore is shared leadership and the implication of shared accountability that comes along with it. Teams are different than staffs, as was discussed early on in this text. Where staffs were individualized, often silo operators within a larger system, teams are called teams because they are reliant on one another. Don't leave the starting gate until this concept is clear and accepted as the norm. Communicate clearly, at this early stage of team development, that "rather than perpetuating the belief that a single individual with enormous leadership abilities is the formal leader who can take the team into future success, we are in need of other individuals—team members—to take on responsibility too"[12] for *shared leadership*.

Another tool to not leave home without is respect—for the differences, the sameness, the variety, the approaches, and the level of investment and understanding that will present differently for every single member of your team. You may have formed some solid ideas by now, I hope, on how to lead a great team. But don't ever forget that you can't just forge ahead with a single message and expect everyone to hear or receive it in the same way. Work with each team member, learn about them, understand and accept them all, so that you can reach each one on her or his own turf.

"Ducks are followers who want clear marching orders. Owls like to learn about your long-term vision. Woodpeckers scan data and nitpick before they decide to accept your argument. Chicken Littles are anxious pessimists who thrive on worst-case scenarios. Most people don't fall neatly into a specific category. But, as you get to know your team members and study how they process information, you can then customize your approach to gain their buy-in."[13] Lucky for you, you are planning to start (or even restart) at the beginning.

Begin your team's journey of greatness with a fresh evaluation for each team member. Create, write, share, discuss, and listen to each and every person, one-on-one, and use those conversations to set the stage for this new, focused endeavor you're beginning. With that foundation in place, next help your team members to consider and articulate their true missions. From that point, you can move forward setting long-term goals, for both the team and for each individual on their own professional path, and together you can move towards greatness.

IF YOU CAN'T SAY IT, SHOW IT

This action list is from an article called "Ten Things Bosses Never Tell Employees." Understandable, once you read them; some of these things would be hard to say. But, if they're true for you, there are ways to show these feelings. Find them.

- "I care about whether you like me." When I come off like a hard-___ who doesn't care about your opinion of me, it's an act. My business is an extension of myself. I want you to like it. And me.
- "I don't think I know everything." I don't offer you advice because I think I'm all knowing or all-powerful. I see something special in you, and I'm repaying the debt I owe to the people who helped me.
- "I think it's great when you're having fun." You don't have to lower your voice or pretend to be working hard when I walk by. I know it's possible to work hard and have a little fun at the same time. Before I got all serious, I used to work that way. When you enjoy what you do, it makes me feel a little better about our team.
- "I want to pay you more." I would love to be the employer of choice. I can't, mostly because of financial constraints.
- "I would love to turn you loose." You can't stand to be micromanaged. That's good, because I hate micromanaging. But freedom is earned, not given. Show me you can fly on your own and I'll gladly focus on something or someone else.
- "There are things I just can't tell you." Even though I would love to, I have limitations and expectations in my position, too.[15]

EXERCISES

-46-

To kick off your team's first year of development, you can host a workday focused on helping them create their individual mission statements.[16] With those in hand and with the clarity of long-term purpose that they represent as a foundation, you can next move through individual evaluations, analyses of strengths and weaknesses of your team members, and the all-important step of goal setting. This week's exercises will help you to do two things: (1) to see how you can lead that workday and process, and (2) to create your *own* mission statement in the process.

1. **Introduce the exercise. Draft** a brief outline here of what you will say to convey how important it is to focus on what each team member is committed to doing over the coming year. Then explain how a personal mission statement will help to guide their actions towards achieving their mission.

   _____
   _____
   _____
   _____
   _____
   _____

2. **Select action words. You'll** provide the team with a list of action words. You can tell them *"every mission requires action and action words are verbs. Review the list and select the three words that most inspire you."* Find, create, collect a list of words, and then select the three that most inspire you. (Throughout this week's homework, you'll actually be creating your own mission statement, which will help you to understand how to lead your team to do the same.)

   _____
   _____
   _____
   _____
   _____
   _____

3. **Identify core values. When** running this exercise for your team, you can say: *"Our actions are driven by our values. To that end, no mission statement would be complete without language to reflect personal/professional values. Review this list of values and select three that speak to you."* Find, create, collect a list of values, and take this next step in creating your mission statement. Select three with which you most strongly identify.

   _____
   _____
   _____
   _____
   _____

4. **Connect values and action.** When presenting this next step to your team, you might say: *"Now that you have selected your values and your actions, it is important to see if they pass the compatibility test. Combine each action you've selected with your values to see if they make sense, when working together in a sentence or phrase. In the event one or more verbs don't make sense, when paired with a value, it is important to determine which of the two words is more true to who you are. Keep that word, set aside the other, and identify a stronger word to replace it."* Do this step on your own now, to continue developing your mission statement.

_____
_____
_____
_____
_____
_____
_____
_____

5. **Identify the professional causes** to which you are committed. Explain this by saying, "*In a library work setting, this portion of the exercise might identify concepts such as catalog integrity, customer service, or safety, depending on each team member's position.*" You can explain this step by saying, "*As you think about what you want your professional life to be about, it is important to think about the causes in which you really believe. Where does your professional passion lie? Review the attached list of causes connected to our organization's purpose and select the three with which you most closely identify.*" Now, find, create, and collect a list of causes (intellectual freedom, literacy, customer service, financial management, etc.) of the many causes or purposes that drive your library's work. Select your three most compelling ones.

_____
_____
_____
_____
_____
_____
_____
_____

6. **Put it all together.** At this point, a mission statement can be written by combining all of the elements selected throughout the exercise. Direct your team members to "*pull together your mission statement by combining the sum of your verbs, values, and causes into a statement.*" Create your mission statement, refine or clarify it if necessary until it makes sense, and use it as an example when you help your team develop theirs.

_____
_____
_____
_____
_____
_____

Don't let these mission statements sit and collect dust. Review them, acknowledge them, and use them in the work you'll do one-on-one to set long-term goals.

Unable to ignore the challenge, while creating this exercise I decided to try it on myself, to see if it really worked. Also, I felt that, since you're being asked to create your own mission statement, to use as an example for your team, it might help if you had my statement, for your own example. Here's what I created:

MY ACTION WORDS – lead, motivate, support

MY VALUES – respect, honesty, commitment

MY CONNECTIONS – commitment to lead, respectful support, honest motivation

MY PROFESSIONAL CAUSES – staff development, leadership skills, clear visions

MY MISSION STATEMENT – I am committed to contribute my energies to develop respectful, honest, motivating leaders who offer a clear vision and then work to support their staff's achievement of it.

INTENTIONAL SUCCESS

| ## WHAT ABOUT TOMORROW?
(SETTING SHORT-TERM GOALS)

From personal experience, I can tell you that if you really stick to the South Beach Diet, you really can drop 10–15 pounds in just the first two weeks! After that, progress continues but at a slower pace, as the impact of your new habits becomes part of an overall nutritional approach. But, oh, those first two weeks! What a surprise! What a confidence builder! Who wouldn't stick with something when sure, quick progress is so visible?

As I was leaving a position where I'd worked with the best manager (still, to date) I've ever known, I was going to be assuming my first significant manager's job. Her advice to me was simple, but caught me off guard a bit. She told me to *give them something early*. I'd be in a honeymoon period, she explained, and should take advantage of that period to make some quick decisions and take actions that would give them each something they wanted. More valuable than words, she said, these decisive actions would demonstrate to them that I was listening, that I would follow up on promises and, most of all, that I cared about their concerns. Now, that made sense!

After working through the creation of individual mission statements and long-term goals, it's time to get down to business and start making some of what you've learned in this book actually happen. It's time for (as South Beach devotees say) Phase One!

Effective team leaders can successfully borrow from the business concept of "executive on boarding. Planning assiduously for one's first 100 days in a new job . . . it's important to get a head-start, especially on what's been going wrong . . . Early wins build credibility and confidence. They confirm that you are, indeed, right for the job [and for the team] . . . and they imbue

HOW CROSS-TRAINING BUILDS TEAM SPIRIT

If you want to build respect for one another's work and to cement a group vision, cross-training can bridge the gap between old, "silo staff members" and successful teams. How? Cross-training

Prevents stagnation

Offers learning and professional development opportunities

Rejuvenates all departments

Improves understanding of the parts and the whole

Leads to improved communication

Erases differences, enmity, and unhealthy competition

Increases knowledge, know-how, skills, and work performance

Improves overall motivation

Leads to—and strengthens—the sharing of goals and objectives[23]

a 'we can do it' spirit."[17] So, short-term, start with conversations that can reveal immediate needs, wants, or hopes and then find a way to make something happen for everyone.

Don't be dissuaded by the many other options available to you, as the team leader, when it comes to things you can start doing right away. Numerous as they are, they're only as useful as the difference they can begin to make right away for your team. The following are just a couple options that might get you started into action. Pick from these—or others—that match what your team needs most right now.

CROSS-TRAINING – One of the best ways to build understanding and camaraderie, both of which can become the foundation of team strength, is by breaking down the walls of misunderstanding between positions, job descriptions, and contribution. Consider including your own position in a round-robin of training, rotating the assignment of team leader on days when you're away. Don't just launch into this without a preamble, though. "Cross-training should be carefully planned and presented as a learning opportunity. Sending people to work in another department at a moment's notice is not what cross-training is about. Employees must 'buy' into the idea. They become 'partners.'"[18] The values to this exercise are many. They range from the simple—some people have actually never spoken to coworkers before, except in passing—to the sublime—"employees who think 'the grass is greener on the other side of the lawn' return to their job with a better attitude."[19]

In one library, the concept of a *welcome desk* provided an opportunity for cross-training in the most basic concepts of the library's work. Everyone, from the director to the maintenance people, was required to spend one hour each week at this central desk, welcoming customers and ensuring all questions were answered. The result was a new appreciation for the work of the library and for the contributions of each staff member. When a security person, for example, was asked how many babies were allowed in the story time room for the next program, he was amazed to hear the limit was thirty! After the program, he complimented the children's librarian, to whom he'd never really talked much before, on the amazing job she did handling the crowd! And that's just how one interaction ended. Dozens of other examples helped to bring the staff closer together and increase their respect and admiration for one another. And all this—in only one hour a week each!

INCREASING INVOLVEMENT – Every team has wallflowers, and no matter how you try to spin it (*they make other contributions that are important*), resentment within groups grows steadily when a portion of the team does a majority of the work. The best way to begin getting everyone involved in sharing the load is to ensure there's something that can appeal to each person's specific interests. Maybe you don't know what that is yet? Maybe you can let them pick?

"Google engineers are encouraged to take 20 percent of their time to work on something company-related that interests them personally. This means that, if you have a great idea, you always have time to run with it!"[20] Imagine!? When you finish and close this book and begin sharing with your team how its development is going to be your biggest focus, how might their appreciation of that idea grow (and their trepidation shrink) if you added that, for one hour each week, they were to work on whatever they wanted—as long as it would somehow help contribute to the team's overall greatness?

KEEPING PEOPLE – Maybe you've been in charge of your team for some time or maybe you're reading this book because you've just moved into a leadership position. In either case, you need to focus, both short- and long-term, on keeping the people around you who can make a difference—even as you're all working out just what that difference will be. After you or a previous leader has worked hard to build your team, it's now your job to keep them—so they can move forward successfully along with you.

One effective way to retain staff is to study why most people leave jobs, and then do the opposite. According to one study,[21] there are six frequent reasons for turnover. Think each day about how each of these can be avoided:

1. People leave because the work or workplace was not as expected. Make sure you're painting a clear and honest picture of what your team is all about and what contributions each person is expected to make to it.

2. People leave because of a mismatch between the job and person. In your early conversations with team members, when you discern their skills, goals, and ambitions, check to make sure there's a balance there. If necessary, provide the

---

TO GET STARTED . . . GET LISTENING

Read these tips to help prepare you to really listen to your team members as you begin the processes outlined in this book. Read through this list. Then read it again. If necessary, copy this page and read through it *again* in the moments just before each opportunity you get to really listen.

- **LISTEN WITHOUT JUDGMENT:** If, for example, you are shocked by what you hear, rather than reacting, ask a question that helps you understand more fully.
- **USE MORE THAN YOUR EARS:** We are remarkable instruments for taking in information, finding patterns, and making meaning. Use everything.
- **CHECK FOR UNDERSTANDING:** Repeat what you heard and ask if you heard correctly. This could be repeated as often as necessary.
- **HIZZLE:** Credited by its creator, Mark Jones, as the transformative power of listening, *hizzling* means hearing, seeing, and loving (in professional application, loving the work or purpose—not the person.)[24]

---

necessary bridges, such as additional training or support, that are needed.

3. People leave because of too little coaching or feedback. Depending on the size of your team, providing ongoing coaching and feedback for everyone can be a daunting and unnecessary task. Create buddy systems, support a mentorship program, and build the largest support network that you can.

4. People leave because of too few growth and advancement opportunities. With your eyes on the horizon, opportunities for growth can always be seen. As the

team leader, concentrate on helping to find and take advantage of those opportunities!

5. People leave because they feel devalued and unrecognized. Almost everything covered this year will help to dissuade your team of this notion, as long as you continually provide the meetings, conversations, evaluations, and listening that's required.

6. People leave because of a loss of trust and confidence in leaders. True team leaders, because of the value they place in others, continually earn and re-earn trust as time goes by. Be who you say you are. Do what you say you'll do. Trust will follow.

Here is, I hope, the worst-kept secret in team leadership. "For most organizations, especially those focused on service delivery, they key to success lies in its people."[22]

The second worst-kept secret? People depend on leaders to move forward.

SUGGESTED READING

Holman, Peggy. *Engaging Emergence: Turning Upheaval into Opportunity*. San Francisco: Peggy Holman, 2010.

EXERCISES

-47-

1. **Make a list of** every member of your staff and, if you can do this based on your current understanding of their hopes and dreams, write next to each name one small "gift" you can give them right away, that would make a difference in their work life. If you cannot think of one, then pause in completing these exercises and go ask them.

   _____

   _____

   _____

2. **List each job description** that falls within your team's sphere of duties. Sketch a plan that will allow a rotation of assignments, to initiate cross-training. (This isn't just sending unprepared people to "work" in another department for a couple of hours; this should include staff creating simple outlines of their work, a sharing and discussion of responsibilities, and a schedule creation—sort of like an old-fashioned dance card—that can only be completed when all team members have rotated through and experienced one another's work.)

   _____

   _____

   _____

3. **Look back at the** list of team members you created for question #1. Put a check mark next to the name of each person who is already actively involved in the team's work. Now, for all those remaining who don't have a check mark, begin drafting ideas that can help you (1) identify their passions for growth, and (2) increase their overall involvement using those passions.

   _____

   _____

   _____

   _____

4. **Gather some statistics to** analyze what the turnover rate has been for your team for the past five years. If available, reread exit interviews to see if you can find clues to why people left. Review the reasons people leave that were listed in this chapter and, on these lines, note the ones you're going to have to be particularly careful to focus on from now on.

   _____

   _____

   _____

   _____

5. **Lots of short-term ideas** have been offered this week. These ideas were meant to prompt you to sort through the myriad of activities and options described in this book and, without getting lost in the enormity of leading great teams, to help you figure out some _right-now_ actions to take to get started. List here at least five things you've decided to put into action right away.

   _____

   _____

   _____

   _____

INTENTIONAL SUCCESS

| ## LEADING TEAMS
It's time to talk about you.

"The journey of a thousand miles begins with one step."[25]

If you think of your career as a leader as your professional journey, the beauty of every new day is that you can start that journey over whenever you choose. After this past year's focus on leading your team to greatness, the moment you close this book you can take another first step. If you remain committed to success, there aren't enough detours, pitfalls, or orange barrels in the world to keep you from your goals. Give yourself time. Imagine how many steps it would *really* take to walk all around the world!

"The truth is that even people we recognize as being hugely successful took a long time to get the breakthrough. I don't know about you but I am continually surprised to find that people want the quick fix when it comes to achieving success. Take the long term view, if success (really) matters to you."[26]

Here are a few final reminders, then, to help you move successfully along your career path. Great teams need great leaders, so you can't spend all your time thinking about your staff and their needs. This is a personal journey you're on, too, so here are some final ideas on how you can stay strong—for you and for them—and avoid those barrels.

GET ALL YOUR REASONS FOR NOT BEING SUCCESSFUL OUT OF THE WAY

"Everyone has them. The things you say to yourself about why you can't have what you want in your career. Your reasons are scary to you, but really they are just a non-productive conversation you keep having with yourself over and over again."[27] Career coach Deborah Brown suggests the best advice is to face your reasons head-on and deal with them. Write down why

BE READY FOR WHAT YOU DIDN'T SEE COMING

Team leadership and development, although a daunting challenge, *can* be successfully accomplished with careful planning, action, and caring. But what happens when surprises pop up? Great leaders stay ready—stay vigilant—stay aware that change will happen and that, when it does, their team will turn to them for guidance, support, and direction. If you practice this approach, you'll be ready to fill that bill.

- Always be willing to look at new information and to modify your beliefs based on current reality, not just what you've done before.
- Have self-esteem that doesn't depend on status.
- Build team relationships that also don't depend on status.
- Be a lifelong learner.
- Stay civilized and maintain goodwill and good manners.
- Remember the mission: keep your team focused on where they are going and why.[33]

TOP TIPS THAT WILL (ALWAYS) HELP YOUR CAREER

1. **PEOPLE:** Look at the person on your right. Look at the person on your left. Look at the person who works a few job descriptions below you and above you. Be a team. Help them and they'll help you and, together, you'll all succeed.
2. **TRAINING:** Admit every day that you don't know everything. Find out what you're missing.
3. **EFFORT:** Take the initiative. Make the first step. Raise your hand and volunteer for the new project. Find answers. Work hard.
4. **ATTITUDE:** Who wants to work around or for someone who does nothing but complain, whine, and worry? Be positive. Fake it if you have to, some days. Everyone is looking to you for encouragement. It's part of your job to provide that.
5. **PREPARATION:** Everyone can tell at a lecture or staff meeting or training event which leaders have carefully and thoughtfully prepared and which are winging it, rushing in at the last minute thinking they're smart enough to pull something together. That doesn't work. Preparation demonstrates and models commitment. Organize your time, first, so you'll have time to do your job well.
6. **DETERMINATION:** Don't give up. Problems are there to be solved and ideas are there to move your team forward. Keep putting one foot in front of the other.
7. **PEOPLE:** Value everyone.

you think you can't take the next step—whether that involves leading a great team or moving on to that elusive next position. "Your reasons are now out in the open. You can deal with them."[28]

MAKE ANNUAL RESOLUTIONS FOR GROWTH—AND KEEP THEM

In the first 2008 issue of *American Libraries*,[29] Library Director Mary Pergander suggested that a unique start to the new year would be to make career-growing resolutions.

For most of us, being able to select and stick to even just a few of these could mean the difference between a year of growth and just another twelve pages in the calendar turned over. Pick some:

1. Can you name three librarian colleagues working in similar roles in nearby libraries? Reach out and connect to them.
2. Read at least one professional journal cover to cover each month. Make copies of valuable articles and share them.

3. Attend a professional training event.
4. Subscribe to at least one RSS feed on a library topic.
5. Learn at least one new shortcut or feature in your integrated library system, on a database, or elsewhere on the Web.
6. Serve on a professional committee.
7. Apply for a grant.
8. Take a vacation.

LOOK OUTSIDE THE LIBRARY ARENA

Since our team members are required to proactively provide services that meet the needs of our ever-changing world, should we all know what they might be? Keep yourself, your skills, and your awareness sharp by watching and reading more than just what the library journals provide. Be expansive in your knowledge, your interests, and your talents. Remember, many "things [that] can guide us come from outside of librarianship. The concepts of flattening organizations, virtual collaborative work, learning organizations and effective team dynamics [can come] from fields such as management, organizational psychology and economics."[30]

USE WHAT YOU'VE LEARNED

The exercises built into this book are not there by accident. Each week, as new concepts or old ideas were introduced and reviewed, it was critical to encourage readers to apply them to the life of their team. This reality is supported by study after study about how we learn and retain and successfully use information. "Talk to most learners in the days after they return from a face-to-face or online session and you will hear what we call the *Learner's Lament:* 'I wish I had time to use what I learned.' If learning is not reinforced soon, much is quickly lost."[31] If you've reached this point in the book, you've spent a lot of time, energy, and effort building skills to enhance your team. Congratulations! Now, don't let that go to waste.

Noted trainer Pat Carterette once called learning a gift which, for her—and potentially for us all—could result in "increased self-confidence, self-awareness, personal responsibility and the

RECIPE FOR SELF-PROMOTION

In 2011, the Human Resources and Trainer Action Council of the Ohio Library Council shared this "recipe" for self-promotion. Inarguably one of the most difficult steps in advancing our careers—and the most important—self-promotion can often make or break your career's progress.

MIX THESE INGREDIENTS FOR LIFE

1 cup PROFESSIONALISM

Stay out of other people's drama, be noticed for the right reasons, stay upbeat, be able to take criticism.

1 cup of PRIDE

Be what you want to become, toot your own horn.

1 gallon of PERCEPTION

Make sure you see yourself honestly, as others see you. (If you don't know how others see you, ask a mentor or coach!) Are you a problem solver or a problem creator?

5 teaspoons of CONFIDENCE

Step up to the plate. Ask for what you want.

2 quarts of INNOVATION

Volunteer.

1 pound of CREATIVITY

Think outside the box.[34]

notion that problems can be viewed as opportunities."[32]

A gift. If leading others is a privilege and learning how to do it well is a gift, then tomorrow I think I'll take that second step around the world. Sounds like a trip worth taking.

SUGGESTED READING

Lankes, R. David. *The Atlas of New Librarianship.* Cambridge, MA: MIT Press, 2011.

Reed, Lori, and Paul Signorelli. *Workplace Learning and Leadership: A Handbook for Library and Nonprofit Trainers.* Chicago: American Library Association, 2011.

EXERCISES

-48-

1. **List the three most** recent "detours" you've encountered in your career. They could be a poor decision, a less-than-perfect relationship with your boss, or anything that has affected the path you've chosen. You got around them somehow. How did you do it? How might you do it better (easier) the next time?

    _____

    _____

    _____

    _____

2. **What are the three** most often repeated reasons you've cited that are keeping you from the next career achievement you desire? Write them down. Face them. Are they real? If so, what can you do to overcome them? Address them openly, resolve them as best you can and move on.

    _____

    _____

    _____

    _____

3. **Pick one resolution that** you can commit to keeping in the coming year. Or, if there's not one on the list in this chapter, come up with one of your own. Put it on a note, affix the note where you can see it, and keep the resolution!

    _____

    _____

    _____

    _____

    _____

4. **Select one resource that** you already or will soon begin watching consistently, that comes from outside of the library arena, which can help you keep your skills sharp and your career in line with future realities.

    _____

    _____

    _____

    _____

    _____

5. **Please, please continue to** set one hour aside each week, even if it's your own time, so you can never stop improving your skills. Right now, write down when and what you'll do during your hour next week. Find another book to work through? Create your own training plan? Don't close this book until you plan what you're going to do next. And, whatever you do, don't give up your hour!

    _____

    _____

    _____

    _____

NOTES

MONTH ONE

1. James Michener, *Hawaii* (New York: Random House, 1959), 1.

2. Charles S. Parry and Marilyn J. Darling, "Emergent Learning in Action: The After Action Review," *The Systems Thinker* 12, no. 8 (October 2001).

3. Boeing Airline Company, Office Instruction, Aero-Space Division, Secretarial Standard No. 901(June 28, 1961).

4. M. Jason Martin, "'That's the Way We Do Things around Here': An Overview of Organizational Culture," *Electronic Journal of Academic and Special Librarianship* 7, no. 1 (Spring 2006), 1.

5. John Lubans, Jr., "Teams in Libraries," *Library Administration & Management* 17, no. 3 (Summer 2003), 144.

6. Ibid, 145.

7. Marti Peden, "Attitude and Accountability" lecture, NEO-RLS Library Career Development Series (2011).

8. "Team-Building Exercises: Planning Activities That Actually Work," *Mind Tools*, www.mindtools.com/pages/article/newTMM_52.htm.

9. Katharine C. Briggs and Isabel Briggs Myers, "MBTI," Form M, *CPP, Inc.* (1998), www.cpp.com.

10. Ibid.

11. Adapted from Don Richard Riso and Russ Hudson, "The Riso-Hudson Enneagram Type Indicator (Version 2.5)," *Enneagram Institute* (1994), www.EnneagramInstitute.com.

12. From Martin Elliot Jaffee, "Management and Meaning: Understanding Personality Types in the Library Workforce," presentation, Cleveland, Ohio (May 2009).

13. Jack Ricchiuto, *Collaborative Creativity: Unleashing the Power of Shared Thinking* (Akron, OH: Oak Hill, 1996).

14. 14. Adapted from Maureen Sullivan, "Tomorrow's Library: Collaboration, Shared Leadership and Service," NEO/Kent State University School of Library and Information Science, September 28, 2011.

15. Ibid, 2.

16. Carmine Gallo, "Five Great Ways to Create a Winning Corporate Culture" (2010), http://hiring .monster.com/hr/hr-best-practices/workforce -management/improving-employee-relations/ corporate-culture.aspx.

17. Ted Nellen's notes on Edgar H. Schein, "Organizational Culture & Leadership" (October 1997), www.tnellen.com/ted/tc/schein.html.

18. Written by K, "Eight to Late: A Quick Test of Organisational Culture" (May 15, 2009), http:// eight2late.wordpress.com/2009/05/15/a-quick-test -of-organisational-culture.

19. Peter Bregman, "A Good Way to Change a Corporate Culture," *Harvard Business Review* (June 25, 2009), http://blogs.hbr.org/bregman/2009/06/the-best -way-to-change-a-corpo.html.

20. Adapted from Kimberly Bolan Cullin and Laura Isenstein's "Transformation in Tough Times" comments. Not published.

21. Jim Collins, *Good to Great and the Social Sectors: Why Business Thinking Is Not the Answer* (Boulder, CO, 2005), 9.

22. "Leading Teams: Make Yourself a Leader, Not a Boss," *Managing People at Work* (June 2005), www .managingpeopleatwork.com.

23. W. Chan Kim and Renee Mauborgne, "Tipping Point Leadership," *Harvard Business Review* (April 2003), 61.

24. Collins, *Good to Great,* 11.

25. Dianne Discenzo, conversation.

26. Robert McNeish, as quoted by George Ambler, "Leadership Lessons from Geese" (July 18, 2006), www.thepracticeofleadership.net/2006/07/18/ leadership-lessons-from-geese.

27. Tim Bridge, PersonaDev.com (2008), www .dumblittleman.com/2008/02/11-solid-ways-to -improve-your-time.html.

28. Don, "Using Time Management to Stay Motivated," Time Management Tips (March 6, 2011), http:// notesoneselfgrowth.com/using-time-management-to -stay-motivated.

MONTH TWO

1. WWW, "The 7 Traits of Highly Effective Teams," *Worldwide Success* (January 17, 2007), www-success .com/blog/index.php/2207/01/17/the-seven-traits -of-highly-effective-teams.html.

2. Audra Bianca, "Organizational Gap Analysis," *eHow.com,* www.ehow.com/pring/about_5304768 _organizational-gap-analysis.html.

3. "Quotation #29901 from Classic Quotes," *The Quotations Page,* www.quotationspage.com/ quote/29901.html.

4. Johanna Rothman, "Hiring for Team Fit," Rothman Consulting Group, Inc., from *Cutter IT Journal* 18, no. 7 (July 2005), www.jrothman.com/Papers/ hiringforteamfit.html.

5. Leo, "Job Description Update FYI," *University of Missouri,* mulibraries.missouri.edu/staff/admin/hr/ jobdesupdate1.doc.

6. Coeli Carr, "7 'Moneyball' Hiring Tips," *Forbes Magazine* (September 23, 2011).

7. Lee Gardenswartz and Anita Rowe, from "The Manager's Recruiting Guide," reproduced from *The Diversity Tool Kit*, Irwin Professional Publishing.

8. From "M.O.S.A.I.C.: Making Our System an All-Inclusive Community," workshop handout, Cuyahoga County Public Library, Parma, Ohio.

9. "Management Tips: How to Write a Job Advertisement," *International Guild of Hospitality and Restaurant Managers, Inc.,* www.hospitalityguild .com/GuidePro/Management/job_advert.htm.

10. Ibid.

11. Ibid.

12. Chris Russell, reprinted from Recruiting Blogs in "Creative Ways to Pimp Your Job Ads," www.jobs .co.za/recruitemnt/recruitment-advice/article/146/ creative-ways-to-pimp-your-job-ads.

13. Hildy Gottlieb, "Writing a Great Employment Ad," from Creating the Future, 2008, www .help4nonprofits.com/UseItToday/UseItToday -Writing_a_Great_Employment_Ad.htm.

14. Daniel Crosby, "How to Write Job Postings That Don't Suck," from *UpstartHR* (October 6, 2010), http://upstarthr.com/how-to-write-job-postings-that -don't-suck.

15. Patrick Neeman, "How to Write a Great Job Requisition: 5 Tips," from Social Recruitment Tips (February 28, 2011), http://blog.jobvite .com/2011/02/how-to-write-a-great-job-requisition -5-tips.

16. Note 8. Supporting workshop handout used in M.O.S.A.I.C. Taken from M. Loden's "Implementing Diversity," Irwin Publishing Co., Chicago.

17. Joan Lloyd, "Team Hiring Can Build Stronger Teams," *Joan Lloyd at Work,* www.joanlloyd.com/ Managing?Team-hiring-can-build-stronger-teams .aspx.

18. "Leadership Quotes," *GreatQuotes.com,* www.great -quotes.com/quotes/category/Leadership.

19. Lloyd, "Team Hiring."

20. Ibid.

21. 21. J. T. Taylor, "Five Levels of Decision Making," *Teambuilding USA,* www.teambuildingusa.com/ article-making-effective-decisions.asp.

22. Laura Lemay, "How to Conduct a Team Interview," *eHow,* www.ehow.com/print/how_7610248_conduct-team-interview.html.

23. Chris Havrilla, "Negative Nellies and Debbie Downers," *Recruiterchicks.com* (July 19, 2011), www.recruiterchicks.com/2011/07/19/negative-nellies-debbie-downers.

24. The HR Specialist: Employment Law, "Workplace Confidentiality: Persuade Staff to 'Think' Privacy," *Business Management Daily* (March 1, 2005), www.businessmanagementdaily.com/258/workplace-confidentiality-persuade-staff-to-think-privacy.

25. John Sullivan, "Attract Reluctant Applicants by Compiling Your Selling Points," *ere.net* (July 23, 2007), www.ere.net/2007/attract-reluctant-appplicants-by-compiling-your-selling-points.

26. Todd Bavd, "Are You Selling Your Applicants on the Job? Then Maybe It's Time to Think Again," *HR Ninja: A Blog by Todd Bavd* (May 20, 2010), www.hrninjablog.com/?p = 1875.

27. Ibid.

28. Kevin Larson, "Rscheearch Shmecsearch," *fontblog* (November 16, 2005), http://blogs.msdn.com/b/fontblog/archive/2005/11/16/493452.aspx.

MONTH THREE

1. Richard Rubin, *Hiring Library Employees: A How-to-Do-It Manual* (New York: Neal-Schuman, 1993), 79.

2. Harold Messmer Jr., "How to Evaluate Job Applicants," *Dummies.com,* www.dummies.com/how-to-evaluate-job-applicants.html.

3. "Henry Ford Quotes," *goodreads.com,* www.goodreads.com/author/quotes/203714.Henry_Ford.

4. Messmer, "How to Evaluate."

5. Rubin, *Hiring Library Employees*, 90.

6. Leslie Lea Nord, "How to Hire Delightful Employees: Role-Play Has a Role," *Public Libraries* 50, no. 4 (July/August 2011), 40.

7. Ibid., 42.

8. Will Manley, *The Manley Art of Librarianship* (Jefferson, NC: McFarland, 1993), 175–76.

9. Nathan Newberger, "How to Master Telephone Interviews," http://worktree.com/tb/IN_telephone.cfm.

10. "The Pre-Interview Test Most Miss; And How to Pass It – Part 2 of 2, www.lorenaslist.com/refresh/templates/blog.php?id = 159.

11. Susan M. Heathfield, "5 Resume Flags for Employers," *About.com Human Resources,* http://humanresources.about.com/od/hire-employees/tp/resume-red-flags-for-employers.htm.

12. Catherine Hakala-Ausperk, notes from "Climbing the Library Ladder II: The Secrets of Resumes, Cover Letters & Interviews That Work!" Northeast Ohio Regional Library System Workshop (September 16, 2008).

13. Susan M. Heathfield, "5 More Red Flags for Employers," *About.com Human Resources,* http://humanresources.about.com/od/hire-employees/tp/five-more-resume-red-flags.htm.

14. Richard Rubin, notes from "Cover Letters, Resumes & Interviews" presentation, Kent State University (April 26, 2011).

15. Kerry David Carson, Paul Phillips Carson, and Joyce Schouest Phillips, *The ABCs of Collaborative Change: The Manager's Guide to Renewal* (Chicago: American Library Association, 1997), 10.

16. Ibid., 133.

17. Robert H. Rosen with Paul B. Brown, *Leading People: The 8 Proven Principles for Success in Business* (New York: Penguin Group, 1996), 45.

18. Collins, *Good to Great.*

19. Jim Collins and Morten T. Hansen, *Great by Choice: Uncertainty, Chaos, and Luck—Why Some Thrive Despite Them All* (New York: HarperCollins, 2011), 1.

20. Career Excellence Club, "Successful Induction: Getting New Team Members Off to a Great Start!" *Mindtools.com,* www.mindtools.com/pages/article/newTMM_99.htm.

21. "Preparing for New Employees: Setting the Stage for Success," Manager/Supervisor Guide for New Staff Orientation" (Fall 2010), Wellesley College, web.wellesley.edu/CMSPortalWeb/ShowProperty/BlueLive/binaries/departments/humanresources/files/current/new-staff_mgr_guid.pdf.

MONTH FOUR

1. Phil Shapiro, "It's Time for Public Libraries to Get Creative," *PC World* (April 26, 2010), www.pcworld.com/article/194960/its_time_for_public_libraries_to_get_creative.html.

2. Ibid.

3. Rubin, *Hiring Library Employees,* 66.

4. Kirsten Olson, "Ten Tips to Hire the Right Candidate with Skills for the New Economy," *HiringMonster.com,* http://hiring.monster.com/hr/hr-best-practices/recruiting-hiring-advice/acquiring-job-candidates/hire-the-right-candidate.aspx.

5. Chris Havrilla, "Getting Naked with Your Hiring Managers," *Recruiter Chicks.com* (June 2011), www.recruiterchicks.com/2011/06/07/getting-naked-with-your-hiring-managers.

6. Rubin, *Hiring Library Employees.*

7. Olson, "Ten Tips."

8. From Ned Parks, "How to Problem Solve, Manage & Lead with Powerful Questions," New Directions Learning & Development (April 14, 2010), www.nedparks.com.

9. "The 5 Whys," *Wikipedia: The Free Encyclopedia,* http://en.wikipedia.org/wiki/5_Whys.

10. Ibid.

11. From a workshop on diversity handout, no author listed, Cuyahoga County Public Library, Parma, Ohio.

12. Shelia Spencer, "The ABC's of Interviewing," *The Toastmaster* (February 2003), www.sciencepeople.com.au/assets/pdf/abc.pdf.

13. Rubin, *Hiring Library Employees,* 86.

14. From Gayatri Trivedi's "Expert Interviewing Tips, Parts 1, 2 and 3," *JobsJournal* (2010), www.jobsjournal.com/articles/312002370/Expert-Interviewing-Tips-Part-1; www.jobsjournal.com/articles/312002370/Expert-Interviewing-Tips-Part-2; www.jobsjournal.com/articles/312002370/Expert-Interviewing-Tips-Part-3.

15. Spencer, "ABC's of Interviewing."

16. Rubin, *Hiring Library Employees,* 90.

17. Carol Tavris and Elliot Aronson, "Cognitive Dissonance: The Engine in Self-Justification," in *Mistakes Were Made (But Not by Me): Why We Justify Foolish Beliefs, Bad Decisions, and Hurtful Acts* (Orlando, FL: Harcourt, 2000), 17.

18. Harold Messmer Jr., "How to Select the Right Applicant for the Job," *Dummies.com,* www.dummies.com/how-to-content/how-to-select-the-right-applicant-for-the-job.html.

19. Tom Mochal, "Develop a Staffing Strategy When Making Hiring Decisions," *TechRepublic* (September 10, 2003), www.techrepublic.com/article/develop-a-staffing-strategy-when-making-hiring-decisions/5062217.

20. Susan Dunn, "How to Choose the Right Job Candidate," *ManagerWise* (December 2011), www.managerwise.com/article.phtml?id=456.

21. Ibid.

22. Rubin, *Hiring Library Employees,* 96.

23. Peter Carbonara, "Hire for Attitude, Train for Skill," *Fast Company* (December, 2007), www.fastcompany.com/node/26996/print.

24. From a workshop on diversity handout, no author listed, Cuyahoga County Public Library, Parma, Ohio.

25. Lou Adler, "10 Great Ways to Make Bad Hiring Decisions," *ERE News & Features* (September 12, 2008), www.ere.net/2008/09/12/10-great-ways-to-make-bad-hiring-decisions.

MONTH FIVE

1. "How Do You Make the Hire?" *Small Business Guide: Business Owner's Toolkit,* www.toolkit.com/small_business_guide/sbg.aspx?nid=PO5_1630.

2. "Tips for Making a Job Offer," *Professional-Resumes.com,* www.professional-resumes.com/top-tips-for-making-a-job-offer.html.

3. Ibid.

4. "How to Negotiate a Salary with a New Employee," *Small Business Resource,* http://freesmallbusinessresource.com/how-to-negotiate-a-salary-with-a-new-employee.

5. "Making a Job Offer," *OfficeTeam: Specialized Administrative Staffing,* www.officeteam.com/joboffer.

6. Allison Green, "10 Things Employers Forget When Hiring," *US News* (November 7, 2011), at http://money.usnews.com/money/blogs/outside-voices-careers/2011/11/07/10-things-employers-forget-when-hiring.

7. Paul Falcone, "Recruiting and Hiring Advice," *Monster.com,* http://hiring.monster.com/hr/hr-best-practices/recruiting-hiring-advice/acquiring-job-candidates/making-a-job-offer.aspx.

8. Rubin, *Hiring Library Employees,* 108.

9. Alice Ihrig, *Decision Making for Public Libraries* (Hamden, CT: Shoestring, 1989), 52.

10. H. Scott Davis, *New Employee Orientation: A How-to-Do-It Manual for Librarians* (New York: Neal-Schuman, 1994), ix.

11. Max Messmer, "How to Introduce a New Employee to Your Corporate Culture," *Dummies.com,* www.dummies.com/how-to/content/how-to-introduce-a-new-employee-to-your-corporate-.html.

12. Sylvie Lapointe, "Ground Rules," *National Managers Community* (October 2004), www.managers-quetionnaires.gc.ca/documents/facile/ground-rules-e.pdf.

13. Ibid.

14. Messmer, "How to Introduce a New Employee."

15. Maureen Sullivan, from a diversity workshop handout, Cuyahoga County Public Library, Parma, Ohio, October, 1997.

16. "Creating Healthy Workplaces," *Managing People at Work* (August 2004), 3.

17. Lapointe, "Ground Rules."

18. "Clarify Expectations with New Employees," *The Purcell Group, LLC,* http://thepursellgroup.com/candidates/career-resources/how-to-manage-your-career/clarify-expectations-with-new-employees.

19. Mark Murphy, "Why New Hires Fail," *LeadershipIQ* (August 14, 2009), www.leadershipiq.com/news-and-research/why-new-hires-fail.20. Becky Schreiber and John Shannon, handout from "CAMLS Skills Track: Coming Together as a Team," 2002.

20. Rubin, *Hiring Library Employees,* 107.

21. Schreiber and Shannon, handout.

22. Ken Blanchard, Jim Ballard, and Fred Finch, *Customer Mania! It's NEVER Too Late to Build a Customer-Focused Company* (New York: Free, 2004), 90.

23. Groucho Marx, "Quotable Quotes," *Good Reads,* www.goodreads.com/quotes/show/76970.

24. Michael Stephens, Office Hours, "The Role of Mentoring," *Library Journal* (September 15, 2011), 38.

25. Ned Parks, notes from "Keeping Your Morale and the Morale of Your Staff Up during These Tough Times," presentation, NEO-RLS Fall Membership Meeting, September 15, 2009.

26. Cecile Bianco, "How Mentoring in the Library Profession May Help You," *Library Worklife: HR E-News for Today's Leaders* 1, no. 10, ALA-APA Allied Professional Association, http://ala-apa.org/newsletter/2004/10/17/how-mentoring-in-the-library-profession-may-help-you.

27. Ibid.

28. "Peak Performance: Working with a First Time Employee," *Managing People at Work* (November 2006), 1.

29. Brooke E. Sheldon, *Leaders in Libraries: Styles and Strategies for Success* (Chicago: American Library Association, 1991), 52.

30. Cleveland Area Metropolitan Library System (CAMLS), notes from "CAMLS Mentoring Project Meeting," 2004.

31. Davis, *New Employee Orientation,* 51, 34–35.

MONTH SIX

1. Diana Pazdera, Hakima Lamari, and Trish Nicol, "Library Skills 101," prepared for the Surrey School District (April, 2007), www.sd36.bc.ca/destiny/.../library%20skills%20101-updated.doc.

2. Ohio Library Council, "Ohio Public Library Core Competencies" (revised January 2008), www.olc.org/CoreCompetencies.asp.

3. Reference and Information Services Division/OLC, "Ohio Reference Excellence, 2nd Edition" (Columbus, OH, 2000).

4. Reference and Information Services Division/OLC, "Ohio Reference Excellence," "Reference Service," 2–3.

5. Reference and Information Services Division/OLC, "Ohio Reference Excellence," "The Reference Interview," 5.

6. Reference and Information Services Division/OLC, "Ohio Reference Excellence," "The Reference Interview," 13.

7. Reference and Information Services Division/OLC, "Ohio Reference Excellence," "The Reference Interview," 15.

8. Beth McNeil and Joan Giesecke, "Core Competencies for Libraries and Library Staff," from *Staff Development: A Practical Guide,* 3rd ed. (Chicago: American Library Association, 2001), 49.

9. "Developing Performance Standards: The Second in a Series of Articles on Employee Performance Plans," U.S. Office of Personnel Management, April 1998, www.opm.gov.

10. Reference and Information Services Division/OLC, "Ohio Reference Excellence," "Reference Tips," 1–6.

11. Carter McNamara, "Suggestions to Enrich Any Training and Development Plans," adapted from *Field Guide to Leadership and Supervision for Non-Profit Staff* (Minneapolis: Authenticity Consulting, 2008).

12. Aesop, from "Aesop's Fables," as posted by *ChildhoodReading.com,* http://childhoodreading.com/?p=3.

13. "Professional Learning Community," from *Wikipedia: The Free Encyclopedia,* http://en.wikipedia.org/wiki/Professional_learning_community.

14. Ellesse, "3 Golden Rules to Slow & Steady Success," *GoalSetting College,* www.goal-setting-college.com/success/3-golden-rules-to-slow-steady-success.

15. Jessica Savitch, "Jessica Savitch Quotes," *Brainy Quote,* www.brainyquote.com/quotes/quotes/j/jessicasav313929.html.

16. Collins, *Great By Choice,* 1.

17. Ibid., 45.

18. Ibid.

19. Ibid., 51.

20. Ellesse, "3 Golden Rules."

21. "Locke's Goal Setting Theory: Understanding SMART Goal Setting," *MindTools,* www.mindtools.com/pages/article/newHTE_87.htm.

22. "List of Catchphrases," *Wikipedia: The Free Encyclopedia,* http://en.wikipedia.org/wiki/List_of_catchphrases.

23. *Merriam-Webster Dictionary,* "Cultivate," www.merriam-webster.com/dictionary/cultivate.

24. "Motivate Staff to Continue Developing Their Skills," *Human Resources at UC Berkeley,* http://hrweb.berkeley.edu/performance-management/cycle/motivate.

25. "Learning Organization Checklist" handout, Foundations of the PCLS Learning Organization (Tacoma, WA).

26. Andrew Sanderbeck, "Just When I Get Comfortable . . . Everything Changes: Proven Techniques and Approaches to Create an Attitude of Change Acceptance, Management and Adaptability," handout, Medina, Ohio, 2011.

27. Art Kleiner, "Why a Learning Organization?" *Learning-org,* http://world.std.com/~lo/WhyLO.html.

28. "Motivate Staff to Continue Developing Their Skills," *Human Resources at UC Berkeley.*

29. "Employee Training Tips," *smallbusiness.dnb.com,* http://smallbusiness.dnb.com/human-resources/careers-job-training/1465-1.html.

30. Pam Schuck, "Change Is Not an Optional Event!" handout, STRIVE Training, Brunswick, Ohio, 2003.

31. Lori Reed, "When the Going Gets Tough, the Staff Needs More Training," *Info Today* (April 2010), 6–11.

32. Roger Connors, Tom Smith, and Craig Hickman, *The Oz Principle: Getting Results through Individual & Organizational Accountability* (New York: Penguin Group, 1994, 2004), 47.

33. Ibid.

34. Steven Smith and Carmelita Pickett, "Avoiding the Path to Obsolescence," *American Libraries Magazine* (September, 2011), http://americanlibrariesmagazine.org/print/5721.

35. Ibid.

36. Surajit Sen Sharma, "Breaking Out of a Career Traffic Jam," *MarketingCrossing.com,* www.marketingcrossing.com/article/lcprintarticles.php?printerflag = P&id = 220382.

37. Renee Montagne and Donna Rosato, "Stuck in a Work Rut?" *National Public Radio* (October 2005), www.npr.org/templates/story/story.php?storyId = 4975156.

MONTH SEVEN

1. "The Miracle Worker," *Wikipedia: The Free Encyclopedia,* http://en.wikipedia.org/wiki/The_Miracle_Worker.

2. Scott Williams, "Coaching: Increasing Employees' Confidence," *LeaderLetter* (Raj Soin College of Business, Wright State University, Dayton, Ohio), www.wright.edu/~scott.williams/LeaderLettter/coach.htm.

3. "Coaching One on One to Improve Individual Performance," *Coach4Growth.com,* http://coach4growth.com/index.php?view + article&catid = 35:coaching-skills/coaching-one-on-one-to-improve-individual-performance.

4. Dave Arch, Bob Pike, and Lynn Solem, *One-on-One Training: How to Effectively Train One Person at a Time* (San Francisco: Jossey-Bass Pfeiffer and Creative Training Techniques, 2000), 7–10.

5. Ibid., 22.

6. Ibid., 46.

7. Williams, "Coaching."

8. Keith Rosen, "Asking the Right Questions When Coaching Employees," *allBusiness.com,* at www.allbusiness.com/print/11510413-1-9a0bs.html.

9. "James T. Kirk Quotes," *thinkexist.com,* http://thinkexist.com/quotation/a-meeting-is-an-event-whereminutes-are-taken-and/1022827.html.

10. Jason B. Jones, "Bad Meetings Are Your Fault," *Chronicle of Higher Education* (August 20, 2009), http://chronicle.com/blogs/profhacker/bad-meetings-are-your-fault/22650.

11. Ibid.

12. Ricchiuto, *Collaborative Creativity,* 78–81.

13. Ibid., 78.

14. Ellen Birkett Morris, "Training Tips for Successful Small Group Work," *TechRepublic.com* (October 12, 2011), www.techrepublic.com/article/training-tips-for-sucessful-small-group.work/1036579.

15. Deborah McGlauflin, "Meeting Facilitation Tips," *Insights in Action,* 2006, www.insightsinaction.com/id14.htm.

16. Samantha Hines, *Productivity for Librarians: How to Get More Done in Less Time* (Oxford: Chandos, 2010), 66.

17. Kenneth W. Davis, "This Week: Stop at 'Fish,'" *Manage Your Writing* (February 7, 2012), www.manageyourwriting.com.

18. Jane Curry, Sue Fullman, Rob Martin, and Diana Young, "Of Frogs and Foam: Writing to Save Our Lives," *Curry Young,* www.curryyoung.com/?p = 666.

19. Karl Walinskas, "Communicate the Write Way: 7 Tips for Written Communication," *Small Business Branding and Marketing Advice and Commentary* (January 27, 2012), www.smallbusinessbranding.com/4093/communicate-the-write-way-7-tips-for-written-communication.

20. Davis, "Stop at 'Fish.'"

21. Catherine Hakala-Ausperk, *Be a Great Boss: One Year to Success* (Chicago: American Library Association, 2011), 1.

22. Walinskas, "Communicate the Write Way."

23. Davis, "Stop at 'Fish.'"

24. John Murphy, "Two Techniques That Will Make You a Faster, More Productive Copywriter," *Murphy Agency Blog* (March 22, 2011), www.themurphyagency.com/two-techniques-that-will-make-you-a-faster-more-productive-copywriter.

25. Gary McClain, "Communication through Writing," *netplaces,* www.netplaces.com/managing-people/communicatoin-and-feedback/communication-through-writing.htm.

26. Rodolphe, "Rumors and Gossip at Work, a Dangerous Game," *hubpages,* http://rodolphe.hubpages.com/hub/gossipandrumors.

27. Ibid.

28. Ibid.

29. "Executive Suites: What Does Your Office Say about You?" *Office Broker News,* http://us.officebroker.com/Executive-Suites:What-Does-Your-Office-Say-About-You%3F.obart.

30. Gary McClain and Deborah S. Romaine, "Translating Body Language," *Managing People,* www.netplaces.com/managing-people/communication-and-feedback/translating-body-language.htm.

31. Randy Rogusky, "Body Language in the Office Speaks Louder Than Words," *The Plain Dealer,* April 28, 2008, http://blog.cleveland.com/business/2008/04/body-language-in-the-office-sp.html.

32. Jena McGregor, "New Study: What You Wear Could Affect How Well You Work," *Washington Post,* March 2, 2012, www.washingtonpost.com/blogs/post-leadership/post/new-study-what-you-wear-could-affect-how-well-you-work/2011/04/01/gIQAssHomR = blog.html.

33. Judith A. Siess and Jonathan Lorig, *Out Front with Stephen Abram: A Guide for Information Leaders* (Chicago: American Library Association, 2009), 45.

34. Ibid.

35. "Notice What Others Miss," *Managing People at Work* (October 2009), 3.

36. Beth Weissenberger, "Gossip in the Workplace," *Business Week,* November 3, 2009, www.businessweek.com/print/managing/content/nov2009/cq2009113_999372.htm.

37. Claudyne Wilder, *The Presentations Kit: 10 Steps for Selling Your Ideas* (New York: John Wiley & Sons, 1994), 239.

MONTH EIGHT

1. Becky Schreiber and John Shannon, "Nine Personality Styles and Their Impact on Leadership Development," workbook, Schreiber Shannon Associates, 1998, 26.

2. Becky Schreiber and John Shannon, "Library Leadership 2000 Institute," handout, 1998, 26.

3. "Peak Performance: Coaching Undependable Workers," *Managing People at Work* (February 2005), 1.

4. Melissa Karnaze, "10 Reasons to Listen to Both Sides of Any Story" (July 14, 2010), *mindfulconstruct.com,* http://mindfulconstruct.com/2010/07/14/10-reasons-to-listen-to-both-sides-of-any-story.

5. Schreiber and Shannon, "Library Leadership 2000 Institute," 27.

6. Ilinda Reese, "Who Moved My Cheese: Change Management," handout, Cleveland Heights–University Heights Public Library, 2004.

7. Jack Ricchiuto, "Coaching In Design & Redesign Projects," handout, *www.DesigningLife.com,* Cuyahoga County Public Library, 2003.

8. Ruth Metz, "Coaching in the Library," *American Libraries* (March 2010), 34.

9. "Resist Playing Counselor to Combatants," *Managing People at Work* (January 2011), 3.

10. Ibid.

11. Harold D. Stolovitch and Erica J. Keeps, *Telling Ain't Training* (Baltimore, MD: American Society for Training & Development, 2002), 35–40.

12. Patrick J. Donadio, "Tips for Dealing with Difficult People," handout, from Communicating with Impact Workshop.

13. Steve Yacovelli, TopDog Learning Group, LLC, "Turning the Page 2.0: Building Your Library Community," for the Public Library Association, 2011.

14. Marie G. McIntyre, "Resentful Employee Hurting His Own Future," *The Plain Dealer: Office Coach,* August 21, 2011, D4.

15. Michael J. Soltis, "The Ten Commandments of Effective Discipline," *Connecticut Business & Industry Association,* 2010, http://www5.cbia.com/hr/the-ten-commandments-of-effective-discipline.

16. Phyllis Neill, "The Four Steps to Effectively Disciplining an Employee," *Ezine,* http://ezinearticles.com/?The-Four-Steps-to-Effectively-Disciplining-an-employee&id = 1322461.

17. Richard E. Rubin, *Human Resources Management in Libraries* (New York: Neal Schuman, 1991) 147–48.

18. Dick Cipoletti, "Effective Employee Discipline: Handling It Properly and Staying Out of Court," *Pocono Business Journal* (May 2010), http://poconobusinessjournal.com/columnist/effective-employee-discipline.

19. Susan M. Healthfield, "Performance Management: Performance Improvement Plan," *About.com,* at http://humanresources.about.com/od/performancemenagement/a/PIP.htm.

20. Meg Delaney and Amy Hartman, "Commando Diplomacy: Building Skills and Tolerance for Having Difficult Conversations and Making Real Progress," at Public Library Association 2012 Conference, Philadelphia, 2012.

21. "Watch Out! After Bad Hire, Prepare to Fire," *Managing People at Work* (October 2009), 4.

22. G. Michael Maddock and Raphael Louis Viton, "Three Types of People to Fire Immediately," *Business Week,* November 8, 2011, www.businessweek.com/printer/management/three-types-of-peole-to-fire-immediately-11082011.html.

23. Soltis, "Ten Commandments."

24. Morey Stettner, "Overcome the Stigma of Firing," *Managing People at Work* (February 2011), 2.

25. McIntyre, "Resentful Employee."

MONTH NINE

1. "Five Levels of Decision Making," *Community Activators,* from *How Leaders Create Hope . . . Training Packets,* www.communityactivators.com/downloads.5LevelsofAuthority.pdf.

2. Ibid.

3. "Paul 'Bear' Bryant: 1913–1983," *KnowSouthernHistory.net,* www.knowsouthernhistory.net/Biographies?Bear_Bryant.

4. Honora Eskridge, "Toward a Philosophy of Management," *Library Worklife: HR E-News for Today's Leaders,* October 2007.

5. "Challenging Work," *NorthCoast 99 2010,* www.northcoast99.com.

6. Ibid.

7. Bob Jewell, "Making & Selling Effective Decisions," workshop notes, Ohio Library Council Annual Conference, Cincinnati, Ohio, October 2004.

8. Ned Parks, "Crash the Barrier: Build the Team," *New Directions Learning & Development,* Library Career Development Series workshop handouts, July 2011.

9. Jeff DeCagna, "Emergence of the Association Enterprise," *Executive Update* (June, 2003), 42.

10. Frances Hesselbein, "Managing in a World That Is Round," *Leader to Leader Institute,* vol. 1996, no. 2: 6–8.

11. "Five Levels of Decision Making," *Community Activators.*

12. Deborah A. Easton, "Empowering Your Staff to Make Decisions," NEO-RLS' A Day for Branch Managers, workshop handout, 2009.

13. Richard E. Rubin, handout/notes from "Employee Motivation, Satisfaction and Commitment" workshop, 2002, 12.

14. Janine Moon, "20th and 21st Century American Work Culture," Workforce Change, workshop handout, 2007.

15. Carrie Ballone, "Leading & Motivating a Multi-Generational Workforce," *LeadStar: Leadership by Angie and Courtney,* www.leadstar.us/pdfs/leading-motivating-a-multi-pdf.

16. Joanne G. Sujansky, "Management: The Five Biggest Traps to Avoid When Leading a Diverse Team," *EHS Today* (August 11, 2004), http://ehstoday.com/columns/ehs_imp_37148.

17. Terri Pasadyn, "How to Lead, How to Follow," notes from workshop handout, 2004.

18. Scott Williams, "Delegating Strategically," LeaderLetter, www.wright.edu/~scott.williams/LeaderLetter/delegating.htm.

19. "What Is Delegating? How Is It Different Than Work Directing?" Free Management Library, http://managementthehelp.org/leadingpeople/delegating.htm.

20. Ibid.

21. Christine M. Riordan, "Sometimes Micromanaging Is Good—and Necessary," *Forbes.com,* July 29, 2012, www.forbes.com/2010/07/29/micromanage-employees-delegate-leadership-managing-staff-print.html.

22. K.T. Bernhagen, "Six Tips for Delegating Success," *The Daily Muse* (September 30, 2011), www.thedailymuse.com/career/6-tips-for-delegating-success.

23. Bill Mayer, "Managing for Change and Continuous Improvement," *American Libraries,* January 25, 2012, http://americanlibrariesmanazine.org/columns/next-steps-change-american-university.

24. Joan Frye Williams, "Innovation and Risk Taking in Libraries," notes from workshop handout, 2006.

25. Susan Pieper, "Do You Have a Passionate Team?" *Rural Library Services Newsletter* 22, no. 6 (November/December 2011), 1.

26. Brooke Bates, "How to Create an Open Environment Where Innovation Thrives," *Smart Business Cleveland,* September 2010, 35.

27. Marti Peden, "Accountability Matters," notes from workshop handout, 2004.

28. Ibid.

29. Cathy Monnin, "The Care and Feeding of Managers," notes from workshop handout, 2011.

MONTH TEN

1. A library director, unnamed.

2. Yogi Berra, "Strategic Planning Quotations," *Woodward Davis,* www.woodwarddavis.com/quotes.html.

3. Mike Schorah, "Why Bother with Mission Statements?" *MikeSchorah.com* (March 2011), www.mikeschorah.com/2011/03/why-bother-with-mission-statements.html.

4. Ibid.

5. "Becton, Dickinson and Company Mission Statement," *MissionStatements.com,* www.missionstatements.com/fortune-500-mission-statements.html.

6. "What Is a Mission Statement?" *infoNet,* www.jiscinfonet.ac.uk/infokits/strategy/mission-vision-values/mission-statement.

7. Fred Koury, "Burn the Ships," *Smart Business Cleveland,* September 2010, 8.

8. "Using Vision, Commitment & Trust," *The Learning Center,* www.learningcenter.net/library/pl-building.htm.

9. Berra, "Strategic Planning Quotations."

10. "Mission Possible: Mission Statement Worksheet," *Bonner Curriculum,* www.bonner.org/resources/modules/modules.../MissionPossible.org.

11. Frances Hesselbein, "Journey to Transformation," *Leader to Leader Institute* (Winter 1998), http://leadertoleader.org/leaderbooks/121/winter98/fh.html.

12. Robert D. Stueart and Barbara B. Moran, *Library and Information Center Management,* 7th ed. (Westport, CT: Libraries Unlimited, 2007), 95.

13. Library board member, unnamed.

14. Maureen Sullivan, personal interview.

15. Jen Hetzel Silbert and Tony Silbert, "Traditional Approaches: Top-Down SWOT!" *AI Practitioner: International Journal of AI Best Practice,* Innovation Partners International, August 2007.

16. Thomas Crouser, Jr., "Tom's Blog: Can You Lead: SOAR, Don't SWOT!" *Can You Lead,* (February 11, 2011), http://canyoulead.wordpress.com/2011/02/11/soar-dont-swot.

17. Ibid.

18. Ibid.

19. Cassandra O'Neill, "SOAR Don't SWOT: Asset Based Strategic Planning," *Nonprofit Boards and Governance Review* (June 13, 2007), http://charitychannel.com/articles/tabid/348/article/202/soar-dont-swot-asset-based-strategic-planning.aspx.

20. Dr. Lionel Boxer, "Appreciative Inquiry (AI) + SWOT = SOAR," *Intergon,* http://intergon.freeyellow.com/ai/aiswot.html.

21. Robert S. Kaplan and David P. Norton, "Linking the Balanced Scorecard to Strategy," *California Management Review* 39, no. 1 (Fall 1996): 52.

22. Paul Averson, "What Is the Balanced Scorecard?" *Balanced Scorecard Institute,* www.balancedscorecard.org/basics/bsc1.html.

23. "Strategic Objectives," *Global Future Report* (April 26, 1999), www.globalfuture.com/planning11.htm.

24. Steve Strauss, "Ask an Expert: Finding What Motivates Your Employees," *USA Today,* May 21, 2007, www.usatoday.com/money/smallbusiness/columnist/strauss/2007-05-21-motivating-employees-N.htm.

25. Jim Loehr and Tony Schwartz, *The Power of Full Engagement: Managing Energy, Not Time, Is the Key to High Performance and Personal Renewal* (New York: Free, 2003), 5.

26. "Setting Performance Goals for Newbies: Pursuing Career Success," *Career-Success-for-Newbies,* www.career-success-for-newbies.com/setting-perfromance-goals.htm.

27. Alan G. Robinson and Dean M. Schroeder, *Ideas Are Free: How the Idea Revolution Is Liberating People and Transforming Organizations* (San Francisco: Berrett-Koehler, 2006), 201–3.

28. Jonathan, "21 Things Not to Do If You Want to Succeed," *Advanced Life Skills: Strategies for Positive Change,* http://advancedlifeskills.com/blog/21-things-not-do-do-if-you-want-to-succeed.

MONTH ELEVEN

1. Peter Drucker, "Famous Quotes on Culture," *culturedyn.com,* www.culturedyn.com/Famous%20Quotes%20on%20culture.htm.

2. Jerry, "What Is Workplace Culture and Why Does It Matter?" *Visionomics,* (February 23, 2011), www.visionomics.com/what-is-workplace-culture-and-why-does-it-matter-2.

3. "What Is Workplace Culture and Why Do I Care," *MoneyInstructor.com,* www.moneyinstructor.com/art/workculture.asp.

4. Kevin Eikenberry, "Workplace Culture—Seven Reasons Organizational Culture Matters," *Doherty Staffing Solutions,* www.dohertystaffing.com/workplace-culture-seven-reasons-organizational-culture-matters.

5. Carmine Gallo, "Five Great Ways to Create a Willing Corporate Culture," *Monster.com,* http://hiring.monster.com/hr/hr-best-practices/workforce-management/improving-employee-relations/corporate-culture.aspx.

6. Susan Heathfield, "Culture: Your Environment for People at Work: What Is Organizational Culture?" *About.com,* http://humanresources.about.com/od/organizationalculture/a/culture.htm.

7. Collins, *Great by Choice,* 36.

8. Ibid.

9. Ibid., 10.

10. "Stepping Up to Superior Supervision," *Managing People at Work* (August 2006), www.managingpeopleatwork.com/ArticleArchive.php?page=83.

11. Ibid.

12. Harrison Barnes, "Can You Be Trusted?" *Jobsjournal.com,* www.jobsjournal.com/articles/312002751/Can-You-Be-Trusted-.

13. Ibid.

14. "Leading Teams: Integrity: It Works!" *Managing People at Work* (July 2003), 4.

15. Ibid., 5.

16. Penny Loretto, "Top 10 Work Values Employers Seek," *About.com,* http://internships.about.com/od/internships101/tp/EmployeValues.htm.

17. Tom Niles, "Three Core Values Great Employees and Employers Must Have," *CRM News,* (April 4, 2006), www.crmbuyer.com/story/49623.html.

18. Sandra Nelson, "Making Connections: Organization Communication in Public Libraries," workshop notes, 2002.

19. Derek Powazek, "You Don't Create Culture," *Signal vs. Noise Weblog* (May 13, 2008), http://37signals.com/svn/posts/1022-you-dont-creat-a-culture.

20. Michael Hammer, "Corporate Culture Quotes," *qFinance.com,* www.qfinance.com/finance-and-business-quotes/corporate-culture.

21. Sami Lange, "Go 'Title Rogue,'" *Library Journal,* September 15, 2012, 32.

22. Ibid.

23. Alison Green, "10 Workplace Myths Busted," *U.S. News & World Report,"* November 16, 2011, http://money.usnews.com/money/blogs/outside-voices-careers/2011/16/10-workplace-myths-busted.

24. Scott Miller, "More Tips for Internal Customer Service," *Entrepreneur* (June 10, 2002), www.entrepreneur.com/article/52768.

25. Peter Bregman, "A Good Way to Change a Corporate Culture," *Harvard Business Review,* June 25, 2009, at http://blogs.hbr.org/bregman/2009/06/the-best-way-to-chage-a-corpo.html.

26. Bob Morris, "How Office Design Can Create a Positive Work Environment," *Allbestarticles,* www

.allbestarticles.com/home/design/how-office-design-can-create-a-postive-work-environment.html.

27. Hines, *Productivity for Librarians,* 29–30.

28. Ibid., 30.

29. Claud Robison, personal interview.

30. Anat Rafaeli and Monica Worline, "Symbols in Organizational Culture," chapter submitted for *The Handbook of Organizational Culture and Climate,"* 1999, at http://iew3.techunion.ac.il/Home/Users/anatr/symbol.html.

31. Hines, *Productivity for Librarians*, 104.

32. Tina, "Create a Positive, Productive Work Space," *Publicspark Blog* (2011), www.publicspark.com/2011/02/08/create-a-positive-productive-work-space.

33. Anne Fisher, "Is a Messy Office Hazardous to Your Career?," *CNN Money,* March 27, 2006, http://money.cnn.com/2006/03/27/news/economy/annie/fortune_annie_10solved/4.html.

34. Jason Daley, "Creating a Culture of Excellence," *Entrepreneur* (February 12, 2010), www.entrepreneur.com/article/204984.

35. "What Makes a Healthy Work Environment?" *Healthy Environments,* Graham Lowe Group, Inc., www.health.gov.bc.ca/environments/workplace/healthyworkplace.html.

MONTH TWELVE

1. Dr. Seuss, *Oh, The Places You'll Go!* (New York: Random House), 1990.

2. "Teamwork," *Teamwork and Leadership,* www.teamworkandleadership.com/2011/08/advice-for-new-leaders-5-tips.html.

3. "Personal Leadership Plans," *what-are-good-leadership-skills.com,* www.what-are-good-leadership-skills.com/personal-leadership-plans.html.

4. Albert Lang, "Executives Say the 21st Century Requires More Skilled Workers," *Partnership for 21st Century Skills* (August 15, 2010), www.p21.org/index.php?option=com_content&task=view&id=923&itemis=64.

5. "Personal Leadership Plans," *what-are-good-for-leadership-skills.com.*

6. James Bruce, "So, I Want You to Lead . . . : Advice to a New Leader," *Educause* (December 2003), 10–11.

7. Maureen Sullivan, "The Promise of Appreciative Inquiry in Library Organizations," *Library Trends* (Summer 2004), www.ideals.illinois.edu/bitstream/handle/2142/1728/Sullivan218229.pdf?sequence=2.

8. "Personal Leadership Plans," *what-are-good-for-leadership-skills.com.*

9. Robert D. Stueart and Maureen Sullivan, *Performance Analysis and Appraisal: A How-to-Do-It Manual for Librarians* (New York: Neal-Schuman, 1991), 2.

10. "Mission Possible: Creating a Personal Mission Statement," Bonner Curriculum, www.docstoc.com/docs/42645203/Mission-Possible-Creating-A-Personal-Mission-Statement.

11. Becky Schrieber and John Shannon, "Relationship Power: Lighting the Fire within Others," workshop handout, 1998.

12. Peter Smith, "Shared Leadership: New Ways of Leading," *OPI Inc.,* www.ope-inc.com/shared_leadership.htm.

13. "Can You Separate Owls from Ducks?" *Managing People at Work* (July, 2008), 4.

14. Becky Schreiber and John Shannon, "Characteristics of Leaders," workshop handout, 2001.

15. Jeff Haden, "10 Things Bosses Never Tell Employees," *Inc.* (February 15, 2012), www.inc.com/jeff-haden/10-things-bosses-never-tell-employees.html.

16. "Mission Possible."

17. "Advice to New Leaders: Get 'On Board' to an Early Win," *AMAnet* (March 19, 2007), www.amanet.org/training/articles/Advice-to-New-Leaders-Get-on-Board-to-an-Early-Win.aspx.

18. Claire Belilos, "Cross-Training as a Motivational and Problem-Solving Technique," CHIC Hospitality Consulting, 1999, at www.easytraining.com/crosstrain.htm.

19. Ibid.

20. Bharat Mediratta, "The Google Way: Give Engineers Room," *New York Times,* October 21, 2007.

21. Carl Robinson, "Why Great Employees Quit: What You Can Do to Keep Them," *Advanced Leadership Consulting* (2005), http://leadershipcomsulting.com/why-great-employees-quit.htm.

22. Michael A. Germano, "Talent Management and Libraries," *Library Management Today,* (2010), www.libmanagetoday.com/library_hr.

23. Belilos, "Cross-Training."

24. Peggy Holman, *Engaging Emergence: Turning Upheaval into Opportunity* (San Francisco: Peggy Holman, 2010), 52–55.

25. "Kernels of Wisdom," Author–Chinese, www.wisdomworld.org/additional/KernelsOfWisdom-Series/step1on1000mileJourney.html.

26. Duncan Brodie, "Leadership Success—Take the Long Term View," *Goals and Achievements,* http://goalsandachievements.com/leading/leadership-success-take-the-long-term-view.

27. Deborah Brown, "There's Always a Reason Not to Do Something in Your Career," *JobsJournal* (February 24, 2010), www.jobsjournal.com/articles/312002752/There-s-Always-A-Reason-Not-To-Do-Something-In-Your-Career/3908/203.

28. Ibid.

29. Mary Pergander, "Be It Resolved . . . ," *American Libraries* 39, no. 1/2 (January/February 2008): 78.

30. R. David Lankes, *The Atlas of New Librarianship* (Cambridge, MA: MIT Press, 2011).

31. Lori Reed and Paul Signorelli, *Workplace Learning and Leadership: A Handbook for Library and Nonprofit Trainers* (Chicago: American Library Association, 2011), 83.

32. Pat Carterette, "Library Leadership 2000: Quilting a Vision for Ohio Libraries . . . and Beyond!" *Public Libraries,* May/June 2010, www

.publiclibrariesonline.org/content/library-leadership -2000-quilting-vision-Ohio-libraries..-and-beyond.

33. Pat Wagner, "'If Change Is So Wonderful, How Come I Am Not Having Fun Yet?'" Hard Times/Smart Choices—Budgets and Decisions, 2004, workshop handout.

34. Ohio Library Council, Human Resources & Trainer Action Council, "Promoting Yourself," 2011, workshop handout.

INDEX

You may also be interested in

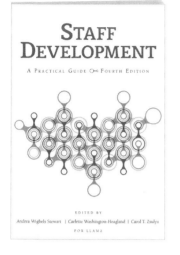

STAFF DEVELOPMENT
A Practical Guide, Fourth Edition

Edited by Andrea Wigbels Stewart, Carlette Washington-Hoagland, and Carol T. Zsulya for LLAMA

This is a volume that every librarian charged with staff development should have at the ready.

ISBN: 978-0-8389-1149-5
232 PAGES / 6" x 9"

THE CHALLENGE OF LIBRARY MANAGEMENT

WYOMA VANDUINKERKEN AND PIXEY ANNE MOSLEY

ISBN: 978-0-8389-1102-0

BE A GREAT BOSS: One Year to Success

CATHERINE HAKALA-AUSPERK

ISBN: 978-0-8389-1068-9

MANAGING IN THE MIDDLE

ROBERT FARRELL AND KENNETH SCHLESINGER

ISBN: 978-0-8389-1102-0

SMALL PUBLIC LIBRARY MANAGEMENT

JANE PEARLMUTTER AND PAUL NELSON

ISBN: 978-0-8389-1085-6

MANAGEMENT SKILLS FOR ARCHIVISTS AND RECORDS MANAGERS

LOUISE RAY

ISBN: 978-1-85604-584-1

JUMP-START YOUR CAREER AS A DIGITAL LIBRARIAN: A LITA Guide

JANE D. MONSON

ISBN: 978-1-55570-877-1

Order today at **alastore.ala.org** or **866-746-7252!**

ALA Store purchases fund advocacy, awareness, and accreditation programs for library professionals worldwide.